Rein Müllerson is Research Professor at the University of Tallinn. He was formerly Professor of International Law at King's College London, UN Regional Advisor for Central Asia and Visiting Centennial Professor at the London School of Economics and Political Science (LSE). He is the author of 12 books on international law and politics.

'This is a compelling book. Rein Müllerson writes with great authority and knowledge, reflecting his experience as a practitioner in international law and relations and as one of the world's leading scholars in this field.'

Lord Raymond Plant,
Professor of Jurisprudence and Political Philosophy,
King's College London

'This book is a thoughtful and at times imaginative reflection on the state of international law today, drawing on literature from law, politics and strategy. It is a thoroughly engaging read.'

Guglielmo Verdirame, Professor of International Law,
King's College London

'Well researched and compellingly written, this book is one of the best recent works on the subject of geopolitics and international law, especially its implications for international relations in the world today. Rein Müllerson has rightly questioned many assumptions taken for granted for so long in the West on such vital issues as democracy, regime change and humanitarian interventions, and it should be a "must-read" for all those who are interested in a more sophisticated understanding of the world today and in seeking a more just world order.'

Zhang Weiwei, Director of the China Institute,
Fudan University, China

GEOPOLITICS AND THE CLASH OF IDEOLOGIES

DAWN OF A NEW ORDER

REIN MÜLLERSON

I.B. TAURIS
LONDON · NEW YORK

Published in 2017 by
I.B.Tauris & Co. Ltd
London • New York
www.ibtauris.com

ISBN: 978 1 78453 972 6
eISBN: 978 1 78672 225 6
ePDF: 978 1 78673 225 5

A full CIP record for this book is available from the British Library
A full CIP record is available from the Library of Congress

Library of Congress Catalog Card Number: available

Typeset by Riverside Publishing Solutions, Salisbury, SP4 6NQ
Printed and bound by CPI Group (UK) Ltd, Croydon, CR0 4YY

MIX
Paper from responsible sources
FSC® C013604

To George Müllerson, with love and gratitude for his contribution.

Contents

Acknowledgements

I warmly thank I.B.Tauris and particularly Lester Crook, Jo Godfrey and Sara Magness for their efforts and enthusiasm in helping me to the completion of the manuscript.

Parts of this book are based on the following previously published articles:

Rein Müllerson, 'Ideology, Geopolitics and International Law', *Chinese Journal of International Law* (2016) 15 (1): 47–73.

Rein Müllerson, 'Democratization: Supply-Stimulated or Demand-Induced?', in Isabelle Buffard et al. (eds), *International Law between Universalism and Fragmentation: Festschrift in Honour of Gerhard Hafner* (Leiden: Martinus Nijhoff Publishers, 2008).

Introduction

The high – some would say naïve – expectation that many, including myself, had after the end of the Cold War has not materialised: the expectation of a world in which law, impartially interpreted and applied, would have primacy over politics. Instead, differing visions of desirable and possible world orders are today accompanied by propaganda warfare, where even international law is used as a tool of hegemonic dominance or, on the contrary, as an instrument to counter such dominance. In place of the Cold War rivalry between the belief in liberal capitalism and communist creeds, today the main competition is between ideologies justifying the continuation and expansion of a unipolar (or non-polar) world with one centre of power, a world that is also becoming more and more homogeneous (liberal-democratic), and a multipolar balance-of-power world where diverse political, economic and ideological systems cooperate and compete. This book argues that, taking into account the very size, and even more so the cultural and developmental diversities, as well as the complexity and increasing reflexivity of the world, the only realistic international system is a multipolar one. Moreover, international law, as a normative system based on a balance of interests and compromises and not necessarily on shared ideology or values (this may underpin domestic legal systems or EU law), can function relatively well only in a multipolar, balance-of-power, international system, which is consciously and conscientiously built and accepted as legitimate. And though the processes of globalisation have a tendency to homogenise the world while making many, if not most, states more heterogeneous, attempts to accelerate these processes are bound to be counter-productive.

The course of history is constantly accelerating in geometrical progression. Changes that, millennia ago, took centuries to bear fruit, today happen within decades. Only 30 years ago we lived in a stable bipolar world; a quarter of a century back the world entered into a 'unipolar moment' where one 'indispensable nation' seemed to order anarchy in international relations. Today, elements of multipolarity are becoming more and more visible, and this multipolarity has so far had more conflictual than co-operational aspects. Such a situation is due, at least to an extent, to the fact that the shoots of the emerging multipolarity are not recognised by those whose interests lie in the existence and prolongation of the unipolar moment and turning it into a unipolar century, while the advocates of multipolarity, instead of practising bandwagoning, have started counter-balancing.[1] Although the historical experience, as well as most theoretical approaches to international relations, proves that sooner or later counter-balancing to a hegemonic power is to be expected, most Western (and especially American) politicians, as well as experts, seem to have been at least closet Fukuyamians (though most of them were usually denying this), who instinctively believed that there was only one right historical trend, that is, liberal-democratic, that only they were on the right side of history. In that respect, liberal-democratic and Marxian ideologies, both of Western origin, are methodologically close and relatively unsophisticated. For example, in their otherwise very interesting, balanced and forward-looking article, Daniel Deudney and G. John Ikenberry observed that '[J]ust as the Nazis envisioned a "new order" for Europe and the Soviet Union designed an interstate economic and political order, so, too, did the liberal West'.[2] So far, so good. However, using the same method that the Marxists had used, these two American professors come to the optimistic conclusion that '[T]he foreign policy of the liberal states should continue to be based on the broad assumption that there is ultimately *one path to modernity* [emphasis added] – and that it is essentially liberal in character', and that '[L]iberal states should not assume that history has ended, but they can still be certain that it is on their side'.[3] This is only a slightly modified and moderated version of the deterministic, unilineal and unidirectional Hegelian, Marxian, Fukuyamian end-of-history argument. Such end-of-history philosophy is used to justify the expansion of liberal democracy all over the world as well as the efforts to perpetuate unipolarity and to make those who are against it seen as being on the wrong side of history.

There is no (not yet, at least) clash of civilisations predicted by Samuel Huntington (though there are certainly visible elements of it), but there is an increasing competition between differing visions of desirable and possible world orders. This is one of the, if not *the*, main obstacles on the path to finding solutions to a series of conflictual situations. Some of the current conflicts or potentially conflictual situations (the 2008 war between Georgia and Russia, the tragedy of Ukraine, as well as tensions in the South China Sea) are direct results of states acting in accordance with their clashing visions of the world, while many others have been exacerbated, and finding solutions to them has been delayed or hampered, since the existing or emerging centres of power consider them secondary in comparison with what, in their view, are their main interests or threats. They are striving either to consolidate the existing balance (imbalance) of power or to change it in their favour. Although the current turmoils in, for example, the Middle East and northern Africa have many variables, both local and regional, the prevalence of conflictual elements in great-power relations (especially US–Russia relations) and limited coordination (with some exceptions, like the 5+1 cooperation on the Iranian nuclear programme) between them have exacerbated the Middle Eastern situation instead of helping de-escalate the conflicts (e.g., Libya, Syria, Yemen, Iraq).

Some of the existing norms of international law, the cores of which are codified in the UN Charter, and which had evolved mostly during a bipolar Cold War world, appeared to indeed be in need of some re-interpretation, or, in the eyes of some, even radical change, at the end of the bipolar world. The 'old' principles, such as the non-interference in internal affairs of states or the non-use of force, had to be re-interpreted to give more room for human rights, including the concept of humanitarian intervention (or R2P, as the new concept became known), as well as to accommodate the surge of interest in international criminal law and jurisdiction. The sovereignty of states was to be sacrosanct no longer, and had to give way to efforts to promote democracy, since the right to democracy came to be seen as a universal human right.[4] In the 1990s, it seemed that this vision was the only one remaining in the ring. It was a vision of international law that corresponded to the Fukuyamian image of the future – the worldwide triumph of liberal democracy and free markets; a kind of Marxian methodology of a linear process of historical necessity which, instead of cumulating in a communist paradise, was called to guarantee a steady march towards liberal democracy. However, in the shadow of this triumphant liberal-democratic dream, China continued its rapid economic growth and, contrary to Deng Xiaoping's 'keep a low profile' policy, also started to flex its military muscles. Russia, which had only barely survived the shock therapy of the 1990s, in the 2000s started the process of recovery and undertook a more sober and less rosy look at the world. Moscow discovered that the erstwhile enemy of the Soviet Union and the Warsaw Pact – The North Atlantic Treaty Organization (NATO) – had not only not vanished in parallel with the disappearance of both the Warsaw Pact and the USSR, but instead had moved closer to the borders of Russia. This was a sobering realisation, and Russia quickly became less conciliatory and much pricklier vis-à-vis the dominant trend.

On the sidelines of the great powers' affairs, the 'democratisation' of the wider Middle East by means of what became known as the 'Arab Spring' soon turned into a chaos in which not only al-Qaeda thrived, but where ISIS (Islamic State of Iraq and Syria, or Daesh) – a much more serious terrorist organisation – found fertile ground. The chaos in the Middle East and northern Africa (especially Libya) is not any more a regional problem; it has already made the whole of Europe much less secure. Today the Old Continent has to find new answers to questions that seemed to have been resolved long ago (tolerance versus intolerance, communitarianism versus integration or assimilation, etc.). Immigration, especially, but not solely, from conflict zones, has become the paramount problem for Europe and the threat of terrorism has increased as a result of the 'war on terror'.

International law, especially in its most sensitive and politically loaded areas, does not work well in a world with unipolar tendencies, since in such a world this legal system (a result of bargains and compromises) and its interpretation is dictated from a single centre. Until the beginning of the 1990s, international law had evolved as a balance-of-power normative system, though the bipolar system was not the best environment for it. The following unipolar moment led to attempts to transform the existing law into a unipolar normative system controlled from a single centre where there could not be any room for counter-balancing or, sometimes, even bargaining. For a while, it seemed that international law may indeed evolve in that direction. However, beginning from the onset of the twenty-first century, it was not only China and Russia – the 'usual suspects' in Western eyes – but other emerging powers which started counter-balancing, and multipolar elements in the system have begun to emerge. The normative effect of these developments has been that while in most sensitive areas the existing norms have become undermined, new ones have not yet crystallised. Hence, today we live in an atmosphere of increased normative uncertainty.

The world does not seem to be ready, if it ever will be, for an international system *à l'Union européenne* (itself in serious crisis) and consequently also for a world law somewhat similar to the *droit européen*. The world is simply too big, complex and diverse for that. Its rich tapestry cannot be flattened into a carpet where one pattern, be it of a Judeo-Christian, Anglo-Saxon, Confucian, Muslim or even secular liberal-democratic pattern, dominates. Therefore, the international law of coexistence, using the distinction made by Wolfgang Friedmann between the international law of co-existence and the international law of cooperation[5], with its principles of sovereign equality, the non-use of force and non-interference in internal affairs, has not at all become outdated. It still has to cautiously help tame the Hobbesian world (being the gentle civiliser of nations, as Martti Koskenniemi wrote[6]), facilitating a move closer to a Lockean one (or maybe Confucian, who knows). There is even a deeper reason for the current crisis of international law. Every legal system, being a normative phenomenon, almost by definition functions well only in situations that could be called 'normal'. In revolutionary periods in any society – be it in France at the end of the eighteenth century or in Russia at the beginning of the twentieth – when normalcy is an exception and expediency rules, law has a tendency to break down. The same happens in international society. Since about the end of the 1980s, the world has been in a revolutionary situation that started with the collapse of the bipolar system via a unipolar moment of the 1990s towards an emerging multipolarity. Until the 'revolutionary dust' settles down, one way or other, and new 'normalcy' emerges, it is difficult to expect that international law could function 'normally'. Some of those legal ideas that were popular in the 1990s (e.g., R2P, the increasingly important role of international criminal jurisdiction) could hardly play a significant role in a multipolar world. It is not by chance that in the 1990s, instead of speaking of 'legality' or 'lawfulness' of behaviour of states, often a much-less-precise term – 'legitimate' – became widely used (e.g., NATO's war against Serbia, though being 'illegal', was nevertheless 'legitimate').

Chapter 1

Geopolitics and International Law through the Prism of Ideology

Confessing My Personal Biases

Having studied, taught and practised international law as well as politics and diplomacy for decades, I have noticed that, often, the more one emphasises the necessity of an objective and impartial approach to the study of social phenomena, including international law and politics, the less one is usually objective and impartial. It seems that only by recognising our inherent and inevitable subjectivity can we become slightly more objective, as complete objectivity is perhaps, in any case, beyond the human nature. Not only our backgrounds, but even the languages in which we think and/or write influence what or how we think, what kind of information we are able to use and tend to accept, and what kind we prefer to reject.

We are what we are due to our upbringing, education, culture and other similar factors. Our individual subjectivity inevitably imposes on our research, research that is supposed to be objective, and therefore I find it appropriate, though maybe unusual in academic research, to make my personal subjectivities and probable biases as clear as possible.

Having been conscripted against my own will into the Soviet Army from the Estonian countryside, I found myself, after many misadventures and adventures, at Moscow University, in the then-capital of the Soviet Union. I became a professor of international law there and later the head of the international law department in the Institute of State and Law of the Academy of Sciences of the USSR in Moscow, where during the years of *perestroika* and *glasnost* I also advised the Soviet leadership, including the first and last President of the USSR, Mikhail Gorbachev, onmatters of international law. About a year before the collapse of the Soviet Union, I returned to Estonia to help it regain its independence, working as the first Vice-Minister for Foreign Affairs. Being invited to the London School of Economics as Centennial Professor (the LSE celebrated its hundredth birthday at that time), I ended up at King's College, London, where I enjoyed teaching and writing until my mandatory retirement age (recently abolished). After a return to Tallinn I had some high administrative posts in universities and now I am wrapping up my career as a research professor at Tallinn University. Throughout this I have worked for the United Nations, being a member of the UN Human Rights Committee, and later had a stint as the UN's regional advisor for Central Asia – a region I had often visited before and since and where I have many friends. Having lived and worked at length in two imperial capitals – one being authoritarian, the other liberal-democratic – I may have absorbed some of the great-power arrogances and their visions of the world. However, being an Estonian, I am also familiar with smaller nations' sensitivities and fears; I understand their points, without necessarily sharing them. Moreover, by nature I am hetero, in the largest sense of the term, which means that I like various kinds of differences. However, I well understand that not everybody is, or even wants to be, like me, and there cannot be anything wrong with it. Having lived, studied and worked in different countries at length I have never felt the need to move in expat circles, as most expats usually do. Why be in Paris and look for Estonians to speak to? I am equally well enshrined in three cultures, which also means that, unfortunately, I am not completely at home in any of them. Moreover, today there is an intensive propaganda war ongoing between these very cultures; a war of such virulence that it forces most people to take sides. It is difficult to always remain unbiased, and it may not even be right to always remain neutral. However, if one is not impartial, how can one remain a researcher? In this book, this dilemma of taking the viewpoint of a researcher versus the position of an activist occasionally arises. If there is 'advocacy journalism', can there also be 'advocacy research'? And is this, in such a case, research?

However, there have always been those who, for whatever reasons, often inexplicable ones, have been able to rise above the circumstances, above the intellectual environment by which they have been surrounded. In the relatively freer West, there were naturally more of them, but there were also quite a few in the East. There were dissidents who were ready to go to prison for views that they often expressed clearly and loudly. There were also highly intellectual persons who articulated their individuality in a less radical way. At Moscow University one of these was my teacher, Professor Grigory Tunkin, about whom I recently published a small review article in the *American Journal of International Law*[1]. I recall a trait which I took away from my close association with him – sometimes, while sitting next to him during various academic discussions, when a speaker explained in the best Soviet tradition just how important his or her dissertation was for the promotion of the USSR's foreign policy interests, and also that this was the first time that so comprehensive a study of this topic had been carried out in the Soviet Union, he used to whisper, and I am not sure whether only to himself or for my ears too: 'it does not matter whether it is first done in the Soviet Union or not, what matters is whether it is true or not; only first in the world matters'. Of course, this does not mean that he had become unbiased. Soviet ideology, notwithstanding that Professor Tunkin had been exposed more than most Soviet scholars also to Western influence, had of course left an indelible imprint on him too. However, he certainly felt the need, if not to break the intellectual bubbles within which we all inevitably find ourselves, then at least to see beyond them.

Already during the changed political climate of the years of *perestroika* and *glasnost*, when I was leading a small working group of lawyers and historians on the legal status of the Kuril Islands in preparation for the 1990 visit of Mikhail Gorbachev to Tokyo, the Soviet leader said something like: 'I don't want the usual gibberish about "eternal Russian territories". I can talk like that myself. I need a memo where not only are our strong points emphasised, but where the arguments, which the Japanese may use, would be highlighted.' As a result, Gorbachev had a document where on the left-hand side of every page were both the strengths and the weaknesses of the arguments of the Soviet (now it would be Russian) position and, on the right-hand side, arguments favouring the Japanese. I do not know whether or how Gorbachev used this information, but I assume that during those talks in Tokyo he revealed to his hosts only what was on the left-hand side of the memo, but Japanese counter-arguments would not come, for him, as a complete surprise. Similarly, while practising law, representing the interests of our clients, we do not reveal to our opponents doubts which we may have on the validity, weight or persuasiveness of our arguments, hoping that they will not be good enough to find those weaknesses in our position. This is the lawyer's approach, where a lawyer first acts as a researcher, but then becomes an advocate.

But the approach of the academic researcher should be different. If there exists what is sometimes called 'advocacy journalism', which, in my opinion, though probably inevitable and sometimes even necessary, is regrettable, then 'advocacy research' is even more deplorable. However, taking into account how scientific research today is mostly funded, some kind of 'advocacy research' seems unavoidable. He who pays the piper also calls the tune. In social sciences, including international law studies, there is, however, an additional factor that gives to our work the characteristics of 'advocacy research'.

On Methods of Research in Social Sciences

Methods of research in social disciplines differ in many ways from those used in natural sciences, and this is understandable. The subject matter of the research dictates the tools and methods used in its analysis and not the other way around. Moreover, research tools are mostly invented, developed and perfected in the process of practical research and not *in abstract*. However, it should be advisable, even necessary, if the social scientists were to try to emulate the methods of the naturalists in at least one important respect – one should attempt to get as far away as possible from the viewpoint of an activist and as close as possible to the viewpoint of that of an impartial researcher. There are few chemists who have a favourite molecule, which they not only study but whose interests, wellbeing and importance they promote at the expense of other molecules. Having spoken on the matter with my natural science colleagues, this seems not to be the case, though even there the objectivity of the research is sometimes skewered to satisfy, for example, interests of either pharmaceutical companies or oilmen.

On the contrary, in the field of social studies, the opposite – that is, not taking sides – seems to be the exception. Too many social scientists seem to have their preferred 'molecules'. I am not speaking of those journalists who all too often have specific agendas that consist not so much of informing an audience as of mobilising public opinion. In the domain of social sciences, taking sides is widespread, almost automatic and subconscious, even among the best social scientists. For example, Paul Saunders – a clear-minded American analyst of the realist school, a critic of Obama's foreign policy – writes: 'What would a realist foreign-policy strategy look like? It would start with the recognition that maintaining America's international leadership – without incurring costs that neither our political system nor our economy can sustain – is the best way to protect US national interests.'[2] Hence, there is a clear agenda – to protect the US national interest, to maintain Washington's global leadership, that is, its dominance, in the world. There is a clear agenda that the 'research' has to justify, underpin and promote. This is exactly the same as it was with the academic research in the former Soviet Union, as described above. And this is so notwithstanding that Paul Saunders, in contradistinction to many other American authors, well understands that without taking account of the positions of the other powers, whose interests and visions of the world may not coincide with those of Washington, the United States can neither carry out its leadership, nor efficiently protect its national interests. Yet, many of those who call themselves, or are by their job description, 'researchers', are blatant activists or apologists. Their approaches are almost invariably either, say, pro-Palestinian or pro-Israeli, pro-Ukrainian or pro-Russian, pro-American or anti-American, pro-Serb or pro-Bosniak and so on and so forth. Moreover, such labels are often used *ad nauseam*, so that they start functioning like self-fulfilling prophecies even where they *ab initio* make little sense (e.g., the population of Ukraine was by mass media quite artificially divided into pro-Westerns and pro-Russians). The intentions of activists may be respectable and their moral outrages may be justified, or even necessary, but such positions are not those of the researcher. Of course, such activism sometimes helps change the world for the better. Often, however, it may lead people astray and contribute to the realisation of negative tendencies.

It has become a commonplace assertion that the first victim of war is the truth. The truth being the first victim of war may have had relatively little impact before the era of mass media. Today, however, the CNN phenomenon and then the internet have increased the importance of this, one may say preemptive, 'killing'. Psychological warfare and propaganda wars have become necessary concomitants of all conflicts; they precede and accompany them. As we discuss below, the warriors in propaganda wars are not all, and maybe not even mostly, cold-blooded manipulators. On the contrary, often they are sincere believers in the righteousness of their cause, like those naïve (from my subjective point of view) suicidal jihadists for whom 72 virgins wait in paradise. Exaggerating the enemies' brutality, demonising them and keeping silent on one's own atrocities, or more often those of unsavoury allies, are widely used tactics. As one example, the latest newspaper article I read on the war in Syria before I sat down to write these lines was an interview by a certain Ziad Majed in the French paper *L'Obs*. Mr Majed, whom the interviewer called a 'spécialiste', said, inter alia, that 'the opposition in Syria will never agree to the alliance with Bashar al-Assad, whose regime has killed more than 90% of the civilians in the conflict'.[3] Where do such numbers come from? Has there been a reasonable and impartial commission, where all sides have been equally represented, which had provided such figures? Can a critically minded person who knows anything about wars, especially civil wars, which are particularly brutal and where civilian casualties increasingly prevail, believe that one side indeed caused more than 90 per cent of the total civilian casualties? Although the Western media does not often show how Alawites, al-Assad's tribesman, are murdered, or how civilians are targeted by the opposition in the areas controlled by the government (a specialty of the Syrian and also Russian media), statements like that given by Mr Majed simply defy common sense. These uncritical figures are taken primarily from two sources – the Syrian Observatory for Human Rights (Mr Rami Abdulrahman in Coventry), and the Syrian Network for Human Rights (Mr Fadel Abdulghani). To believe them, not only is Bashar al-Assad evil incarnate (which he may well be, together with some of his opponents – rival civil war factions often deserve one another), but all of his opponents, even including al-Nusra and ISIS, are not so bad after all. If one were to believe Mr Majed, al-Nusra terrorists, though affiliated with al-Qaeda, are freedom-fighters since they are fighting alongside 'moderate' opposition, which in 2014 created the Army of Conquest to fight the government in Baghdad. There is no doubt that all sides in the Syrian conflict are guilty of targeting civilians. But as an article in the French *Libération*[4] confirms, statistics on casualties have mostly come from opponents of al-Assad's government, who started collecting data on victims of the regime (not on victims of the opposition) from the very start of the conflict. As the newspaper observes, 'for them it was also an information battle against the regime that was in denial of repressions'. At the same time, the Syrian Observatory for Human Rights, that is, Mr Rami Abdulrahman, who has been accused of trying to monopolise information sources coming from Syria, has claimed that 'information provided by other organizations had been either erroneous or unreliable'. Yet, notwithstanding all of this confusion, 'experts' still chime the mantra that more than 90 per cent of civilians in Syria are killed by the government, and newspapers in even liberal democracies which boast of their impartiality still republish such implausible claims. When, on 30 October 2016, the rebels against the government of Syria bombarded western Aleppo from the eastern part of the city, killing no less than 46 civilians, including 16 children, most Western information agencies condemning these unspeakable atrocities failed to mention who had committed the crime. Therefore, as Renaud Girard writes, most of the readers, viewers and listeners had an impression that it was done by the 'regime' or the Russians – the 'usual suspects'. The French journalist calls for putting an end to such a Manichean manipulation of journalism: where one side, in this case the government – named inevitably as the 'regime' – is evil, while the rebels are mostly considered as victims. He observes that though the President of Syria is a cruel dictator, 'in case of free elections he would, instead of having 90% of votes, most probably only 51%'. Such Manicheanism in journalism has an additional danger: it makes one believe that if somebody militarily destroyed a hated dictator, peace, liberty and prosperity would reign in places like Syria.[5]

Beside such obvious media support of one side of a conflict, there are subtler, more professional and therefore less obvious means of information manipulation. Often it is done by professional journalists and, hence, the term 'advocacy journalism' has emerged. There is probably no way of avoiding this in journalism. The worldview of journalists working for the *Guardian* in Britain or for *Libération* in France usually differs from the worldview of those who write for the *Daily Telegraph* or *Le Figaro*. Where we stand depends on where we sit, and even the best journalists not only record facts but also analyse and comment on them, and even then are often swayed by which facts they choose to use. Worryingly, there is a kind of advocacy journalism that may become really dangerous.

There are indeed situations where impartial and detached reporting may seem almost impossible, even immoral. For example, Christiane Amanpour, one of the most famous, and probably also one of the best, journalists in the world, once claimed: 'When you're neutral in a situation like Bosnia, you are an accomplice – an accomplice to genocide.'[6] Of course, from the standpoint of the law she was completely wrong, but from a more humane point of view one may understand her indignation. At the same time, as has been observed by some of her colleagues, 'Bosnia is also where she earned her mistrust of some of her colleagues. They complain that she oversteps the traditional bounds of objectivity and takes advantage of the freedom CNN gives her to bash whomever she considers guilty of that day's atrocities – in Bosnia usually the Serbs'.[7] Indeed, the Yugoslav wars of the 1990s, and especially the run-up to the NATO bombardment of Serbia over Kosovo, were accompanied by one of the most biased media coverages that free press has ever undertaken; it was like artillery fire in preparation of attack by the tanks and infantry. I do not use quotation marks for the words 'free press', since the best Western European media is still the freest available, which unfortunately does not mean that it is without bias. Such bias may come either automatically or through careful calculation. Sometimes accusing all sides in a bloody conflict of atrocities, which may more often than not be the case, can destroy any mobilising effect. On whose behalf to intervene, whom to bomb, if all sides are evil? Therefore, it is often felt necessary to single out a particular guilty party, whose crimes are meticulously recorded and reported, sometimes exaggerated, and where any benefit of the doubt is de-emphasised for the party who is *a priori* marked as guilty. At the same time, atrocities of the other party are either downplayed or justified as expressions of unavoidable frustration. And who to single out for condemnation and who to spare often depends on geopolitical calculations. As a short illustration, let us take the run-up to the NATO bombing of Serbia in 1999. First, there was a propaganda campaign to demonise one party and a concerted victimisation and sometimes even glorification of the other party. NATO's spokesperson, Jamie Shea, particularly excelled in this respect, as someone who later became known as NATO's 'spin doctor'.[8] While the atrocities of the Serbs were all meticulously reported (and there is no doubt that they did indeed occur), sometimes exaggerated, and any doubts as to the 'who' and 'how' were ignored, similar acts by the Kosovar Albanians, specifically of the KLA (the so-called Kosovo Liberation Army), which mirrored and often exceeded the atrocities of the Serbian side, were often downgraded or received only limited media coverage. And this was done notwithstanding that, shortly prior to NATO's Allied Force operation against Serbia, President Bill Clinton's special envoy to the Balkans, Robert Gelbard, had described the KLA as, 'without any questions, a terrorist group'.[9] The KLA had long been engaged in

> tit-for-tat attacks with Serbian nationalists in Kosovo, using reprisals against ethnic Albanians who 'collaborated' with the Serbian government, and bombing police stations and cafes known to be frequented by Serb officials, killing innocent civilians in the process. Most of its activities were funded by drug running, though its ties to community groups and Albanian exiles gave it local popularity.[10]

The then British Foreign Secretary, Robin Cook, told the House of Commons on 18 January 1999, only a couple of months before the NATO bombing operation against Serbia: 'On its part, the Kosovo Liberation Army has committed more breaches of the ceasefire, and until this weekend was responsible for more deaths, than the security forces. It must stop undermining the ceasefire and blocking political dialogue.'[11] Later, it was revealed by Gabriel Keller, a deputy head of the Kosovo Verification Mission (KVM), that:

> every pullback by the Yugoslav army or the Serbian police was followed by a movement forward by [KLA] forces [...] OSCE's presence compelled Serbian government forces to a certain restraint [...] and UCK [i.e., KLA] took advantage of this to consolidate its positions everywhere, continuing to smuggle arms from Albania, abducting and killing both civilians and military personnel, Albanians and Serbs alike.[12]

And yet, such revelations, from people who knew what was happening on the ground, were drowned in a sea of misinformation, sometimes true but often exaggerated, aimed at discrediting the Serbian side. It is not surprising that an entity created by way of illegal use of force by NATO acting in coordination with the KLA (being considered by the West earlier to be a terrorist organisation) and led today by warlords turned-'respectable'-politicians, is not at all, to put it mildly, a success story. Besides a multitude of internal problems tearing the society apart, it is also making a significant contribution to the spread of terrorism. As a French newspaper recently found: 'Surprisingly, with its 1.8 million inhabitants – 95% of whom are Muslims – Kosovo is the greatest European per capita contributor to ISIS. This extremism is to a great extent linked to the monies that came in the 2000s from the Gulf region, particularly from Saudi Arabia'.[13] That is why the world is in need of researchers who study, for example, states or other international actors as molecules, which may have different sizes, agendas and functions, but to which the researcher does not have any emotional attachment or revulsion. It is certainly difficult, for many impossible and for some even repulsive to have such a detached approach to morally and emotionally loaded issues, which indeed may call for action and mobilisation. However, there are usually enough, and often too many, activists for 'good' (and sometimes not so good) causes, but there are far fewer researchers in the field of social studies. Therefore, in my research I try, as much as possible, to approach all actors involved in different crises and conflicts as molecules, with roles, interests and versions that do not influence me emotionally.

Why International Law?

Why would one feel the need to analyse the interrelationships between these three phenomena – geopolitics, ideology and international law? What has made the study of the relationships between them not only necessary but also urgent? And why I? Why should I write on such a topic? Do I have the necessary qualifications for such multidisciplinary heavy lifting?

Such a study, as if both by definition and necessity, presumes an interdisciplinary approach. One may believe that such an endeavour has to be undertaken by a collective of experts or researchers, not by an individual author who certainly lacks a deep enough understanding of all the issues and problems that must be raised in such a wide-ranging work. And there is certainly quite a lot of merit in such an assertion. However, human beings are not yet able to meld their individual brains, as predicted by technological futurist Ray Kurzweil (now Director of Engineering at Google) in 'The Singularity is Near' and excitingly described by Ramez Naam in his science fiction trilogy *Nexus*, *Crux* and *Apex*. I would therefore agree with Ian Morris who, when introducing his inter- or rather multidisciplinary approach in the amazingly wide-ranging study *Why the West Rules – For Now*, makes a point that 'the interdisciplinary, single-author model probably is the worst way to write a book like this – except for all the other ways.

To me it certainly seems the least bad way to proceed'.[14] Of course, to carry out such an endeavour, one must not only read on a wide range of topics, but also communicate and discuss with colleagues from various domains. I have found discussions with colleagues from different countries, who specialise in various disciplines such as history, philosophy, international relations and even foreign languages, to be especially fruitful.

As to why international law is a focus of my study, the answer is relatively simple: for several decades I have been involved with this *métier* in various capacities as researcher, teacher and practitioner of law. I studied international law and started writing on it during the Cold War, which was a period of intensive geopolitical rivalry between the East (led by Moscow, sometimes in alliance with but more often in competition with Beijing) and the West (under the uncontested leadership of Washington, if not to count some aspects of the policies of the France of General de Gaulle). And of course, this rivalry was all explained and at the same time confused by the competition of the two ideologies – the liberal-democratic and free-market ideology versus the state-centred communist ideology – and international law was often used as an instrument of this ideological struggle. The geopolitical and ideological lines were clear and if you were not with us you were against us; no nuances were readily recognised or accepted, especially in the East.

There is no absolute truth; international law is full of uncertainties and ambiguities, and relative indeterminacy is one of its characteristics (otherwise international lawyers would soon be out of a job). International relations has been and remains a domain better epitomised by Niccolo Machiavelli and Thomas Hobbes than Immanuel Kant, though covered with a veneer of Lockeanism. However, it is still possible to, and there is a dire need to, study international phenomena, including their most important normative component – law – as impartially as possible.

In the last chapters of the book we will concentrate on some of the most important areas of international law, which today are under huge strain from current geopolitical rivalries. To find out why international law is not working as most of us would like it to, it is necessary to see through ideological fog, or, using John Rawls' famous thought experiment of moral philosophy inversely, not to stay behind but, on the contrary, to lift 'the veil of ignorance' that serves to hide geopolitical games where the actors use, among other tools, international law.

Why Geopolitics?

In his 2014 article in *Foreign Affairs* entitled 'The Return of Geopolitics', Walter Russell Mead writes that 'geopolitical rivalries have stormed back to center stage'.[15] As if the process of NATO enlargement, the bombing of Serbia over Kosovo in 1999 or the Georgia–Russia war of 2008 had all been something different, not related to or caused by geopolitical rivalries. 'Geopolitics is Back and Global Governance is Out'[16] was the title of the article by Stewart Patrick and Isabella Bennett published in May 2015 in *The National Interest*. They observe that, in its 2010 National Security Strategy, 'the White House described a new global era in which the primary objective of statecraft was no longer to temper geopolitical rivalry but to manage shared dilemmas of interdependence'. As the document had stated, 'Power, in an interconnected world, is no longer a zero-sum game.' Alas, lament the authors, 'neither the Russians nor the Chinese' (among others) got the word. 'From Eastern Europe to the Middle East to the South China Sea, great power frictions are not only exacerbating regional insecurity but also bleeding over into other realms, handicapping joint efforts to address transnational threats like cyber-insecurity.' Patrick and Bennett correctly single out and highlight the focal points of global geopolitical confrontations – Ukraine, the Middle East as a whole and Syria in particular, as well as the South China Sea and wider East Asia generally. However, can it really be so that it is only, or even mostly, the Russians and the Chinese who had not got the message? Or maybe they had got the message but not from the fine pronouncements of the National Security Strategy – rather, from deeds? Moreover, it is such sentiments, even if uttered sincerely (though not all politicians are always economical with the truth at all times and on all issues – one should always take their words 'with a pinch of salt'), but which gloss over actual or potential controversies in the hope that these are the words that influence the world and not the other way around, which first deceive those who utter them. For example, in his speech in Tallinn on 3 September 2014, President Obama, among many other things, declared that 'we reject any talk of spheres of influence today'.[17] This statement was especially well received by the audience in Estonia, and understandably so. This country, like quite a few of its neighbours, had not only and for some length been within the Soviet sphere of influence, but had been both occupied and annexed directly by it in 1940. However, this is only one side of the coin, or rather one face of a cube. Is it difficult to understand that today's Russia sees things, and not without reason, very differently? It sees that Estonia has become a small but active cogwheel in a huge military-political mechanism, which extends the sphere of American influence in Europe up to Russia's borders. Naturally, Washington does not acknowledge any rival spheres of influence, since for this 'indispensable nation' the whole world is the undivided sphere of its influence. And this is a matter of geopolitics that has to be explained and serviced by, and often hidden behind, an ideological veneer. Mathieu

Slama does not exaggerate when writing that 'what has to be understood is that the United States, like Russia, defends its conception of geopolitics that serves its interests: universalism for America and sovereignty and multilateralism for Russia'.[18] And to these two geopolitical interests correspond these two ideological visions: universalisation and increasing uniformity versus a world of multipolarity and sovereignty.

Returning to the title of Patrick and Bennett's article 'Geopolitics is Back and Global Governance is Out', mentioned above, it is necessary to understand that geopolitics has never left the scene, while global governance has been more of an idea or ideal – rather similar to the ideas propagated earlier by the World Federalist Movement, with the UN General Assembly as a world parliament and the Security Council as a world government – than a practical reality. There may be something close to this ideal of global governance at the regional, that is, European, level centred on the institutions and the law of the European Union. This is not to deny that in some specific, relatively narrow or politically less-sensitive areas we may allow ourselves to speak of global governance and, occasionally, when its permanent members have been able to put aside their particular ambitions, even the Security Council has risen to the level of responsibility that is expected from it. Also, it is hard to deny that the human rights movements, which today – due to the multitude of crises, many of which can be rightly defined as global – are undergoing difficult times, have had their successes, and the overall tendency in this field since World War II has been positive. Even international criminal justice, considered by many as one of the indicators or attributes of global governance, has become, since the end of the Cold War, a practical reality of international relations. However, notwithstanding some temporary early successes and unjustifiably high expectations (most of my students in London in the 1990s wanted to write their theses on international criminal law), the jurisprudence of nearly all international criminal jurisdictions testifies that international relations, due to their inherently political nature, are not ready (if they ever will be) for any significant criminalisation.

To an extent, the comprehensive and broad movement towards global governance, with its multitude of books and journals bearing the term, has been due to the expectation of a continuation of a unipolar world, one which existed in practice for a while in the 1990s. And though, as we will discuss further in the book, it is not at all excluded – and it is highly desirable that the world would be better governed, and that one day there would be much more global governance than today – geopolitics has never left the scene. In the 1990s we had geopolitics of a unipolar world, and now we have shifted into geopolitics under competing global visions (unipolar versus multipolar, homogeneous versus heterogeneous). So, what is this persistent phenomenon – geopolitics – which refuses to go away, which refuses to yield to global governance?

While working on this book, and having already published an article entitled 'Ideology, Geopolitics and International Law'[19], I still had doubts as to whether the term 'geopolitics' would be too narrow, too specific, even outdated (notwithstanding its declared forceful second coming), and therefore also somewhat misleading for the purposes of studying the relationships that international law has with ideology and the realities of international relations and politics; that is, with factors that at the end of the day determine the nature, potential and limits of international law.

In a way, international law is part of the reality of international relations, both in the sense of the influence that it wields or indeed because of the lack of its expected impact; it is also, as we will discuss in detail further, a part of the ideology that extends to these relations. In that respect, international law is a phenomenon that also belongs to both of the other two phenomena under study – geopolitics and ideology. In a sense, it also bridges them. Further reflection led me to the conclusion that notwithstanding all the limitations that all approaches and theories, including those that put geopolitics at the centre of their analysis, necessarily possess, and despite the baggage that the term 'geopolitics' carries from the past with some unsavoury names and unjust conquests, the term nevertheless well explains many facts, developments and tendencies in today's relations between states and other entities involved in international politics.

Let us take, as examples, some of the most prominent current or recent situations and conflicts where geopolitical explanations would have significant illuminating power: the tensions in South East Asia and specifically in the South China Sea between the United States and China, as well as the role of regional actors in these tensions; the 2008 armed conflict between Georgia and Russia in the Caucasus; the conflict in and around Ukraine; and of course the whole bundle of conflicts in the Middle East. Although in many of them personal ambitions, religious extremism, nationalism or simple human stupidity (*homo sum, humani nihil a me alienum puto*) have all contributed to the aggravation of situations pregnant with explosions, at the centre of all of them are geopolitical calculations (or miscalculations). Below, we will come back to these and other conflicts and discuss them in more detail. Here I would like to emphasise that geography – economic, physical and political – plays an important role in all of the above-mentioned situations. Had Georgia not been so close to Russia, Washington would not have given to it any more thought than to Western Samoa. Although Ukraine is much bigger than Georgia or Western Samoa, and therefore could be of interest to American businesses even if it were geographically placed elsewhere, its main strategic attraction to the United States is its location (as the estate agents in London emphasise, there are three factors to be taken account of when choosing your property: location, location, location). Zbigniew Brzezinski writes:

> Ukraine, a new and important space on the Eurasian chessboard, is a geopolitical pivot because its very existence as an independent country helps to transform Russia. Without Ukraine, Russia ceases to be a Eurasian empire. However, if Moscow regains control over Ukraine, with its 52 million people and major resources as well as access to the Black Sea, Russia automatically again regains the wherewithal to become a powerful imperial state, spanning Europe and Asia.[20]

Although the population of Ukraine is less than that (even before the loss of the Crimea), it is still a big enough country to not be neglected. But pay attention to the subtitle of Brzezinski's work – *American Primacy and its Geostrategic Imperatives*. It is not only that Russia should not control Ukraine (otherwise it would be, in the opinion of Brzezinski, an empire), but for the continuation of American primacy it is necessary that America controls Ukraine. The expansion of NATO after the end of the Cold War, the demise of the Warsaw Pact as the counter-balance to NATO in Europe and the collapse of the Soviet Union are also, in substance, geopolitical phenomena, and though the concept of the promotion of democracy and even theories of democratic peace have been used as justifications to NATO's expansion, these very rationalisations themselves reveal their supporting ideological roles in geopolitical expansions. Geopolitical expansions may take various forms, starting from the occupations and annexations of territories, through the creation of formal empires, varying in their formality, to the creation of military-political alliances ruled more or less from a single centre. The words 'empire', 'primacy', 'domination' and 'hegemony' may mean similar things, like 'zones of influence' or 'areas of vital interests'. The substantial point is that a strong Russia would necessarily extend its influence beyond its own borders, as does a strong United States and as will an increasingly powerful China. China's policies in the East and South China seas are not primarily economic, though this aspect is naturally present, but geopolitical – namely the 'access denial' strategies vis-à-vis the United States, whose 'pivot to Asia' is also guided primarily by geopolitical considerations and is principally aimed at Chinese containment. China's claims and actions in the South China Sea do not primarily target its overseas neighbours, and neither does China intend to impede freedom of navigation (it would only be natural that it should be China that would guarantee this in the South China Sea, not the United States). The main objective behind Chinese claims here is to counter American presence close to the Chinese mainland, which may become a potential existential threat for Beijing if Washington tries to militarily contain China's rise, not limited to economic matters.

Without a global geopolitical approach to the study of the conflicts and developments in the South China Sea, it would indeed seem that at the core of the situation are bilateral tensions between China and its South Asian neighbours. In this scenario Washington would indeed appear as an impartial mediator, concerned primarily with the peaceful resolution of these tensions and upholding the norms of the law of the sea, including the freedom of navigation. And clearly Washington would very much like the situation to be seen in such a light. Therefore, only by looking at the bigger picture can we see that the main problem does indeed lie in bilateral relations – not between China and its neighbours, but between a rising China and a United States trying to control and contain this rise.

The Chinese behaviour in this respect is similar to the United States' response to the attempt of Premier Khrushchev to introduce medium-range missiles with nuclear warheads to Cuba in 1962. Although the Soviet behaviour at that time did not breach any norms of international law, Washington considered the Soviet weapons and their adequate carriers to be a potential existential threat to America. In case of any serious crisis between the two superpowers, these missiles would have dangled as the sword of Damocles over Washington. Similarly, the Russian annexation of the Crimea in 2014 was carried out to a great extent because of the foreseeable risk of having American or NATO forces in the peninsula. Although there may not have been any intention on the part of Moscow to attack the United States from Cuba in 1962, or on the part of NATO to attack Moscow in 2014, intentions may change but geography remains. Jean-Yves Le Drian, the French Minister of Defence under François Hollande and Foreign Minister under Emmanuel Macron, believes that the 'denial of access' policy is one of those landmark evolutions that mark a change in the effectiveness of military power – change that favours non-Western countries vis-à-vis the militarily superior West. He writes: 'It is so already in the Baltic Sea and the Black Sea and in the seas surrounding the mainland of China, where local powers install sophisticated systems in order to make for Western countries the cost of the deployment of their forces, in case of crisis, prohibitively high'.[21] It is, indeed, all geopolitics.

There are many examples showing that geography matters not only in terms of international politics but also to the law itself. Let us take, for instance, the history of the emergence, practices and the legal status of exclusive economic zones. In the 1970s, the waters beyond territorial seas (today up to 12 nautical miles) were considered as 'high seas' open to all, not only for navigation but also for other uses and exploitations, including for economic purposes. Yet already then, some states, especially so-called 'developing countries' with long coastlines, near to the territorial waters of which the boats of more developed nations used to trawl, had started to claim and extend their own rights, even sovereignty (today these are considered 'sovereign rights'), and enforce them, far further away from their own coasts than was permitted by international law. Though developed countries with large fishing industries tried to counter these claims and protect the freedoms of the high seas (e.g., the famous 'Cod Wars', or 'militarised territorial disputes', as they in reality were, between the United Kingdom and Iceland), ultimately they were forced to give up their policies, notwithstanding the fact that they were, both economically and militarily, far superior to their counterparts. One of the reasons for such a retreat was geography. As these disputes concerned activities close to the coasts of developing countries and usually far away from those of economically developed fishing states, it was much costlier for the latter to enforce their rights than for the coastal states to enforce their claims, notwithstanding that they were made in violation of the then existing law of the sea.

Let us take another example. Although the United States militarily is still considerably more powerful than China, the 'denial of access' policy of the latter vis-à-vis Washington in the seas surrounding the Middle Kingdom seems to seriously worry Washington, and rightly so, since this policy is exercised by China close to its mainland and far away from the borders of the United States. Washington tries to compensate this geographic disadvantage not only by the presence of its Seventh Fleet at China's doorstep, but also by forming alliances with other states in the region. Finally, Ukraine is much closer in many respects, including geographically, to Russia than to the United States. Therefore, Russia needs spend far fewer resources to contain

Washington's advances there. For the same reason, Moscow has a much greater stake in Ukraine than does Washington.

In this book, I do not intend to concentrate on the history and definitions of geopolitics, though, obviously, some clarifications are necessary. In my opinion, geopolitics is one of the central and crucial characteristics and layers of international relations, as well as a certain prism through which to see and study those relations. As Pascal Boniface writes, 'geopolitics is one of the ways to understand the world'.[22] Dominique Moïsi defines geopolitics as 'a set of strategic, geographic and historical observations, reasonings and arguments that help us better understand conflicts'.[23] Although geopolitical approaches and explanations do not explain everything, their particular usefulness in the context of our study is, as we will discuss below, that the realities of geopolitics, that is, geopolitical reasons behind concrete foreign policy moves and acts, are often hidden behind ideological justifications, and even international law can be used to hide or justify geopolitical objectives and motivations. It has to be noted that, as we believe, no theory or approach can, on its own, explain complicated social phenomena comprehensively and, at the same time, precisely enough. David Deutsch was right in observing : '[W]e prefer simpler explanations to more complex ones. And we prefer explanations that are capable of accounting for detail and complexity to explanations that can account only for simple aspects of phenomena'.[24] However, at least in international law, and I believe in social sciences generally, there seems to be a kind of sliding scale: the more rigorous a theory the more it leaves unexplained, and the more comprehensive a theory the less rigorous, and therefore also of less valuable in practical terms, it becomes.Bertrand Russell analysed a somewhat similar problem in philosophy:

> No one has yet succeeded in inventing a philosophy at once credible and self-consistent. Locke aimed at credibility, and achieved it

> at the expense of consistency. Most of the great philosophers have done the opposite. A philosophy that is not self-consistent cannot be wholly true, but a philosophy which is self-consistent can very well be wholly false. The most fruitful philosophies have contained glaring inconsistencies, but for that very reason have been partially true.[25]

Therefore, we simply need more than one theory in order to explain and understand any complicated phenomenon. Different theories may be seen as petals of a flower which individually explain some aspects of complicated reality, be it international relations or international law, while at the centre of the flower there may be, not a grand 'theory of everything', but a capitulum on which different theories or theoretical approaches can find common ground. Therefore, a geopolitical approach to international relations and law should be complemented by other approaches and theories. Depending on time, space and issues to be explained, the relative significance and usability of specific approaches may vary. It is believed to be Johan Rudolf Kjellén, Professor of History and Political Science at the Universities of Göteborg and Uppsala, who was the first (in 1905) to use the term 'geopolitics'. Among those who were the pioneers of contributing to an elaboration of various aspects of geopolitical approaches to international relations were German Friedrich Ratzel (1844–1904), American Alfred Mahan (1840–1914) and Englishman Halford John Mackinder (1861–1947). The approach gained unsavoury connotations when Karl Haushofer (1869–1946) used geopolitical arguments to support and justify Nazi expansionism in Europe. Carl Schmitt (1888–1985), whom his detractors used to call the 'Crown Jurist of the Third Reich', in his *The Nomos of the Earth in the International Law of the Jus Publicum Europaeum*[26], which was published after World War II, also adhered to geopolitical explanations of both international relations and international law.

The end of the twentieth and the beginning of the twenty-first century has seen a revival of interest in Schmitt's writings. His critique and criticism of liberalism, and the last 100 pages of his *Nomos* specifically, have sometimes been used to attack American 'imperialism' in the post-Cold War world. Yet, others have denounced such attacks as superficial appropriations of Schmitt's ideas, while some still deny the relevance of these ideas on grounds that Schmitt, himself an advocate of imperialism, cannot at the same time be also a reliable critic of it.

Of course, in real life one does not necessarily exclude the other. The Russian pre-1917 international lawyer of Estonian origin Friedrich Martens was, at the turn of the twentieth century, an ardent enthusiast of Russian colonialism (imperialism), and also welcomed the 'white man's burden' in general terms.[27] At the same time, he was very critical of the 'excesses' of British, French and especially Portuguese, Belgian and Spanish colonialisms in Africa.[28] While greatly exaggerating the benefits of Russian colonialism, Martens was quite correct in his critical analysis of other states' imperial conquests. Similarly, Schmitt's controversial background, though it too must be taken into account where appropriate, should not be used to deny some of the deep insights of this original thinker, as well as their illuminating usefulness and explanatory value for the study of today's international relations, especially from the point of view of geopolitics. Being an anti-liberal and conservative thinker, Carl Schmitt extended his anti-liberalism and conservatism to international relations and law, particularly in his *Nomos*. For example, Anna Jurkevics, using Hannah Arendt's comments in the margins of her copy of the *Nomos*, argues that because of Schmitt's neglect of justice, and his emphasis on the role of conquest in the emergence of nomos (law), he himself was an imperialist, and as such was in contradiction with himself.[29]

However, even if all this were true, and there is certainly a lot of truth in it, this does not mean that there cannot be any 'scholarly use of Schmitt's conception of *nomos* as a tool of critique against an American "empire" in the post-9/11 era'.[30] Similarly, David Chandler, writing about what he calls 'the superficial nature of current uses of the work of Carl Schmitt'[31] believes that 'the management of inter-imperialist rivalry, the fundamental theme of Schmitt's *Nomos*, is not the dominant concern of the present'.[32] This is certainly not so, and already by 2008, when Chandler's article was published, one could discern what today has become quite obvious – American unipolar dominance is being challenged both in Europe and in Asia and we have already entered into a world of, if not an 'inter-imperialist rivalry', then at least one where the empire faces multiple challenges. Therefore, I tend to agree with Martti Koskenniemi's reading of the *Nomos*,[33] which questions: 'How should one, then, read *Nomos* in view of the present European-American controversy?'[34] And he responds: 'One alternative is to suggest that his critical analysis is largely correct. The United States is embarked on a morally inspired crusade, opposed by a Europe that invokes the formal law of sovereign equality under the United Nations Charter. There is undoubtedly something right in such an analysis'.[35] However, before quoting Koskenniemi further, a clarification is needed. Koskenniemi's article was published in 2004, during the period when, in the run-up to, during and after the American invasion of Iraq, Europe – at least what then US Secretary of Defence Donald Rumsfeld called the 'Old Europe' – was still strongly opposed to Washington's imperial ambitions. Today's Europe seems to be short of leaders who can say 'no' to Washington – an attribute President de Gaulle expected from those who sought to become his successors.[36] Challenges are mainly coming from China and Russia, who not only invoke formal principles enshrined in the UN Charter, but also take forceful steps to balance the power of the United States – steps that sometimes impinge upon international law. To counter such accusations, Russia has started referring to American justifications of Washington's (NATO's) violations to validate its own breaches, even though earlier Moscow had been the fiercest critic of the actions (e.g., the use of force against Serbia in 1999 in violation of international law) – it was only later that they became considered by the Kremlin as precedents justifying Russia's behaviour. Europe has not been so innocent itself either; already in 1999, NATO allies participated in the bombing of Serbia over Kosovo. Koskenniemi considers the *Nomos* to be 'less a history of international law, than political manifesto against the moralization of the warfare that Schmitt saw as a cynical instrument to justify the enormous destruction that Western technological superiority was inflicting on its adversaries'.[37] Of course, while Schmitt's nostalgia for a halcyon period of 'limited intra-European warfare' may only raise eyebrows today, one may nevertheless condemn 'a present period of hypocrisy and danger in which nothing stands in the way of the hegemonic pursuits of a single superpower'.[38] Indeed, is not the Schmittean 'friend–enemy' test reflected exactly in George W. Bush's famous 'you're either with us or against us'? Today it is France that seems to have become the Mecca of geopolitical studies. As Pascal Boniface writes, 'geopolitics has occupied the bookshelves in bookshops, in libraries; it is omnipresent on TV screens, newspapers and radio; it seems to be everywhere'.[39] It may indeed be that geopolitical explanations, shunned for years as something associated with, appropriated and abused by the Nazis, or considered by liberal thinkers as unbecoming (the belief that not mentioning something will make the unmentionable disappear), are today applied even there where they may not be the most appropriate.

However, geopolitics, as a practical reality of international relations, has never left us, and today, unlike during the idealistic 1990s, it has become much more difficult to conceal these realities behind well-meaning words.

Dominique Moïsi characterises the current geopolitical situation and challenges as follows: 'The feeling of chaos we experience vis-à-vis the lack of order in today's world is a result of the interaction of four phenomena'.[40] In his opinion, the first of these phenomena is the fact that for the first time since the middle of the eighteenth or maybe even the end of the sixteenth century, the West has lost its uncontested superiority, as well as its monopoly of being a single model for the rest. He specifies: 'The United States is not anymore able to play the role of the world gendarme while China is not ready and does not even desire to play such a role'.[41] Zhang Weiwei, a renowned Chinese intellectual and the former interpreter for the Chinese leader Deng Xiaoping, confirms the point: 'China is unlikely to enjoy policing the world together with the US, as doing so, from the Chinese point of view, tends to make enemies around the world and, furthermore, this does not fit the Chinese mentality or Chinese way of behaving'.[42] However, as Professor Zhang observes in his latest book:

> With the rise of China, Xi Jinping has gone from strategic ambiguity to strategic clarity on a number of key issues (such as the South China Sea, where China has engaged in land reclamation projects to advance territorial claims disputed by other countries). This is based on self-confidence, and also reflects the new consensus reached within China that with the rise of China, the country should be proactive in its strategic and foreign policy. In fact, many countries, including major Western ones, have expressed the hope that China take up more international responsibilities and provide more international public goods.[43]

The calls sometimes coming from the West that a stronger China will have to take on more responsibilities and behave like 'a responsible stakeholder', paraphrasing the then US Deputy Secretary of State Robert Zoellick[44], sound a bit disingenuous, since a strong China will inevitably have its own, and often, though not necessarily always, different from Western, understandings of the concept of 'a responsible stakeholder'. Hugh White is right that:

> we should not mistake China's reluctance to shoulder the burdens of leadership, as they are defined by Washington, for reluctance to exercise power in pursuit of its own agenda. From Beijing's perspective, Washington's definition of the responsibilities of leadership reflects American interests, not necessarily China's. China will not shoulder the burden of protecting the US-led international order where that does not suit its interests, but it will happily use its power to serve its own interests where it can. The Chinese are quite ready for prime-time, but they will sing their own song.[45]

The second phenomenon consists of the explosion of the Middle East and the implosion of several states in the region. The third is the return of a Russia that is taking revenge for recent humiliations. The fourth phenomenon is the lack, for various reasons, of political leadership in the West. Here, Moïsi, correctly, in my opinion, singles out one of the most serious deficiencies of liberal democracies – 'the characteristics that are necessary to become elected are not the same that are necessary to get things done'.[46] The problems of liberal democracies, as we will discuss below, are not, of course, limited to those related to endless elections (though there are whole books dedicated to the topic[47]). The problems are more general. But it is true that liberal democracies, as if by their very nature, have difficulty with producing political leaders who would possess both brain and spine when a crisis hits or radical changes are needed. Mathieu Slama, in writing on the popularity of President Putin, not only in Russia but in other parts of the world, observes: 'It is obvious that the success of Putin is to a great extent due to the fact that he represents a kind of political animal that has become extinct in Europe. Liberal democracies have this natural tendency – and this is a significant weakness – to build their politics on an essentially legal basis, to promote political managers who may be very competent but who lack symbolic, almost metaphysical, dimensions of power'.[48] If political managers may adapt to everyday management of well-running and stable societies, revolutionary times – and there is no doubt that we are in the middle of such a period – call for political leadership.

So, how could we define geopolitics? I think a single definition of the term is impossible, but there are several elements that most dealings with the matter cannot avoid. First of all, as the term indicates, it combines the notions of geography and politics; it is about international politics that takes geographical factors seriously. Alexander Orakhelashvili's remark that 'geopolitics is about projection of power in space'[49] is important as it combines both geography and politics. Pascal Boniface observes that the term 'has the merit of putting geographical factors in perspective. However, these factors should not lead us to geographical determinism'[50], he warns. And geography itself has a rather broad meaning. First of all, it combines size – both territorial and demographic – as well as location. Moreover, economic geography, including the presence or absence of natural resources, cannot be excluded from geopolitical analysis. Pascal Boniface is correct that 'the economic rivalries are an intrinsic part of geopolitical rivalries'.[51] Most importantly, geography means location. Tell me who your neighbours are, I will tell you who you are. Though this is not always true, geographical location from the point of view of geopolitics is not any less important than from the point of view of estate agents in London. Physical geography also plays an important role. Robert Kaplan is right that 'even if we can send satellites into the outer solar system – and even as financial markets and cyberspace know no boundaries – the Hindu Kush still constitutes a formidable barrier'.[52] It is also interesting to note that in Europe, after the end of the Cold War, acute military conflicts arose first in the two mountainous regions of the continent – the Balkans and the Caucasus.[53]

And yet, what is put in is not always more important than what is left out. So, is there anything important that is left out in a geopolitical approach? This approach concentrates attention on states, specifically the 'great powers', their influence and rivalry, and thus squarely belongs in the realm of realism within international relations studies. Despite its importance, it would be wrong to forget that there are other and differing approaches that do not necessarily contradict, but rather complement geopolitical studies, such as liberal international relations theories, constructivism and institutionalism, critical and feminist studies and so on. Of course, geography does not explain everything. North Korea's (DPRK) behaviour vis-à-vis its neighbours and the world community as a whole cannot be explained by its geography, though it also plays some role. In this case it is the characteristics of the political regime that are decisive in explaining the actions of this totalitarianism. Geopolitics, as one of the ways of looking at international relations, has limits that are inevitable, and necessary corollaries of its strengths. Other approaches complement and explain different facets of these relations.

In the light of the above, as well as having reflected upon different definitions of geopolitics, I would like to propose for the purposes of my own analysis the following working characterisation of geopolitics. Geopolitics is one of the central features and characteristics of international (interstate) relations, where geographical factors (location, size, resources and even landscape and climate) play significant roles in determining the foreign policy behaviours of states. Geopolitical rivalries or cooperation may have global dimensions even when playing out regionally, or taking place mostly at a regional level. This is primarily the domain of major and relatively independent players, though others often become involved in various capacities (usually as allies or 'bandwagoners'). Geopolitics is also a way of looking at and studying these relations when these features and characteristics are put at the centre of analysis. When using geopolitical approaches, it is necessary to bear in mind that there are also other approaches that may better highlight different aspects of the phenomena under study, yet when using other approaches, it must be kept in mind that geopolitics is always there, at least in the background.

Why Ideology?

Of course, everybody has an ideology, either as an eclectic sum or a more or less systematic set of opinions about ourselves, about the world and our place in it. *The Oxford Dictionary* defines ideology as 'a set of beliefs, especially one held by a particular group, that influences the way people behave'.[54] In that sense we are all ideologues, consciously or not, religious or secular or somewhere in between. In a way, all religions are transcendental ideological systems. Marxism has been a powerful secular ideology, one that is currently undeservedly suffering from its past and unwarranted 'success'. Today the dominant ideology is liberal democracy, and not only in the West. Religion, instead of withering away, as Marxism and other secular ideologies had predicted, is having its second coming. The 'opiate of the people' has always had its healing functions, if used in moderate doses, and yet it may poison and kill if consumed in excess. The same applies to all ideologies. Every ideological system strives towards purity and self-sufficiency; a certain rigidity is its necessary characteristic. Giving stability to our worldviews, and helping us avoid endless doubts in complicated situations, ideology, by making our choices easier, may also lead us to the wrong ones, for ourselves as well as for everybody else, especially when we are dealing with a topic such as international politics. In complicated situations which call for, often said yet rarely practised, 'outside-the-box' thinking, not only are facts often interpreted in the light of preconceived biases, but often facts that do not fit into these biases are simply ignored. Martin Seliger has defined ideology as 'a set of ideas by which men posit, explain, and justify ends and means of organized social action, irrespective of whether such action aims to preserve, amend, uproot, or rebuild a given order'.[55] This may be called a neutral definition of ideology. Marxists' approach to ideology as 'false consciousness' or Theodor Adorno's classification of ideology as 'a socially necessary illusion'[56] depict ideology as sets of ideas that are, as if by necessity, false but nevertheless widespread, persistent and dominant. Of course, dominant ideologies, be they dominant within a given society, within a group of societies or even in the world as a whole, are by definition dominant yet not necessarily or by definition false.

There are also non-dominant ideologies – ideologies whose aim is to get rid of a specific form of dominance (e.g., male dominance in many societies), or all and every form of dominance. Such ideologies are progressive and their aims are positive, yet this does not yet mean that they may not be false (or at least partly so). Moreover, as ideologies function in social, economic and especially political domains, the questions of their falsity or verity are often a relative issue. They either support or undermine certain positions and views on matters of great interest for substantial groups of people. Ideology starts playing a negative role when it replaces (and it practically always, at least at the end of the day, does replace) critical thinking, and people find themselves in an ideology trap where views are expressed, decisions endorsed and made not on the basis of facts, but on preconceived convictions that are considered inherently right, even sacred. In such cases, dominant ideologies serve as instruments in the perpetuation of dominance. Later in the book, we will see how these ideological battles transform into propaganda wars in international relations, affecting even such a seemingly neutral institution as international law.

During the Cold War, ideology played a significant role in international relations. Competing ideologies had to support, justify and explain geopolitical competition between the superpowers. However, even then its role was probably overrated. It was, as it still sometimes is, felt by 'us' necessary to be seen as oceans apart from 'them', though in reality we may have been much closer and more similar than we would have liked to think ('we' were not as perfect as 'we' thought and 'they' were not as evil as we depicted 'them'). Be it as it may, the Cold War's end seemed as though it would bring an end also to the confrontation of ideologies. However, today we see an intensification of clashes between different ideologies. For example, certain widespread denominations of Sunni Islam clash virulently not only with Shiʿa denominations, but with practically every non-Sunni (and even with other Sunni) worldviews. Whether the recognition of such a conflict contributes to its intensification, or, on the contrary, helps soften and overcome actual or potential clashes, is an issue discussed below. Here, I would like to concentrate shortly on the current ideological antagonism between the United States (to an extent also the West as a whole) and Russia.

Fyodor Lukyanov, editor-in-chief of *Russia in Global Affairs*, believes that between Russia and the United States 'there is no conceivable and structured ideological conflict but an acute irritation with each other that is combined with non-concurrence of their value systems and psychological perceptions'.[57] Indeed, though there is some non-overlap in the value systems of the majority of Russians and the majority of Americans, it is not as significant as the differences in the value systems between, say, the Americans and the Chinese, or particularly between the Americans and the Arabs in the Middle East (of course, here I am generalising and therefore also simplifying). In the case of American–Russian relations we have the worst kind of ideological struggle (mutual demonisation), whose main, if not only, purpose is to service their geopolitical rivalry. Hence, there we see the vilification of the opponent, information wars and needless verbal provocations, which make cooperation even on the most urgent issues extremely difficult, as every moderation, compromise and even the smallest attempts at cooperation are seen by extremists on both sides as concessions to the Devil. Certain trends towards ideological conservatism in today's Russia are to be seen, at least partly, as exaggerated attempts to mark and distinguish Russia's specific way of development from Western liberalism, and as a reaction not only to the West's geopolitical expansion, but also its attempts to impose its values (that are not necessarily alien for the majority of Russians) on Russia. Moscow blames the West, and particularly Europe, for abandoning its Christian values, and acting as though it is ashamed to recognise its Christian heritage (as Europe did, for example, when adopting the Treaty of Lisbon of 2007). Russia also criticises Europe for its excessive consumerism and tolerance of everything, including non-traditional sexual practices, but especially for its attempts to impose these values on others, including on itself. As Sergei Karaganov, one of Russia's eminent opinion formers, writes, Russia's ideological response in international relations to such attempts is 'the overall support for state sovereignty, cultural originality and uniqueness, an emphasis on pluralism that goes against the universalizing policies carried out by the West during the last decades with the aim of the creation of a universal ideology'.[58] French author Mathieu Slama is also of the opinion that 'it is clear that "Putinism" corresponds to a certain spirit of time, the spirit of resistance vis-à-vis excesses of globalisation'.[59] At the same time, comparing Vladimir Putin and Alexander Solzhenitsyn, Slama suggests that the prevailing ideology in Russia has deep roots in history and culture, and it rejects as alien those ideologies of Western origin – Marxism–Leninism and liberal democracy. However, today's Russia is more democratic than many in the West assume and arguably also no less democratic than it was during the chaotic years of Boris Yeltsin's presidency. Recently, Timothy Frye of Columbia University, in an article entitled 'Why IR Theory Gets Russia Wrong'[60] also, in my opinion, gets Russia very wrong. Writing that '*personalist non-democracies* [emphasis added] such as Russia were especially likely to experience rocky political transitions', he observes that nevertheless 'compared to other countries, Russia is too rich and well educated to be so non-democratic. A long line of research suggests that a country's income and education levels are correlated with the type of government'. The answer to this contradiction – a personalist non-democracy that possesses practically all the necessary conditions to be democracy – is that Russia is a democracy, just not a Western-style liberal democracy, and democracy that is too personalised in the person of President Putin. Both of these characteristics – a far lesser emphasis on liberal values, especially if compared with the West, and the personification of political authority – aptly correspond to the historical legacy of Russia and cannot be changed overnight, even if need be, though it is this personification of authority which may indeed create problems for Russia in the not-so-distant future. At the same time, neocons, and even some liberal interventionists, not only verbally attack Russia and demonise President Putin, but also criticised President Obama for being soft on America's 'enemies', Russia in particular. President Obama and his Secretary of State were accused by neocons at home as well as by all kinds of hawks abroad for not bombing Bashar al-Assad in Syria, for concluding a nuclear accord with Iran, for not being forceful enough with Russia in Ukraine. 'We are being completely outfoxed in Syria by Putin,' complained the former US ambassador Nicholas Burns. 'We are being humiliated. We've lost our strategic foothold, and we've abdicated our leadership.'[61] Another former US ambassador (to the United Nations), John Bolton, who became famous (infamous) by saying that cutting off 10 floors of the 38-storey UN building in Manhattan would not make any difference, agreed: 'Washington allowed this descent into chaos, despite its repeatedly proclaimed policy of removing Assad and aiding the moderate opposition, because to do anything meaningful to advance its policy would have endangered the precious nuclear negotiations with Iran'.[62] These neocon attacks, aimed primarily at Russia and China, but also against the policies of President Obama, were indicative of an ongoing ideological struggle turned propaganda war in international relations, which may be seen as a moralising crusade from which no president, whatever his or her personal preferences, can be completely free. In spring 2007, when Barack Obama was still a presidential candidate, I read that Reinhold Niebuhr was one of his favourate philosophers.[63] Then I too, though somewhat belatedly, discovered for myself this hugely original thinker. Although his *Irony of American History* may be of more direct relevance to those who study or practise international relations, I believe that his *Moral Man and Immoral Society* is no less illuminating to the field. Where the subject matter is the relations between nations (specifically chapter 4, 'The Morality of Nations'), it reads like a moral man writing about an amoral substance. Niebuhr writes: 'The selfishness of nations is proverbial'.[64] And he continues:

> Since there can be no ethical action without self-criticism, and no self-criticism without the rational capacity of self-transcendence, it is natural that national attitudes can hardly approximate the ethical [...] For self-criticism is a kind of inner disunity, which the feeble mind of nation finds difficulty in distinguishing from dangerous forms of inner conflict. So nations crucify their moral rebels with their criminals in the same Golgotha [...] While critical loyalty toward a community is not impossible, it is not easily achieved. It is therefore probably inevitable that every society should regard criticism as a proof of a want of loyalty.[65]

The reason for this, as Ernest Gellner put it, is that 'the political effectiveness of national sentiment would be much impaired if nationalists had as fine a sensibility to the wrongs committed by their nation as they have to those committed against it'.[66] I find the thought that the applicability of moral norms, which play an extremely important role in interpersonal relations, declines the further we move from inter-personal relations towards inter-communal relations, while international (interstate) relations are on the vanishing end of the applicability of norms of morality, extremely important. Therefore, the excessive use of moral arguments and justifications in international relations, though naturally not completely excluded, should always be taken with caution. The point is not that the concept of morality is not applicable in international relations, but that in this specific field moral arguments are far more often used naïvely or hypocritically than in personal relations. Moreover, the world is too complicated and colourful to be adequately expressed in black and white colours: democracy versus authoritarianism, absolute evil versus absolute good. The French philosopher Luc Ferry has recently written about current bloody conflicts:

> The truth, in contrast to what the majority of small-scale moralists think, is that many bloody conflicts in today's world are tragic in the sense of Greek tragedies where the opposing sides represent not of the good and the evil, right and wrong, but quite legitimate, though differing, claims. Had I been a Western Ukrainian of Polish origin, I would have probably wanted my country to join the European Union and even NATO. However, had I been from East Ukraine, from a Russian-speaking family, I would have almost certainly wanted my country to be closely attached to Russia. Had I been a Palestinian boy of fifteen from the occupied territories, I would without doubt be an anti-Semite; by contrast, an Israeli of the same age from Tel-Aviv would almost certainly despise Palestinian organisations.[67]

And though among the world's rich palette of ideologies, practices and trends there are also those that represent so-called absolute evil and deservedly call for moral outrage, most often in today's conflicts either between or within nations, rare are those where one is absolutely right while the other is absolutely wrong. At the time when I was writing these lines, both Russia and the United States had presidents – Vladimir Putin and Barack Obama – who were both strong leaders, clever and rational individuals, even sincere (to the extent a politician can afford to be sincere). Yet, they see the world in very different terms. They had differing visions of the past, present and desirable future of their own countries as well as the world as a whole. And it was normal since it was inevitable. Not only were their personal backgrounds different; neither were the domestic challenges facing their respective countries the same; and internationally, while the US tried to perpetuate the unipolar moment of the 1990s where Washington had been the unconditional leader of the world, Moscow was struggling to leave behind for good the humiliating 1990s, when the country was on the brink of not only losing its great power status but even existing as a sovereign state. What would be wrong is the burning desire to impose on others one's own understanding of the world. President Obama's favourite philosopher was certainly a realist in terms of international relations theory. At the same time, he was also a highly moral person. His criticism of Idealism and Idealists in foreign policy was not an exercise in cynical realpolitik; it was a criticism stemming not only from pragmatism, but also from the moral high ground. 'And the irony is increased', writes Niebuhr in *The Irony of American History*,[68]

> by the frantic efforts of our idealists to escape this hard reality by dreaming up schemes of an ideal world order which have no relevance to either of our present dangers or our urgent duties. Our dreams of bringing the whole human history under the control of the human will are ironically refuted by the fact that no group of idealists can easily move the pattern of history toward the desired goal of peace and justice. The recalcitrant forces in the historical drama have a power and persistence beyond our reckoning.[69]

And just how currently relevant and topical is the following observation:

> Today [the book was first published in 1952] the success of America in world politics depends upon its ability to establish community with many nations, despite the hazards created by pride of power on the one hand and the envy of the weak on the other. This success requires a modest awareness of the contingent elements in the values and ideals of our devotion, even when they appear to us to be universally valid; and a

> generous appreciation of the valid elements in the practices and institutions of other nations though they deviate from our own.[70]

It is difficult to tell how much of President Obama's relative moderation in matters of foreign policy, openly criticised by neocons and bemoaned by liberal interventionists, was due to Niebuhr's influence, or how much by the dictates of other factors and concerns. However, notwithstanding the pressure from Republican hawks or those abroad who would like to use the American military for their own ends, Obama did not easily yield to their provocations and demands. Instead of taking the Saudi king's advice, as revealed in American documents published by WikiLeaks, of 'cutting the head of the snake'[71], that is, attacking Iranian nuclear facilities, Obama directed the efforts which led to the establishment of the 5+1 nuclear deal with Iran. When President François Hollande of France, in the autumn of 2013, called for an attack on Syria over the alleged use of chemical weapons by the forces of Bashar al-Assad, after, in the opinion of the opponents of the government of Syria, the latter had crossed Obama's 'red line' in their use, the US president instead chose to enact Russia's proposal, leading to the destruction of Syria's arsenal of chemical weapons. Whether this decision was inspired by Reinhold Niebuhr, doubts as to who had used chemical weapons in Syria (it is still not confirmed that it was the forces of al-Assad, or that they had been the only ones who had done so), or understanding that attacking the governmental forces of Syria would primarily aid the jihadists to come to power in Syria, Barack Obama, in this case, behaved far more responsibly than hotheads in America, France or the Middle East willed him to do. One of the other reasons Obama did not rush into, and finally rejected, a military attack against the government of Syria was the absence of evidence for the suggested 'slam dunk'[72] scenario, whereby it had been troops loyal to President Bashar al-Assad that had used sarin gas against civilians in August 2013 in the Damascus suburb of Ghouta. As Jerry Goldberg writes, 'Obama was [...] unsettled by a surprise visit early in the week from James Clapper, his director of national intelligence, who interrupted the President's Daily Brief, the threat report Obama receives each morning from Clapper's analysts, to make clear that the intelligence on Syria's use of sarin gas, while robust, was not a "slam dunk"'.[73] After the Iraqi disaster, where the American, just like the British, intelligence community were coerced by political leadership to adopt 'dodgy dossiers' on the presence of weapons of mass destruction in Saddam's Iraq (it had been George Tenet, the then CIA Director, who had told George W. Bush that it was a 'slam dunk' case that Saddam Hussein possessed non-conventional weapons), it was understandable that the American intelligence services were not pleased with the prospect of being manipulated, once again, by trigger-happy neocons and liberal interventionists in order to drag America into another military adventure. Moreover, as Seymour M. Hersh, a veteran American investigative journalist, reported in April 2014, American intelligence officials had traced those attacks to radical jihadists in apparent collaboration with Turkish intelligence.[74] Another American investigative journalist, Robert Parry, who had broken the Iran–Contra affair under Ronald Reagan's watch, concludes:

> It's now clear that if Obama had launched a major bombing campaign against the Syrian military, he might have inadvertently cleared a path for Al Qaeda's Nusra Front or the Islamic State to seize control of Damascus, touching off an even more devastating human catastrophe. But 'regime change' in Syria was a neocon obsession, even if it carried the risk of terrorist groups gaining control of a major Middle Eastern nation.[75]

When in late autumn 2016 it was becoming clear that the troops of Bashar al-Assad, with the help of the Russian air force, would liberate Aleppo from terrorists and their so-called 'moderate' allies supported by the West, France tabled a Security Council resolution calling to end the bombardment of the Eastern Aleppo – the stronghold of the terrorists, referring to the humanitarian concerns. It was clear for every competent person that Russia could not afford to have such a resolution passed and therefore Moscow vetoed it. French scholar and reserve colonel Caroline Galactéros writes that the hastily tabled French draft was meant by Paris, London and Washington

> to fuel the international indignation against Moscow. The American request, made by means of the French proposal, to stop bombing Eastern Aleppo 'for humanitarian reasons' would have allowed the Islamists (al-Nusra and its allies) to consolidate their positions, serving the civilian population as human shield. Meanwhile they would have continued shelling the Western Aleppo and prevented Damascus and Moscow to radically change the balance power in their favour.[76]

And she adds: '"The West" is not waging war against the Sunni Islamism. It nourishes, advises and trains it'.[77] The victory of Donald Trump (notwithstanding, but in a way probably also due to, the media bias against the 'outsider' of the political elite) was a shock that, together with the June 2016 Brexit and similar developments in many, if not in most, European countries, reflects a revolutionary situation, as mentioned above, in liberal democracies. Likewise, there is a revolutionary situation also in international relations that started with the collapse of the bipolar world, went through the unipolar 'moment' of the 1990s and has now entered a much longer stage of the formation of a multipolar, balance-of-power world.

The gist of the crisis of liberal democracy consists in inherent dialectical controversies between liberalism and democracy, relationships that may be characterised as *frère–ennemi* relations. Already for decades, liberal elites in most Western countries have labelled those democrats whose policies (and/or personalities) they do not like as populists (let us recall that Ralf Dahrendorf has noted that, '*one man's populism* is another's *democracy*, and vice versa', though he has also claimed that 'while populism is simple, democracy is complicated'). At the same time, democrats (populists) call liberals arrogant elitists who are alienated from the people, from their needs and ways of thinking, consider them as losers and ill-informed (recall Hillary Clinton's characterisation, though later retracted, of Trump's supporters). And there is quite a lot of truth in both accusations. In a way, and simplifying a bit, both Brexit and Trump's victory are triumphs of populism over elitism (or, if you like, democracy over liberalism).

Although it may sound counter-intuitive, it seems that in foreign policy (if not in the doctrines, then at least in instincts), President Obama's successor Donald Trump is not so far away from his predecessor. The differences between Obama's foreign policy and the foreign policy orientations of Hillary Clinton, had she entered the White House as President, would in fact be more marked. Similarities between Obama and Trump are substantive, not in tone and style. In the latter, they are worlds apart. Trump's choice of Rex Tillerson – the former CEO of ExxonMobil Corporation – as Secretary of State is a sign that seems to indicate that, in the foreign policy of his administration, pragmatic calculations will prevail over behaviour driven by ideology.

Although the Democrats skilfully, though in vain, tried to play a 'Russian card' against Trump (can somebody of sound mind believe that Trump can be Putin's puppet or vice versa?), and Trump himself attacked Obama's foreign policy during the presidential campaign, what Trump has promised to do is in substance not so far apart from what Obama did or tried to do (clear exceptions being the Iran nuclear agreement and the attitude to the Paris climate deal – COP 21 – though even on these matters Trump may be, hopefully, forced to backtrack). As Leon Hadar put it in *The National Interest*,

> it is important to recognize that both the liberal internationalist Obama and conservative nationalist Trump are pragmatists and not ideologues by nature when it comes to foreign policy issues [...] They have rejected the grand Wilsonian designs of promoting democracy and nation building pursued by George W. Bush under the influence of his neoconservative advisors, and believe that Washington needs to readjust its global strategy to the changing international balance of power and under the pressure of diminishing economic and military resources.[78]

Renaud Girard observes in the same vein that 'in international politics, Donald Trump and Barack Obama have this in common: they are American nationalists who do not trust ideologies. Both are far away from the ideological neoconservatism of people like George W. Bush, who believe that the West can expand everywhere democracy, if necessary using military force'.[79] In that respect they both differ also from 'liberal interventionists', whose representative has been Hillary Clinton. While Obama gave his consent to the 2011 Libya intervention (mandated by the Security Council as a humanitarian action in its Resolution 1973 but carried out by NATO as a regime-change operation), he has later recognised it as his most serious foreign policy mistake.[80] Therefore one could only welcome the statement of the British Prime Minister Theresa May during her January 2017 US visit that there is no 'return to the failed policies of the past. The days of Britain and America intervening in sovereign countries in an attempt to remake the world in our own image are over.' Indeed, rejection of regime-change strategies would be better for America and for the world as well. Finally, it is obvious that Donald Trump, especially if compared with Hillary Clinton, has much less experience in the domain of international affairs. However, knowledge is not tantamount to understanding. Moreover, expert knowledge often comes with a price tag whose name is ideological indoctrination or self-indoctrination. Often experts know a lot but, carrying blinkers that have come in the form of the ideological wrappings of knowledge, understand very little. Was it knowledge or the lack of understanding of international affairs that forced Hillary Clinton as a senator in 2003 to vote for the invasion of Iraq – an act which became the biggest contributing factor in the emergence of ISIS – or as Secretary of State in 2011 leading 'from behind' the intervention in Libya with disastrous consequences, which we feel today and probably will even for years to come? To understand complex realities, knowledge must come from different sources. Open-mindedness and readiness to change one's mind are qualities more important than knowledge that may sometimes even serve as a blinder. Moral Realism, as advocated by Reinhold Niebuhr, not the moralising of *prêchi-prêcha*, as the French call it (though no politician, especially in liberal democracies, can completely avoid it[81]) that is often an expression of naïvety and/or cover for particular interests, would be an ideal towards which to strive in foreign policy. The call by the French thinker and journalist Renaud Girard that 'it is urgent that the West returns to realism in foreign policy' is critical indeed. And he questions: 'How many human lives we would have saved in the Middle East if the United States had not invaded Iraq in 2003 with the crazy idea of establishing democracy in the whole region'.[82] It reminds me of a piece of foreign policy analysis made by Condoleezza Rice in 2006, then the Secretary of State. Speaking of the developments in the Middle Eastern region, she claimed, without any sign of irony or hesitation in her voice, that 'what we're seeing here, in a sense, is the growing – the birth pangs of a new Middle East'.[83] Birth pangs indeed, but of what? Nothing turned out at all as she had predicted. Today, thousands upon thousands are continuing to die, not only in the Middle East but also Europe and elsewhere, as a result of these birth pangs. Has she, or anybody else, been held responsible, even if only politically and morally, for advocating and supporting these 'birth pangs', which have birthed but monsters? Condoleezza Rice, after being so terribly wrong in 2006 on Middle Eastern matters, nowadays – that is, in March 2016 – in a public lecture entitled *Challenges of a Changing World*, instead of covering her head with ashes, she teaches young Ukrainians in Kiev how to build democracy at home and fight the Russian aggression abroad.[84] And she is not an exception, but more a confirmation of the rule: right or wrong, but one of 'us' invariably ready to confront 'them'. The rule that is common in many societies, in the East and the West, in the North and the South.

Morality is an interpersonal phenomenon that may be extended to relations between larger human groups with difficulty. The larger the group the more challenging it becomes to speak of their relationships in moral terms. Attempts to do so are often caused by a mixture of hypocrisy and naïvety. 'All nations are tempted – and few have been willing to resist the temptation for long – to clothe their own particular aspirations and actions in the moral purposes of the universe'[85], wrote Hans Morgenthau. And Robert Kaplan believes that 'simply because a nation is a democracy does not mean that its foreign policy will necessarily turn out to be better or more enlightened than that of a dictatorship'.[86] In his opinion, 'the tendency to dominate is a natural element of all human interactions'.[87] If morality is a concept and behaviour in interpersonal relationships, then the further we go from interpersonal relationships into inter-group relationships, the less room is there for morality. Something similar is happening with the concept of democracy. Democracy is a concept and set of practices of political communities, primarily states; its applicability to inter-state relations is also rather questionable. Morality does not necessarily flourish better in democracies than under authoritarianisms, though there is a difference. If in democracies morality is more often than not diluted by the hypocrisies of elites, in dictatorships moral relationships are often brutally suppressed, and therefore also distorted. Inter-state relations are the relations that are the furthest away from the applicability of concepts of both morality and democracy. As we will discuss in some detail below, the closest we get to the notions of democracy, and in a way also to morality, in international relations is through the recourse to the concept of the balance of power. As the democracy deficit within the European Union – a relatively close-knit community of liberal democracies – shows, it is difficult to extrapolate to larger and more heterogeneous entities the concept of democracy, elaborated for small and relatively homogenous communities, that is, nation-states. Such an admission would also be moral, since it is further away from naïvety and less covered by the fog of hypocrisy. The British referendum of 23 June 2016, where the majority of the electors (51.9 per cent for Brexit, 48.1 per cent against) chose to vote for leaving the European Union, and the repercussions of this momentous event all over Europe reveal *inter alia* the absence of democracy within the EU and the alienation of not only the so-called unelected Brussels bureaucrats from the peoples of Europe but a serious rift between the political elites and the majority of people in most European liberal democracies. As Alexis Brezet, the editor-in-chief of *Le Figaro*, writes, 'the Brexit demonstrates that Europe has to recreate itself, change its governance, policies and philosophy'.[88] One interesting and important practical question is whether authors like Niccolo Machiavelli, Thomas Hobbes or Samuel Huntington, who have been criticised for being on the 'wrong' side of history, having concentrated their attention on the negative aspects of the phenomena they studied, have in some way also contributed to the perpetuation of these negativities, and whether optimists, like John Locke or the early Francis Fukuyama, who concentrated their attention on the positive aspects of and potentials in social realities, have also contributed more to the advancement of positive changes in practice. Or, to put it differently, do theories that concentrate on positivities and avoid, if not discounting then at least not emphasising, negativities contribute more to the betterment of the world? Does depicting the world as it is also contribute to its perpetuation? Or does elaborating and promoting utopian scenarios contribute to their realisation in practice? Did Huntington's belief in the coming clash of civilisations, which was meant to replace the militarised ideological stand-off between two competing social systems, contribute to the emergence of the clash itself as a kind of self-fulfilling prophecy? Or maybe, on the contrary, could Huntington's vision have served as a warning to help avoid the undesirable, yet possible and foreseeable? Is somebody Machiavellian because the world is Machiavellian or is the world Machiavellian because there are too many Machiavellians in the world?

I have no definitive answers to these questions. And probably they do not even exist. The world needs utopians, who see opportunities that others do not, and it needs realists that see the world as it is, not necessarily approvingly. Unfortunately, the domain of international relations is more Machiavellian than Lockean, and therefore a geopolitical analysis which looks beyond ideological fig leaves, revealing that which actors endeavour to conceal behind words, strongly contributes to an effective functioning of international law.

Chapter 2

Processes of Homogenisation and Heterogenisation in the World

Hegemonic Ideology in the Service of Geopolitical Domination

'The construction of hegemonic ideology is usually central to projecting dominance into the future, and multilateral institutions are often very useful for this purpose',[1] writes Nico Krisch. In his article, Krisch concentrates on the use of international law as a multilateral institution for the construction and spread of hegemonic or dominant ideology. In the latter chapters of this book we will return to the issue of the use (and abuse) of international law for the purposes of dominance, as well as for challenging dominance in international relations. Here, however, we would like to concentrate on some more general issues regarding ideology in service of geopolitical dominance. Dominance is rarely voluntarily accepted, especially if it is not depicted as inevitable, natural and necessary – and not only by those who dominate but, and particularly, by those who are dominated – a kind of 'white man's burden' for all of humanity. For dominance to be effective, it is indeed not sufficient that it be accepted as natural within societies that are dominant internationally. For example, the British educational system and mass media in the nineteenth century were very successful in fostering an atmosphere of the natural superiority of what the Americans started calling the WASPs (white, Anglo-Saxon, Protestant males) over everybody else in the world. However, such an ideology had little chance of being spread and adopted among the peoples of the colonies, be it in Asia among the peoples of the Indian Raj or in Africa. There was, nonetheless, a segment of the population in practically all of the colonies which considered that, by becoming more like their white colonisers, they would at least be superior vis-à-vis their own compatriots, even if never equalling their colonisers in status.

The French philosopher Alain Badiou was not wrong when he discovered some of the roots of our current wave of terrorism in the subjective division of some parts of the world population into three groups or categories: the Western civilised middle class – the liberal-democratic group that still thinks itself superior, but is afraid of losing its privileges and more comfortable lifestyle; those desiring to live like Westerners (*le désir d'Occident*) – desperate to imitate the Western lifestyle; and 'fascist nihilists', who envy the West but, being unable to find a place within it, end up as destructive, and self-destructive, hating all things Western.[2] Hence, the dominance, as well as the desire of the dominated to join or replace the dominators, are all potentially destructive phenomena which sooner or later tend to explode.

The racist ideologies of the Nazis had even less chance of being accepted by those who were not considered 'Arian' than the ideologies of the colonisers, although there were even quite a few individuals among those nations which were considered as being amenable to 'arianisation' who more or less voluntarily accepted Nazi dominance. All such exclusivist ideologies shared by politically dominant groups had little chances of becoming widespread; and they did not even have the pretence of universality – they were not even meant to be universalisable. However, there have been, and there are, different dominant ideologies that are intended to be universal, and which in the appropriate circumstances may indeed become widespread and accepted by all peoples. This is true for proselytising missionary monotheistic religions, as well as for certain secular ideological systems.

During the Cold War, there were two competing secular ideologies that were meant, *inter alia*, to service the geopolitical competition between the two superpowers. These ideologies – liberal-democratic free-market and communist – were both universalising, proselytising, missionary and potentially non-exclusivist. After the collapse of the USSR, only one of them remained, since China, though ruled by the Chinese Communist Party, had in reality become a capitalist economy. Although China's capitalism differs considerably with its Western variant, China has not shown any signs of trying to spread its ideology beyond its borders. Liberal-democratic ideology, servicing the geopolitical interests of the only remaining superpower and its allies, on the contrary, has attempted to spread forth as the only and uniquely correct way of being; all others being 'on the wrong side of history'.

However, because of both its links with dominance, and the natural survivalist instincts of other ideologies and their carriers, this dominant ideology soon began to face challenges from various rivals. If the dominant ideology had little chance of being widely accepted, albeit for different reasons, in China or in the Middle East, Russia attempted in the 1990s to follow the Western ideological model. It is possible to understand the reasoning – Russia, geographically a Eurasian power (probably the only genuinely Eurasian country), is culturally largely a European nation. The Europhilic tendencies in Russian culture have traditionally been strong, and the first (and the last) President of the Soviet Union, Mikhail Gorbachev, often spoke of a 'common European house' stretching from Lisbon to Vladivostok. Similarly, President Putin has more than once, especially during his first two presidential terms, spoken of Russia as a European country, as of a country of European traditions.[3] Hence the acceptance of liberal-democratic ideas and market reforms came relatively easily to Russian society. However, as this dominant ideology was linked to, and serviced by, the geopolitical hegemony of the United States, and the reforms emanating from the ideology were brutally, inconsiderately and thoughtlessly implemented (the so-called 'shock-therapy'), their failure and the backlash that followed were almost inevitable. As Zhang Weiwei, one of the foremost contemporary Chinese thinkers, observes: 'The shock therapy by the US in Russia is now widely viewed by the Russians as the "third catastrophe" (the earlier ones being the Mongol invasion in the 13th century and the Nazi invasion during the Second World War)'.[4] Russian political scientist Sergei Karaganov believes that 'the West in its euphoria of the victory in the Cold War started imposing, sometimes by force, its policies and values (Afghanistan, Iraq, Libya) and lost. The support for the "Arab spring" even more destabilised the Middle East and as a consequence also diminished the attractiveness of democracy'.[5] Indeed, in the Russia of the 1990s there was no therapy, only shock, and it almost killed the patient. This is why Russia today is challenging American dominance, and why Moscow attempts to contain and roll back NATO's advance, both military-strategically and ideologically. This is also why the Russian political elite is currently trying to find intellectual inspiration in the writings of those philosophers who did not belong to the *Pléiade* of Europhiles.[6] The return to so-called 'traditional values', and the increasing role of the Russian Orthodox Church in Russian society, enact the same ideological purposes of countering the dominant Western liberal-democratic narrative. Here, the ideological transformations in Russia go hand-in-hand with, and are pushed by, the efforts of the West, and specifically of the United States, to coerce Russia not only to accept the dominant narrative, but also to follow Washington's lead on political, economic and military matters. One liberal Russian thinker (not the same thing as a Western-style liberal), Dmitri Trenin – the Director of the Moscow Carnegie Centre – recently well summarised the current and possibly future trends of his country's evolution (and God help us avoid revolutions, whatever be their colour):

> The guiding idea for Russia, which until recently has been a European idea, has to be replaced by a Russian national idea that does not at all mean self-isolation (*repli sur soi*) or a return to old roots. The idea has to be national, since individualism, notwithstanding its importance as an engine of progress, cannot be absolutized. Big collectivities of human beings – peoples, nations – remain significant actors of global politics. States, particularly big and independent ones, continue to be the principal elements of international society. The national idea of Russia in the most general terms is an idea of an independent and self-sufficient country having its own specific place in a global world and guaranteeing the security of and decent quality of life for its citizens and being able to produce global and regional goods.[7]

Russia's assertiveness in its foreign policy and increasing authoritarianism at home are, to a great extent, conditioned by and are responses to Western, particularly American, attempts to coerce Russia to follow the line drawn in Washington. Such attempts are often counter-productive, especially vis-à-vis great powers. The following anecdotal episode is indicative in that respect. One of President George W. Bush's assistants had explained to Ron Suskind, an American journalist and best-selling author, how reality is created in today's world: 'We're an empire now, and when we act, we create our own reality. And while you're studying that reality – judiciously, as you will – we'll act again, creating other new realities, which you can study too, and that's how things will sort out. We're history's actors [...] and you, all of you, will be left to just study what we do.'[8] This statement is not only arrogant, but also illusory, as Washington's ability to control and guide realities, even those unleashed by its own hand, is rapidly diminishing; at best it may have characterised a rather short unipolar moment[9] which followed the demise of the Soviet Union. Though the manner in which the assistant phrased it is an expression of extreme arrogance combined with ignorance and naïvety, many intelligent and knowledgeable Americans share the thought process. In the summer of 2012, for example, the *International Herald Tribune* published an article by Yale law professor John Fabian Witt, 'The Legal Fog between War and Peace.' In the article, the author, among many interesting and knowledgeable insights into the use of unmanned drones, also wrote: 'Inside the United States Government, lawyers like Jeh C. Johnson in the Pentagon and Harold Koh in the State Department, along with hundreds of other lawyers in the Justice Department, the White House and elsewhere, are creating new systems for regulating the targeting process'.[10] I personally know well and hold in great esteem Yale Professor Harold Hongju Koh – who at the time was the State Department Legal Advisor – and do not think that he, even if together with his colleagues from the State, Defence and Justice Departments, was creating *international* legal rules for drone targeting (and Professor Witt's article is about international law). Harold is too clever and professional for that. But if Professor Witt does not mean by 'and elsewhere' the foreign, defence and justice ministries of China, Russia, France, Germany, Brazil and many other countries, which have not delegated to the government of the United States the onerous task of legislating international law for the whole world, his comment – in substance, though not necessarily in tone – differs little from what President George W. Bush's aide had told Ron Suskind. Such a mindset is not harmless, and though it may sometimes indeed help to create new realities, they often have nothing in common with what even Washington would have intended to create.

The American Dream for the Whole World

Many nations, both big and small, have their own dreams. In China today they often speak of a Chinese dream, and everybody has, of course, heard of the American dream. However, since the collapse of the Soviet Union, there is only one nation in the world whose dream is dreamt for everybody (discounting so-called Islamic State's dream of Islamisation of the world). In all US national security projections, the emphasis is on the continuation and strengthening of American supremacy, the perpetuation of the dominance of the United States[11] – but at the same time there is a genuine belief by many, both within the political elite as well as among ordinary Americans, that such dominance is good for the planet and for all societies, as long as they 'correctly' understand their own interests, provided they have the 'right' understanding of the good and the bad. If the American 'Manifest Destiny' of the nineteenth century was an ideological tool that justified and led the territorial expansion on the North American continent, the current 'manifest destiny', having mostly exhausted its nineteenth-century territorial component, is directed towards the expansion of the American way of life, and by extension American interests all over the world. All recent US national security strategies are based on the assumption of continuing American economic and military superiority, which should help Washington shape the world and not be shaped by it; no strategic competitor is allowed to rise.[12]

The collapse of the Soviet Union and the end of the bipolar world created a situation that had never existed before. Of course, there had been dominant powers before, but their hegemony had always been limited geographically. The empires of Alexander the Great or Rome may have dominated almost all territories that were known or that mattered, but they all still controlled less than a tenth of the world. The British dominance of the nineteenth century was not only constantly contested, especially in Europe, but also relatively limited geographically, even though it may have been true that the sun never set on the British Empire. The Cold War period saw probably the greatest territorial expansion of hegemonic dominance the world had ever seen. But this was a duopoly – the two hegemonic powers shared, though reluctantly, their self-proclaimed 'responsibilities' for world order. And even then there were contested territories (Afghanistan, Korea or Vietnam), as well as territories that simply didn't matter much. Today, for the first time in the history of humankind, a single power intends to dominate the planet.

'All presidents from both political parties have proclaimed the applicability of American principles to the entire world'[13], writes Henry Kissinger. So, in his 1993 address to the United Nations General Assembly, President Bill Clinton expressed no doubts in claiming that 'Our overriding purpose must be to expand and strengthen the world's community of market-based democracies' because the principles of political and economic liberty were universal 'from Poland to Eritrea, from Guatemala to South Korea' and their spread would require no force.[14] Developments in different parts of the world soon showed President Clinton's generalisations to be both naïve and arrogant. It would be almost funny had it not been so sad that Eritrea, being so optimistically, even if only in passing, mentioned by Bill Clinton in his UN speech, and having only just seceded from Ethiopia, became one of the most totalitarian and repressive states in the whole world, today competing with war-torn Syria and other hot-spots in sending refugees to Europe.

The Geopolitics of Attempts to Create a Uniform World Led from One Centre

After the collapse of the Soviet Union and end of the bipolar world, where both the United States and the Soviet Union had aspired for a worldwide hegemony, Washington sought to create a world in which there would be only one superpower, one indispensable leader. If the Soviet Union, in trying to extend its domination, was driven primarily by ideological considerations – it tried to convert the dominated (even domination was subordinate to conversion) into socialists and communists – the United States cared much less about the convictions of their followers. In contradistinction to the United States, or to Czarist Russia for that matter, Soviet foreign policy did not, and even was not meant to, serve the immediate economic interests of the USSR; on the contrary, more often than not, Soviet foreign policy was a significant burden on its economy. Soviet expansionism was motivated primarily by political, military-strategic, and most importantly ideological considerations. Eastern European 'people's democracies', firmly under Soviet control, and especially the so-called 'countries of socialist orientation' (Cuba, Angola, Mozambique, Mongolia and Vietnam),with their Soviet-imposed, artificial, ineffective planned economies, were much more of a drain on Soviet resources than a source of any profit. However, for the Kremlin, it was not profit, but the spread of socialist ideology and Soviet political influence that was the primary motivation of its foreign policy. This may also partly explain why America had more allies than the Soviet Union. Washington not only had like-minded partners in Europe, but also buddies whose values and worldviews were light-years away from the values propagated by the Americans. Such differing accents between the foreign policies of the United States and the Soviet Union may be explained by differences in their socioeconomic systems – the former was, and is, a capitalist, market-oriented system; the latter was a totalitarian, ideologically and politically oriented system. Simplifying slightly, we may say that if the former makes money by using all available means, including any political and military tools at their disposal, the latter spends money in order to gain long-term political and ideological influence. The ideology of the Soviet Union was a utopian and warped one, that sought to ultimately make the whole world communist. In doing so it often acted counter-productively to its real material needs by imposing its own ineffective political and economic systems on its client regimes in Eastern Europe, Asia, Latin America and Africa, which Moscow supported and maintained at the expense of billions of dollars. After its collapse, Russia seems to have learned the lesson. Today it more or less tries to act in accordance with its national interests (as they are understood by the Kremlin, of course), and it is more often than not the United States, together with its allies, which is carried by ideological zeal (though if you scratch ideological slogans deep enough you will always discover tangible economic interests). However, a small caveat may be necessary. Russia, as a country of state capitalism, sometimes subordinates the interests of her private capital to the interests of the capitalist state as a whole, as they are understood and defined by those in the Kremlin. If in Russia, *grosso modo* and, with some exceptions, the Kremlin dominates Russian capitalists (what is good for the Kremlin is good for Russia), in America, it is big business and financial capital that controls the White House and Capitol Hill (what is good for Ford is good for America).

It is not only interesting but also important to emphasise that today the only power striving for global dominance – the United States – has become as, if not more, ideological than the USSR was at its most. Washington seeks to not only create one world led from one centre, but a world that conforms to the currently dominant economic, political and social system (though it may well be that after the ambiguities of the 'Arab Spring', as well as the doomed efforts to liberalise and democratise Afghanistan, the American political elite will become less enthusiastic about pushing ahead with these uniforming aspect of its 'global dream'). Stephen Kinzer makes a valid point in observing that 'spreading democracy, Christianising heathen nations, building a strong navy, establishing military bases around the world, and bringing foreign governments under American control were never ends in themselves. They were ways for the United States to assure itself access to the markets, resources, and investment potential of distant lands.'[15] Today we may also observe that Washington's ultimate aims when promoting democracy in different parts of the world and effecting regime change are primarily economic. It remains to be seen whether the relative moderation ofPresident Obama (relative only to his predecessors – that is to say, Presidents Clinton and George W. Bush) in matters of regime change and the pragmatism of President Trump and his foreign policy team, led by Rex Tillerson, will manifest a trend of reaching an understanding that the world is too big and too diverse to be governed from one centre. Such a turn would be beneficial both for the world and for the United States of America.

In the 1990s, there was an attempt, though not a very committed one (at least nothing close to the efforts spent on the Marshall Plan), to integrate Russia into an American-led international order, to persuade and even force it to follow Washington in its foreign policies and to conform to American ideals in its domestic affairs. These efforts failed not only because they were not undertaken seriously enough by the West, but more because countries such as Russia cannot be integrated into an international system in terms that are prescribed by the self-proclaimed integrator. British expert Richard Sakwa wrote as far back as 2008: 'The international system today does not have a mechanism for integrating rising great powers. This applies to China, as well as to Russia and some other countries'.[16] I believe there is a deep truth in this remark, which is not only limited to countries as big as Russia or China. Although Russia is culturally much closer to the West than the Middle Kingdom, and Russia's history has, for many centuries, been one of European history, it cannot be integrated into existing European structures in terms prescribed by the structures themselves. If I were allowed to use French, which, like Russian but unlike English has *les verbes pronominaux* (возвратые глаголы) it would be better to say that *La Russie doit plutôt s'intégrée qu'être intégré* (Россия должна скорее интегрироваться, чем быть интегрирована). That is to say, the conditions of its integration should have been negotiated as between equal partners, and not imposed on a 'take-it-or-leave-it' basis. The Chinese intellectual Zhang Weiwei has, for example, written that China as a civilisational state 'has exceedingly strong and historic cultural traditions. It does not easily imitate or follow other models, be they Western or otherwise [...] A civilizational state can exist and evolve independently of endorsement or acknowledgement from others'.[17] Moreover, he observes that 'if a civilizational state like China follows the Western model, the country will experience chaos and break up. Indeed, in retrospect, if China had followed the Western model rather than adhering to its own path, the country could have disintegrated just like the Soviet Union and Yugoslavia'.[18]

In the same vein, Vladimir Putin in his 2012 pre-election article wrote that 'Russia has practically always had the privilege of pursuing an independent foreign policy and this is how it will be in the future'.[19] Such a statement, and noting the words 'practically always', may have been a response to President Yeltsin's failed attempts to have Russia accepted by Washington, and by the West in general, as an equal and independent player that may possess its own interests, but that could nevertheless be a partner of, and on good terms with, Washington and Brussels. This remark also expresses the truth that nations react differently to attempts to 'civilise' them, to induce them to correspond to the dominant trend. Quite a few follow the lead happily, while others do so only grudgingly, whereas some still become prickly, and pushing them would be counter-productive. One could have hardly expected Russia to exercise the politics of bandwagoning, which many smaller states have happily (or not so happily) done and continue to do today. Dmitri Trenin writes that

> in principle, a country of the level of economic, social and political development of Russia is able to become integrated into the contemporary Western world if one of the main conditions is met, that is, if there is the consent of the elites as well as the majority of the population to be assimilated into the extended West under the aegis of the 'grown-ups', i.e. of the US, EU, NATO, and remaining at the periphery of the system.[20]

Knowing Russia, one can only agree with Dmitri Trenin in that if such a choice were possible and realistic for the countries of Central and Eastern Europe, and in principle for Georgia,

Moldova and even for Ukraine, 'for Russia, taking account of her size, imperial past and inherited mentality of her elites as well as the majority of the population' such an integration/ assimilation (using the language of geopolitics, I would also call it bandwagoning) is not realistic.[21] In the 1990s, I was shocked to read that the then Russian Foreign Minister Andrei Kozyrev had said that post-Soviet Russia did not have any specific or particular national interests, that its foreign policy would in the future be guided only by universal interests and human values. Already then I wondered how such a person could be the Foreign Minister of a country with the size and history of Russia, or any other country for that matter. However, being concentrated at that time on other matters, I lost sight of this naïve comment, but it never left my mind completely. Although being personally familiar with the lightweight nature of Andrei Kozyrev as a politician and diplomat, such a statement went over the top and looked simply unbelievable. Later, while reading Dimitri Simes' insightful book *After the Collapse: Russia Seeks its Place as a Great Power*[22] which, *inter alia*, explained the context for Kozyrev's statement, I became even more flabbergasted. Allow me to quote from a spring 1992 conversation that took place between the former US president Richard Nixon and Andrei Kozyrev. This exchange of views reveals much of what transpired in Russia in the 1990s, and why Russia's foreign policy today appears too prickly to the West. Dimitri Simes, who was present at the conversation, recalls:

> Nixon asked Kozyrev how his government was defining Russian national interests. Kozyrev [...] replied that in the past Russia had suffered greatly from focusing too intently on its own interests at the expense of the rest of the world. Now was the time, he added, for Russia 'to think more in terms of universal human values'. 'Well,' Nixon responded wryly, 'that is a very commendable sentiment on the Minister's part. But surely

> there are some particular interests which Russia considers important as an emerging power?' Kozyrev was not persuaded. [...] 'Perhaps, President Nixon, as a friend of Russian democracy you would be willing to help to identify them?' Kozyrev inquired with a shy smile.
>
> The former president somehow kept his poker face. 'I would not presume to tell the minister what Russian national interests should be. I am sure that in due time he will find them on his own. *But I would like to make one point. Russia cannot and should not attempt to walk in lockstep with the United States on all foreign policy issues. As a great country, Russia has its own destiny* [emphasis added]. We want Russia as a friend, and we tremendously appreciate your personal friendship, Mr Minister, but I know that anyone in Russia who tries to follow foreign advice too closely is bound to get into trouble. And we do not want this to happen to our friends'.[23]

And out of the Foreign Ministry building in Smolenskaya Square, in the centre of Moscow, and in President Nixon's limousine, Dimitri Simes, asked by Nixon what he had thought about the conversation with the Minister, responded that such a blindly pro-Western policy makes Kozyrev vulnerable to public indignation and possibly makes the United States guilty by association. And then comes Nixon's hit: 'That is exactly the point. He is a nice man. But you need a real son of a bitch to do this job right, Dimitri. [...] You need to be able to see straight, but also to be ruthless to build a new country on the ruins of the empire. I can't see the Russian people respecting wimps like that'.[24] Exactly. I am not sure of the categorisation of the Minister as a nice man, but certainly as somebody not qualified for the job. Unfortunately, few American politicians have been able to see international relations in such a clear, straight and, I would also say, surprisingly philosophically profound way. Most are all too content to rely on those foreign diplomats or politicians whom Nixon would have categorised as wimps and lickspittles, though it is difficult to believe that they necessarily respect them. In the 1990s, the United States treated Russia like Germany had been treated by the victorious allies after World War I, as 'Weimar in velvet gloves'[25], using Karaganov's expression. In my opinion, Putin and Lavrov could be much more reliable friends (or formidable enemies) to the United States than Yeltsin and (especially) Kozyrev. In fairness to Yeltsin, however, it must be conceded that at certain crucial moments, such as in August of 1991 when facing a *coup d'état* attempt, or in 1999 by choosing Vladimir Putin as his successor, he behaved as a statesman, and even visionary. In parallel with half-hearted efforts in the 1990s to tie Russia to the American bandwagon, there soon resumed attempts to contain Russia. Two of the most prominent examples of this policy have been the expansion of NATO to the borders of Russia and the unilateral withdrawal of the US in 2002 from the ABM (Anti-Ballistic Missile) Treaty, under the pretext of threats from 'rogue' states. Hubert Védrine, the former Foreign Minister of France, does not miss the point in writing that the West in the 1990s missed the opportunity to fulfil the high expectations and hopes of the creation of a real 'international community', a real 'unity of nations' instead of the disunited 'United Nations':

> Vibrant hopes and expectations that emerged after the disappearance in December 1991 of the Soviet Union, hopes especially among the peoples of the West that considered itself to be the winners in the Cold War, remained unfulfilled. The West never tried, as Henry Kissinger has regretted, to really integrate Russia into a new world security structure. Thus, during the last twenty-five years the United States has often in its hubris abused what has been believed to be its absolute power (*toute-puissance*).[26]

This, as we discuss below in detail, is one of the root causes of some of today's most serious conflicts, in Europe and beyond.

Homogenisation of the World through the Heterogenisation of Individual Societies

Today, for an ever-expanding world population of over 7 billion, all of Planet Earth may have become smaller than Eastern Africa was for the first groups of *Homo sapiens*; these days, there are no places without humanity's trace, hospitable or not. Although in the course of this journey from Africa to all corners of the globe the human race gradually became more and more diverse, it nevertheless remained the same species, and its members have retained characteristics that are common to all humans, and a degree of genetic variance that is astonishingly low (we differ on average by about one-in-a-thousand base pairs); even expanding human communities retained many traits that are familiar to all societies. Most social groups that have ever existed have, for long periods, consisted of closely knit traditional communities, and only recently have some of them, particularly in the West, become so individualistic that concerns have been raised over the weakening of societal bonds holding those communities together.[27] For nearly all of human evolution, communitarian ways of living have been, and for many societies still are, much more natural than ways emphasising individualism, or the rights and liberties of the individual vis-à-vis the community where they live. For millennia, *Homo sapiens* did not see themselves as individuals, as personalities separate from social groups, whose integral parts they were. Alexis de Tocqueville was right that 'the word "individualism", which we have coined for our own requirements, was unknown to our ancestors, for the good reason that in their time every individual necessarily belonged to a group, and no one could regard himself as an isolated unit'.[28]

Universalists – that is, proponents of a universal history for humankind, be they Marxists or liberal democrats – tend to underestimate the differences acquired during the journey out from an African village. At the same time, strong cultural relativists, in emphasising the differences, fail to appreciate the universalities that have existed in all or most human communities, and which in a globalising world have a tendency to grow in importance. If the differences are readily evident and striking (the colour of one's skin, the slant of one's eyes or the clothes we don), commonalities, more often than not, are to be discovered in the enactment of close proximity and communication. Our common humanity is deeper, but therefore also better hidden than our differences. As Michael Walzer once aptly put it: 'Every human society is universal because it is human, particular because it is a society'.[29]

As American social psychologist Jonathan Haidt has demonstrated, in today's world there coexist three categories of societies: those with the ethics of autonomy, those with the ethics of community and those with the ethics of divinity. In the first category the individual runs prime with her wants, needs and preferences; in the second, concepts such as duty, hierarchy, respect, reputation and patriotism prevail; while in the third lies the idea that people are, first and foremost, only temporary vessels within which a divine soul has been implanted.[30] If individuals from different societies are able to transverse the boundaries of their ethical communities, to step outside of their 'moral matrix', and even be sometimes able to straddle and enjoy more than one of them, communities themselves change much more slowly, and changes that are instigated and pressed either from above or from the outside may have lasting negative effects. Haidt concludes his essay with a warning against moral monists: 'Beware of anyone who insists that there is one true morality for all people, times, and places – particularly if that morality is founded upon a single moral foundation'.[31]

Today's dominant universalists, the proponents of the world-wide triumph of free-market liberal democracy, are attempting to instil uniformity by supporting differences between individuals as part of ideological individualism at the expense of differences between societies, differences that may legitimise collectivistic ideologies. It is interesting, and in my opinion also important, to emphasise that while the Western mass media, educational systems and systems of indoctrination in general have promoted the idea of social diversity, the diversity of societies, differences between societies organised as states (liberal or non-liberal, democratic or meritocratic,[32] free-market or state controlled, etc.) are much less accepted, if not actively discouraged or even suppressed. Although one may find examples of references to the benefits of having diverse cultures, literatures or cuisines, positive comments on the existence of diverse political, ideological or economic systems have become virtually taboo in the West. Such attitudes have turned almost subconscious; this is how subtle and effective indoctrination works – most people do not suspect that their words or deeds may manifest the rejection of diversity. As an example, *The Economist* in July 2007 made an interesting observation regarding the late Russian Prime Minister Viktor Chernomyrdin: 'Russia's ambassador to Ukraine, is no Western-style democrat. Nor does this (now wealthy) founder of Gazprom and ex-prime minister pretend to be'.[33] It is as though somebody who is not a Western-style democrat, and does not even 'pretend' to be, is almost likened to a proud drug dealer who does not even pretend to be a law-abiding businessman. For completeness it should be mentioned that there are indeed too many of those, who, for various reasons, profess to be liberal democrats, yet who either do not understand the phrase or who cynically exploit the leading narrative in order to receive support from dominant powers.

There are a lot of other indicators which demonstrate how warped the dominant narrative has become. Only those who behave and think in a way as prescribed by Western political correctness are considered on the right side of history. This mind-set has penetrated many non-Western societies where quite a few have become, to paraphrase Alain Badiou, overwhelmed by the *désir de l'Occident*. In November 2015, Georges Malbrunot, a French journalist, in an article on Iran, quotes an anonymous Iranian intellectual, who deplores that, unfortunately, President Rohani of Iran 'is not Iranian Gorbachev; at best he could become our Deng Xiaoping'.[34] There is something disturbingly distorted in the idea that Mikhail Gorbachev had been a more successful reformer than China's Deng Xiaoping. One need only to compare today's China and Russia, and their respective economies and influences in the world (especially if we also take into account their respective starting positions). Such a mind-set goes against simple logic, to say nothing of a deeper comparative analysis of Deng's and Gorbachev's reforms and, specifically, their results. Such a myopia may be explained by the dominant narrative, mostly Anglo-American in origin, which claims that there is only one correct way of life, one adequate political and economic system – liberal democracy and free markets. Such a one-dimensional and negative approach to diversities between societies, which attempts to homogenise the world, is in stark contrast with the acceptance and even encouragement of diversity within societies, similar to biodiversity in some respects. It may even lead one to conclude that such purposeful and forceful encouragement of diversity within societies is done in order to homogenise the world in accordance with one dominant liberal blueprint. Therefore, one may well agree with French economist Hervé Juvin when he observes that: 'Behind permanent references to the need to respect diversity hides a completely different phenomenon; the creation of a conformist humankind through the extinction of diversity'.[35] The encouragement of diversity at the level of the individual may indeed accelerate the extinction of diversity globally through the elimination of differences between societies. This not only puts an end to social, political and economic experimentation, in the process of which new alternative routes of development and responses to new challenges could be found, but it is bound to cause, *inter alia*, a counter-tendency wrought with the danger of civilisational clashes. Even the idea of the universality of human rights, notwithstanding the good intentions of most of its advocates and regardless of the positive results these ideas produce, has its dark side. Whether done purposefully to destroy societies that do not conform, or in the sincere belief that what is good and true for us is (or should be) good and true for all, such a forced homogenisation of the world by way of a heterogenisation of individual societies tears apart many countries, destroying societal bonds that had developed during centuries and are not amenable to rapid change.

There are two contradictory, competing processes going on in today's world, which sometimes cancel each other out: the world as a whole is slowly and rather painfully becoming more and more homogeneous, while most individual societies are increasingly becoming more heterogeneous. The homogenisation of the world is not something completely new. Empires, both ancient and modern, contributed to this process, even though they did not strive to homogenise their imperial space to the extent that nation-states have tried to do. The end of the bipolar international system, as well as the opening up and rapid development of China, increased the rate of global homogenisation. In many ways it was a spontaneous process. Interacting and interpenetrating societies borrow from each other that which they believe works best; the flow of goods, ideas and practices across state boundaries make interacting societies, in some important respects, more similar to one another. This is but one manifestation of globalisation. It and others, such as the promotion of Western-style liberal democracy and market economies, raise questions not only of the universality (unidirectionality) of mankind's history, but also pour doubt on values that are professed to be universal. We can see this reservation today in the backlash to the enthusiastically welcomed 'Arab Spring', or to the attempts to democratise the 'wider Middle East', either by invading Iraq or socially engineering Afghanistan.

The Syrian civil war has significantly contributed to the waves of migration, which are both an aspect and result of the globalisation process (and should be referred to as an immigration challenge as opposed to a refugee crisis, refugees being only part of the phenomena), contributing to both of these tendencies – the assimilation of the world and the dissimilation of individual societies. Until recently, most migration waves have had predominantly economic explanations (through both push and pull factors), while armed conflicts have been the cause of *refugee* flows. Furthermore, we can see that environmental factors are starting to play a role here too. Ian Morris had warned even before the current Middle Eastern turmoil that,

> [G]lobal warming threatens to make even the most lurid fears of anti-immigrant activists come true by the 2020s. Tens of millions of the world's hungriest, angriest, and most desperate people may be fleeing the Muslim world for Europe, and Latin America for the United States. The population movements could dwarf anything in history, reviving the kind of problems that the steppe highway (on which the hordes of Alexander the Great, the Huns, Chingiz Han, and others moved either to the West or to the East) used to present.[36]

Globalisation, and migration waves specifically (a source of homogenisation in the world), leads to the heterogenisation of individual societies. In most societies all over the world, there are increasingly more goods, ideas, practices and people of foreign origin. If foreign-made material goods are, as a rule, accepted welcomingly (though there are also exceptions), foreign values, practices and specifically the carriers of those values and practices tend to harbour resentment from significant segments of indigenous populations.

These controversial parallel processes of homogenisation and heterogenisation have already created some serious problems. The world has become interconnected, but also unmanageable. Everything is related to everything else, and more often than not our conscious and planned actions have unforeseen and unintended consequences. Undesirable events in one part of the world have immediate repercussions elsewhere. Economic and financial crises, terrorist attacks, environmental pollution and uncontrollable immigration waves are major negative consequences of globalisation.

The refugee flows to Europe from Syria, Afghanistan, North Africa and elsewhere, though having specific causes, are one of the currents in the ongoing wave of global migration. It is to be expected that even the resolution of the conflicts which caused them – not an easy task, not at all certain and in any case not a temporary problem – may only slow the general flow of people from developing and poorer countries to more developed and richer ones. Global inequality is the main cause of the current migration wave. Likely, three grand strategies will be necessary for Europe. First, truly integrating those migrants who are already in Europe and who will inevitably arrive in the future. And by integration we mean at least partial assimilation (follow the maxim: when in Rome, do as the Romans do). For example, under the aegis of the European Council for Tolerance and Reconciliation, a working group of experts[37] has prepared a draft *European Model Law for the Promotion of Tolerance and the Suppression of Intolerance*,[38] that alongside clauses that are intended to promote tolerance of different forms of social diversity, pluralism and identity, as well as the observance of human rights without any discrimination, nonetheless foresees necessary limitations on tolerance, which may be summarised as 'no need to be tolerant of the intolerant'. One of the purposes of the *Model Law* is to 'promote tolerance within a pluralistic society (there are no non-pluralistic societies in Europe, and not many globally) *without weakening its common bonds*' (emphasis added). Calling for protection from any form of 'intolerance based on bias, bigotry and prejudice' towards vulnerable social groups, including foreign migrants, the *Model Law* provides that 'foreign migrants for their part, have to adhere to the principle of coexistence of diverse groups within a pluralistic society'. Secondly, regulating, controlling and curbing migration flows through establishing EU–external border controls. Thirdly, undertaking genuine efforts to diminish global inequalities, as well as helping resolve ongoing conflicts, but doing that without incompetent and ruinous interference in the developing world. Although the democratisation of Western European societies went in parallel with their homogenisation, and the latter supported the former, today attempts at ethnic, cultural or religious homogenisation are wrought with serious dangers, besides the obvious fact that some of the methods of homogenisation used centuries ago are today considered genocide, crimes against humanity or ethnic cleansing. An important point to note is also that, historically, it was not, say, the exclusion of ethnic or religious minorities or the expulsion of the Jews or the Huguenots that made some societies prosperous and dominant; on the contrary it was tolerance (often such tolerance was strategic, not humanistic) which was instrumental in the coagulation and ability of the empires of Rome, Genghis Khan, later the Dutch and the British empires, and in the twentieth century the United States, to prevail over other societies. Amy Chua has persuasively shown that 'throughout history, no society based on racial purity, religious zealotry, or ethnic cleansing has ever become a world-dominant power'.[39] If the desire for ethnic or racial purity leads to genetic diseases, the search for intellectual or ideological purity may cause social schizophrenia. In any case, today, in contradistinction to the Western Europe of the period when the concept of the nation-state arose, the dominant tendency in most societies is the rise of diversity. Policies of ethnic, religious, cultural or linguistic homogenisation will inevitably clash with this dominant trend, and therefore will eventually fail, but before their failure becomes certain they will create upheavals in societies that try to follow those bygone principles, and bring suffering on those individuals and groups who are the targets of this homogenisation. At the same time, countries facing massive migration flows cannot afford to have within them communities that differ hugely in their values and convictions, and exist as if in parallel worlds. Even voluntary apartheid, leading to the parallel existence of non-integrated communities which often live next-door to one another, is dangerous and unacceptable. Integration of different ethnic, religious or linguistic groups within the same country without some homogenisation and assimilation is simply not possible.

On the other hand, the purposeful and forceful homogenisation of societies different and differing from one another, be it through the imposition of the concept of the universality of human rights, the forced liberalisation of financial markets or cultural dominance, is an affront to the cultural diversity of humankind, to say nothing of the disastrous practical effects of those more forceful methods of homogenisation. Even the existence of a single international language, especially if it is the language of an economically, politically and militarily dominant power, is dangerous.

On Deficiencies of Western Export Items

While the West is exporting its values and practices to the rest, in Europe itself there is not only the refugee crisis, but also a crisis of both liberal democracy and capitalism in general. It seems that free markets and liberal democracy, phenomena that have facilitated one another, are also increasingly in a state of rivalry and competition. The freer the market, the greater the economic inequality; the greater the economic inequality, the lesser the democracy. Cambridge economist Ha-Joon Chang has even written that '[F]ree market and democracy are not natural partners',[40] though it must be emphasised that Professor Chang is not speaking of 'market economy' as such, but of a 'free market' or rather 'unbridled markets', as advocated, for example, by Milton Friedman and his followers, and as exemplified by the policies of Ronald Reagan and Margaret Thatcher, as well as those of today's neoliberals. However, one of the most persistent and market-friendly advocates of political freedoms, Karl Popper, incisively wrote already more than half-a-century ago that:

> Even if the state protects its citizens from being bullied by physical violence (as it does, in principle, under the system of unrestrained capitalism), it may defeat our ends by its failure to protect them from the misuse of economic power. In such a state, the economically strong is still free to bully one who is economically weak, and to rob him of his freedom. Under these circumstances, unlimited economic freedom can be just as self-defeating as unlimited physical freedom, and economic power may be nearly as dangerous as physical violence.[41]

It was true then; it is even truer today, since economic inequality is on the rise practically everywhere.[42] Economic inequality both *de facto* and inevitably increases political inequality, while political equality applies brakes to widening economic inequality. Strong democracy attained by curbing inequality almost inevitably bridles market freedoms. Democracy seeks to make a society more equal, while unbridled markets increase inequality. The result of such constant balancing is that in Western European liberal democracies (more accurately in social democracies), these two spheres – the political and economic – in the process of supporting one another, have constantly tempered each other's excesses. In that respect, the US differs considerably from Europe. Cambridge Professor John Dunn writes that

> America today remains a society uncomfortable with every surviving vestige of explicit privilege, but remarkably blithe in face of the most vertiginous of economic gulfs, and comprehensively reconciled to the most obtrusive privileges of wealth as such. Behind this outcome lies the continuing vitality of its economy, the real source of the victory of the partisans of 'distinction, or the English school of economists'.[43]

Or, as Joseph Stiglitz puts it, 'instead of government tempering the excesses of the market, in America today the two have been working together to increase income wealth disparities'.[44] There the market has prevailed over democracy, while, say, in Sweden, long governed by social democrats, there has been less room, as Dunn puts it, for 'distinctions and opulence',[45] – democracy has exercised greater constraints on the market. Today, when there are serious doubts as to 'the continuing vitality' of the American economy, one may question whether an equality of opportunity without much effect on the equality of the outcome is not too narrow a concept. Moreover, as Stiglitz well explains in one of his latest books,[46] 'the American dream', 'the land of equal opportunity' has become a complete myth and social, both upward as well as downward, mobility has all but stopped working. Without equal opportunity, however, 'equal rights' also becomes an empty slogan instead of enforceable rights. This has had a nefarious effect also on the political sphere, where the 'current system seems to operate on a "one dollar one vote" instead of "one person one vote" basis'.[47] Paul Krugman puts it forcefully when he writes: 'Extreme concentration of income is incompatible with real democracy. Can anyone seriously deny that our political system is being warped by the influence of big money, and that the warping is getting worse as the wealth of a few grows ever larger?'[48] Zhang Weiwei, speaking about Western, particularly American, democracy, observes:

> The 'separation of powers' is merely confined to the political domain, but in a modern state, at least three powers (political, social and capital) from the three domains (political, social and economic) are interacting with each other, thus shaping the trajectory and the fate of that country [...] In the case of the United States, predominance of the capital power over political and social powers apparently has led to the decline of 'the American Dream'.[49]

In the last chapter of this book we come back to the importance of the issue of separation of powers within states and balance of power in international society, but here it is important to note that the balance between political, social and economic domains in societies is indeed not less, and may in fact be more, important than the separation of powers in the political sphere. John Dunn also observes that within the liberal-democratic movement 'the partisans of the order of egoism', that is, capitalists, have defeated 'the partisans of equality'[50], that is, democrats. One of the important reasons for equality's defeat at the hands of economic egoism has been that, in the long run, the uncompromising instruments used in institutionalising equality, and the rigidities inherent in its pursuit, have blunted equality's appeal as a goal.[51] Both the 1789 French and especially the 1917 Russian revolutions, where, differently from the American revolution of the eighteenth century, the aim was not as much, as Hannah Arendt puts it, 'freedom from oppression,' as 'freedom from want', and one of the fundamental requirements therefore was *égalité*, have contributed to the existing balancing between democracy and liberalism. Arendt emphasises that 'the inescapable fact was that liberation from tyranny spelled freedom only for the few and was hardly felt by the many who remained loaded down by their misery. These had to be liberated once more, and compared to this liberation from the yoke of necessity, the original liberation from tyranny must have looked like child's play'.[52]

The fact that radical attempts to liberate people from 'the yoke of necessity' and create more equal societies have led to tyranny, should in no way compromise the values of equality and freedom themselves. It is possible to abuse all values and norms, but this doesn't mean that we should therefore reject them. What is needed is a critical approach, one able to distinguish between values and their abuses. Advanced liberal democracies today have, in principle, abolished the 'yoke of tyranny', and have alleviated the 'yoke of necessity' for most of their people, but we need to be wary of complacency, since not only does poverty fester in even the wealthiest of European societies, but the 'war on terror', combined with uncontrolled migration and identity crises, threaten to bring back also the 'yoke of tyranny'. For many other societies, both tyrannies still constitute formidable challenges, and even mature democracies have to constantly strike new balances between freedom and equality. Wolfgang Streeck, writing on 'the crises of democratic capitalism', whose heydays, in his opinion, were the years between the end of World War II and the end of the 1960s, observes that 'more than ever, economic power seems today to have become political power, while citizens appear to be almost entirely stripped of their democratic defences and their capacity to impress upon the political economy interests and demands that are incommensurable with those of capital owners'.[53] Since the collapse of communism, the conflictual aspects of the 'capitalism–democracy' association are becoming more and more visible. Therefore, one may be justified in questioning whether the expiry date of at least some of those Western political and economic institutions that are packaged for export has not already passed. Even if we answer this question in the positive – and there are serious grounds for such a conclusion – this would not yet mean that democracy has no future. However, Professor Hui Wang from Tsinghua University in Beijing, believing that 'we need to rethink the parochial [i.e., Western] notion of democracy'[54], emphasises that:

> If constitutionally defined political rights cannot effectively pave the way for democratic participation by citizens; if these political rights cannot check the inequalities that exist with respect to race, gender and class; if these democratic rights cannot restrict monopolies, power and domination; if they cannot limit the increasingly market-like behaviour of political power or the growth in the authority of the market, then we must consider a broader and more complete concept of democracy.[55]

This conclusion, from a Chinese scholar who has been rather critical of contemporary Chinese realities, is wise and should be taken account of: China certainly needs both political and economic reforms, but not through copying the West, which itself is in dire need of political and economic transformations.

American philosopher Daniel Dennett, who states that his sacred values are obvious and ecumenical, lists them in alphabetical order as 'democracy, justice, life, love, and truth'.[56] Is democracy really ecumenical and sacred? Does it have any intrinsic value at all or is its value wholly instrumental? As

Dennett himself observes: '[B]iology insists on delving beneath the surface of "intrinsic" values and asking why they exist, and any answer that is supported by the facts has the effect of showing that the value in question is – or once was – really instrumental, not intrinsic, even if we don't see it that way'.[57] David Held has written that

> [W]ithin democratic thinking, a clear divide exists between those who value political participation for its own sake and understand it as a fundamental mode of self-realization, and those who take a more instrumental view and understand democratic politics as a means of protecting citizens from arbitrary rule and expressing (via mechanisms of aggregation) their preferences [...] According to this position, democracy is a means not an end.[58]

Therefore, if democracy does not deliver that which people need (economic growth, stability, personal and societal security), its fate may be even more fragile than that of autocratic regimes. Amitai Etzioni observes that

> [F]rom the extensive literature written on the question of what caused the fall of the Weimar Republic and the rise of the Third Reich, it is reasonable to conclude that liberal democracy lost legitimacy because it failed to address peoples' need to physical and economic security.[59]

Notwithstanding that people cannot be satisfied with a democracy that does not deliver, the concept, in our opinion, not only has instrumental, but indeed intrinsic value (though we should not call it sacred, as often even those who strive most ardently for it do not know what to do with it once they have it; sometimes they even start to long for the certainties of a stable autocracy). The gist of democracy's intrinsic value is that humans (at least most of us and, we believe, in principle, at a minimum all adults of sound mind), once their immediate needs for survival are met, are not content in an environment where somebody else is deciding what is to their benefit, what they are permitted to do and what they should or should not be doing. There have always been those who are never sated by material fulfilment and yearn for spiritual, intellectual or emotional gratification. Although democracy has this intrinsic value, as it is only in democracy that human beings attain maturity, become citizens instead of subjects, its primary value is instrumental – it must contribute, and often does, to the realisation of other values such as material prosperity, social stability, personal freedoms, security and scientific or artistic creativity. However, one should not underestimate the human desire for emotional comfort, which is sometimes and for some provided by relieving them from the need to constantly take difficult decisions and make their own choices. Some people prefer that somebody else – parents, a political party, the government or God, oftentimes through clergy – take over the burden. Many feel comfortable only amongst their co-religionists, or in the military.[60]

There are logical arguments favouring democracy over other forms of governance, such as 'a human being can be fully human only when he or she fully participates in the political life of his or her country', or that democracy is 'a fundamental mode of self-realisation', or even that 'only democratic governance can put an end to famines'. These and other similar arguments are put forward by thinkers such as Jürgen Habermas and Amartya Sen.[61] However, such reasoning cannot persuade those who prefer pragmatic or emotional arguments to logical or rational reasoning, as many people do. One such argument is best expressed by the late Richard Rorty, the greatest pragmatist philosopher, who wrote in 2007:

> [F]ollowers of Dewey like myself would like to praise parliamentary democracy and the welfare state as very good things, but only on the basis of invidious comparison with suggested concrete alternatives, not on the basis of claims that these institutions are truer to human nature, or more rational, or in better accord with the universal moral law, than feudalism or totalitarianism.[62]

As Cambridge philosopher Simon Blackburn writes,

> Rorty opposes the tradition which descends from Locke or Kant to recent writers such as Jürgen Habermas and John Rawls, which seeks to prove that a democratic and liberal state is the only rational mode of social organisation. For such writers, someone who chose to live in an illiberal or undemocratic state would be trampling on his own reason. It is irrational to sell yourself into the mental servitude that a theocratic state demands. But for Rorty, this Enlightenment attitude with its talk of irrationality is useless. The right pragmatist observation is that theocratic states seem not to work very well, by comparison with liberal democracies – it is theocracies who lose refugees to us, and not vice versa. We can cope, and theocracies cannot.[63]

There are certainly strong points to Rorty's arguments, though most of those millions who leave their war-torn and poverty-ridden countries behind do not travel to the West in search of democracy and liberalism. Often they bring with them highly undemocratic and illiberal habits and traditions, and may even attempt to advance them in countries that have given them refuge. Of course, it is possible to argue that Western societies are prosperous because they are democratic, though it may well be the other way round – it could be prosperity that leads to democracy. The truth is, probably, somewhere in-between, and where the chicken and the egg are located depends on concrete circumstances. Personally I enjoy living in a liberal-democratic country, and I believe that notwithstanding all of its imperfections it is what's best for myself and for my family. Yet, it would be a mistake to make the following extrapolations from this personal observation. The first would be the belief that everybody is like me. We would call this the 'Bush fallacy', as it was President George W. Bush who expressed most clearly and most frequently the belief that those truths which are self-evident to Americans were true for everybody and everywhere.[64] Such a worldview is deeply engraved in American consciousness. Even President Bush Senior, in urging Deng Xiaoping to understand the widespread outrage in America to the 1989 Tiananmen tragedy, wrote to China's paramount leader: 'It is not a reaction of arrogance or of a desire to force others to our beliefs but a simple faith in the enduring value of those principles and their universal applicability'.[65] If such a belief in the universality of one's own values, and acting upon such belief, does not reflect some kind of arrogance (alloyed with naïvety), then what is arrogance?

The second extrapolation is that as democracy, specifically liberal democracy, is, in principle, good for everybody (and having studied the issue in some depth in several countries, I am no longer so certain), it can be easily attained. In fact, when and how to get there is the most crucial question. One of the greatest contemporary philosophers, Jürgen Habermas, insightfully observes that it is necessary to 'relativize one's own views to the interpretive perspectives of equally situated and equally entitled others', and that

> the 'reason' of modern rational law does not consist of universal 'values' that one can own like goods, and distribute and export throughout the world. 'Values' – including those that have a chance of winning global recognition – don't come from thin air. They gain their binding force only within normative orders and practices of particular forms of cultural life.[66]

Therefore, whenever an attempt has been made to impose a Western model of development on non-Western countries it has involved mass terror.[67]

Alastair Crooke, comparing Islamic and Western societies, observes that

> [I]t is this clash of two views of the human being: one view – the western one – privileges 'individuality', and defines this 'individuality' as the appropriate organizing principle around which society should be shaped. The other view – the Islamist vision – sees the human to be integral to wider existence; intractably linked, and not separated as 'an individual', from others and the world that surrounds him or her; which sees the human as a multi-dimensional creature – larger than the sum of his or her desires and appetites, whose ability to access innate moral values, as the basis of his or her responsibility to the community, becomes the organizational principle of economics, society and politics.[68]

Therefore, democracy in the Middle East, or in the Far East for that matter, cannot be analogous to its Western variant; though in the long run (and free from external coercion), different societies may become, in certain important respects, more similar to each other. While Muslim and other non-Western societies may begin to value individual liberties more, at least some Western (and especially Anglo-Saxon) societies will have to tame their excessive individualism, and borrow some communitarian ideas and practices either from the East or from their own past or, even better, find innovative ways to face yet-unknown challenges. In any case, as Hubert Védrine emphasises, 'democracy and human rights will progress in future much less through the prescriptions and interference from the outside by the West than depending on the internal dynamics of individual societies'.[69] Sergei Karaganov, analysing the widening gap between the European and Russian value systems, and, believing that unlike the Europeans, Russia has no plans to export its values to others (this seems to be true though we often hear that Russia tries to undermine its neighbours' liberal democracy; first, there is often no liberal democracy to be undermined and secondly, it is not liberal democracy of Russia's neighbours that the Kremlin is worried about but their aspirations of joining the anti-Russian NATO), concludes that there is no need for either the Europeans or the Russians to attempt to try and like one another in order to have good neighbourly relations, their ideological differences notwithstanding. Nevertheless, he concludes: 'It may well be that in the coming decades their respective philosophies may once again change. Europe may become more nationalistic and realistic, while Russia would become more tolerant'.[70]

The belief in the theory of democratic peace, and acting on this belief in the most implausible of places, like Afghanistan or Iraq, is one of the reasons why there is so much chaos and turmoil in so much of the world, and why US hegemony has become weaker and shorter than it would have otherwise been. Empires have lasted as long as they have lasted because they generally accepted diversity, and their falls were hastened largely by imperial overextension or by attempts to homogenise (e.g., Russification in the Russian Empire at the end of the nineteenth and the beginning of the twentieth century) within imperial space. The world is simply too big, complex and diverse for its rich tapestry to be flattened into a carpet where one pattern, be it Judeo-Christian, Anglo-Saxon, Confucian, Muslim or even secular liberal-democratic, dominates.

Chapter 3

The West versus Russia or vice versa?

Competing Narratives in Europe

In Europe today, there are two competing narratives as far as relations with Russia are concerned – the Euro-Atlantic or pro-American narrative, and the European, some may say pro-Russian narrative (though it may be called pro-Russian only because it is not anti-Russian). However, the competition between these two narratives is not taking place on equal terms, due to the fact that the Euro-Atlantic narrative is considerably more massive and aggressive than any pro-European or pro-Russian narrative (though the former may have now started to become a victim of its own successes, while the latter is improving). In its efforts to completely suppress alternatives, the Euro-Atlantic narrative has gone so far that many in the West have started questioning: is it really possible that our governments are always right (including when invading, e.g., Afghanistan, Iraq or Libya), while Russia is automatically wrong, even when it acts in the same way as Western powers do (e.g., in Syria), since it inevitably and always has ulterior, that is, dishonourable, motives? This is just how Russia is, and only those Russians who stridently and publicly declare their hate for Putin are honourable in the eyes of the West.[1] Russia's propaganda machine, and especially that part of it which reaches beyond its borders, is still in its relative infancy. Yet, NATO, the EU and Washington are all ratcheting up their propaganda machines, allegedly to counter Russian propaganda. Bearing in mind the apt comment of the former US Secretary of Defence Robert M. Gates, who said that any future Secretary who advises his President to send land armies into Asia, the Middle East or Africa 'should have his head examined'[2], it is possible to make parallels with those who sincerely believe that Russian media is all one singular and effective propaganda machine, while in the West the media is concerned wholly with the truth. And yet, one may still read, in an article rather pretentiously entitled 'Propaganda vs. Information Policy', that 'whereas Russia has propaganda, the EU has an information policy', or 'unlike Western media organisations, RT[3] is not concerned with the truth'.[4] The propagandistic message of the West is less obvious and therefore usually also more effective. In that respect the quoted article resembles the most primitive examples of Russian propaganda, but the spread of such materials in the West shows that Russian propaganda (or information policy) is starting to bite. This is not because Russian propaganda is more effective than Western. Western propaganda is much more sophisticated, experienced and widespread and therefore it may even not look like propaganda at all. In 1928, Edward Louis James Bernays, one of the pioneers of the American propaganda machine, in his book *Propaganda*, considered that manipulation of public opinion was a necessary part of democracy (though later he preferred instead of the word 'propaganda' the term 'public relations', therefore becoming known 'as the father of public relations'). Bernays wrote:

> The conscious and intelligent manipulation of the organized habits and opinions of the masses is an important element in democratic society. Those who manipulate this unseen mechanism of society constitute an invisible government which is the true ruling power of our country [...] We are governed, our minds are molded, our tastes formed, our ideas suggested, largely by men we have never heard of. This is a logical result of the way in which our democratic society is organized. Vast numbers of human beings must cooperate in this manner if they are to live together as a smoothly functioning society [...] In almost every act of our daily lives, whether in the sphere of politics or business, in our social conduct or our ethical thinking, we are dominated by the relatively small number of persons [...] who understand the mental processes and social patterns of the masses. It is they who pull the wires which control the public mind.[5]

Today, the West has reason to worry not because Russian propaganda is more effective than Western propaganda, but because of the widening chasm between the dominant Western ideological narrative and global realities. It is an increasingly troubling development to critically minded and intelligent people in many Western, especially European, societies. There are, of course, many conscientious, courageous and highly professional journalists and experts in the mainstream media in the West. Sometimes dissident voices can be heard, though not often enough. However, there is an intellectual background – both temporal and spatial – in every society that determines the dominant narrative, and today, by means of globalisation generally and the spread of the English language as a major component specifically, the Western narrative has an innate advantage.

Dominique Moïsi, one of France's most inspiring international relations specialists, has recently published a very interesting book on the interaction and mutual influence between geopolitics and popular TV series.[6] He asks the question: 'Though TV series are not the monopoly of the United States, is not the mirror that they offer to the world as a whole deformed by the uncontested Anglo-Saxon domination of the world'?[7] His analysis of the TV series, which is not limited to the Anglo-Saxon ones, clearly shows that the answer to this question is a resounding 'Yes'. But Moïsi goes on to write that though such series may help audiences better understand the world, 'he is not naïve enough to believe that they could not lead to the denial of the reality of the world and contribute to the disinformation about this reality, thereby becoming part of a deliberate propaganda machine, as is happening under authoritarian regimes'.[8] I have to wonder whether a person of such high intellectual standards and of such critical mind as Dominique Moïsi does not understand that propaganda in liberal democracies is no less omnipresent and pervasive than in authoritarian 'regimes' (already the use of the adjective 'regime' when referring to authoritarian governments and the adjective 'government' when referring to democracies is the result of a kind of indoctrination accepted almost automatically by most of those involved in international relations studies or practices). In liberal democracies propaganda is much more sophisticated and difficult to recognise as such. Therefore, it is usually also more effective. The most serious difference between authoritarian and democratic propaganda machines is that in democratic regimes those who recognise, bypass and oppose its tools are not killed or sentenced, but usually only marginalised, while under authoritarian governments critics may lose both their liberty and their life. No doubt, this is a vital difference but this does not mean that in liberal democracies there is only objective reporting, while propaganda (public relations) exists only under authoritarian governments.

We all live with our personal histories and in societies with their own information bubbles. We can never be completely free from these determinants, and most people feel at home within these bubbles and happily flow with the dominant trend. It is even comforting, particularly for those who are not intellectually curious, to presume that those who have opinions differing from their own are biased and naïve, while those who think as they do see the world clearly and objectively. Everyone is in such a vicious circle. Often, the more we learn, the more indoctrinated we also become. Every form of education is, at least to an extent, also a form of indoctrination and brainwashing; the difference often is in the degrees. We cannot be free from our cultures, yet cultures also indoctrinate and brainwash – there is no ideologically neutral culture. But without culture we would be simply savages. Is there any way out of this impasse?

Yes, there are ways to soften the impact of indoctrination without losing the benefits provided by our cultural bubbles, but these ways are all difficult, sometimes uncomfortable, and even using them in their combined maximums we do not completely escape all indoctrination. Firstly, there are educational systems that are better than others in developing critical thinking in the young. If one is able, and is tired of marching with the herd, one should try to access such institutions. Secondly, it is necessary to try to have as many points of reference as conceivable, as many vantage points as possible; for that, it is necessary to live in or at least visit various societies, to learn their languages, especially of those societies that differ markedly from the society where one was raised. And though I myself, like many academics whose native language is not English, mostly write and even think in English, and often speak it at home, I understand that the use of only one international language imparts a somewhat one-sided and even distorting view of reality. Languages are not neutral.

A language carries a subconscious worldview. Martin Heidegger has said that 'we speak the language, but the language speaks us'.[9] Zhang Weiwei is right when observing in this context that 'the language we use actually reflects our way of thinking and behaving. The Chinese language seems to underline the fact that seeking commonality from diversity is a trait of Chinese culture'.[10] And thirdly, we have to submit our own views, our certainties and even our most dearly held principles to what Karl Popper called a 'falsification' process[11] – for the sake of objectivity we must submit our own views and positions to at least as much scrutiny as we would those of our opponents.

Russophobia as a Form of Brainwashing

In the summer of 2015 I had the pleasure of reading Guy Mettan's book on the topic of Russophobia in some Western countries; it is not often that somebody so competently and comprehensively analyses the historical roots of the current negative attitudes towards Russia in the West. Written by a Swiss intellectual and journalist, it demonstrates these attitudes as held among Western political elites (as related, for example, to the Ukrainian crisis, the Olympic Games in Sochi or the 2008 war between Georgia and Russia) as well as their historical roots. However, when I first read that 'in fact, Russophobia, in contradistinction, for example, to the French Anglophobia or Germanophobia, is a phenomenon that is somewhat similar to anti-Semitism' and that 'like the latter, it is not a transitional phenomenon related to concrete historical events; it resides in the brain of the person having such phobia independent from the behaviour of the victim'[12], I took it to be a statement too far. However, today, when one global crisis after another threatens to engulf humanity, when in Paris, one of the most beautiful cities in the world, a severe terrorist attack coincides with a meeting of COP 21, which is trying save the planet from overheating, and political elites, experts and journalists from many Western (or aspiring to be Western) countries seem to have nothing better to do than to concentrate their virulent criticism on Russia, I must admit that in that context even Mettan's remark does not look overblown. It seemed only natural that, after the tragedy in Paris, President François Hollande sought to create a wide coalition (*une coalition unique*) to fight ISIS. It was also to be expected that his immediate ports of call in the aftermath of the tragedy were to be Washington and Moscow. This was a sincere, inevitable and humanely natural response to the clear and present danger to France, to Europe and even to the world as a whole. But President Hollande was soon brought back down to Earth. First, President Obama was not at all enthusiastic about such a wide-reaching coalition. As François Fillon, then still a presidential candidate in France, rightly observed, 'the willingness of having an alliance with Russia was quickly forgotten vis-à-vis the opposition of the Americans who have been persistent in their desire to make out of Russia the principal enemy, as well as of Europeans led by Germany, which does not have any other foreign policy but that of the White House'.[13] Then Turkey, under President Erdogan, whom the Western media had earlier scolded for his authoritarian tendencies, his muzzling of the media, his imprisoning of journalists and his attacks on the Kurds instead of ISIS as well as his blackmailing of the European Union via visa-free travel and other concessions in exchange for not sending so many refugees to Europe, had nothing better to do than to shoot down a Russian Su-24 bomber. Soon after, US Vice President Joe Biden, to placate his NATO ally, welcomed Turkey's bombardment of the Kurds, announcing that the PKK and the Islamic State were equal threats to Turkey.[14] And this notwithstanding that impartial observers wrote that 'Recep Tayyip Erdogan, after deliberately breaking the peace process with the PKK last July, has launched a real war against the Kurds. Until this day, the military operations led by Turkey have caused at least 186 deaths among the civilians, mostly women and children'.[15]

I have no direct access to intelligence materials and therefore I cannot claim with any authority (as most who write on the matter cannot) whether the Russian aircraft had entered Turkish airspace or not, whether warnings were given or not, but these are – though important – not the most crucial questions. The world of the secret services and what they do and don't divulge to policy-makers is in some ways similar to that of poker players, where everybody keeps their cards close to their chests. Bluffing, poker faces and keeping packs of marked cards up the sleeve are all tools of the trade. However, there is also a chessboard level of world politics, where all of the figures are on the table for all to see. At this level, decision-making depends more on vision, intelligence (in the better sense of the word), open-mindedness and the ability to think outside the box and without ideological blinders, and not solely on information provided by intelligence services. At this level, it is not so terribly important to know where the Russian military aircraft was when it was shot down. What is crucially important is that the Russian bomber was targeting those (even if not solely) who had not long before cold-heartedly killed 130 innocent people in Paris, and also, of course, more than 200 Russians above the Sinai Peninsula. No one in their sound mind could have thought that Russian planes were threatening Turkey.

And Russia responds. As Michael A. Reynolds observes, 'if Turkish President Recep Tayyip Erdogan thought last November that by downing a Russian Su-24 bomber near the Turkish–Syrian border he could contain Vladimir Putin's Middle Eastern ambitions, he is certainly regretting it now'.[16]

The economic sanctions that Russia placed on Turkey were small potatoes. Russia, which from as far back as Czarist times, and all the way through the Soviet Union, has been the strongest supporter of the Kurds (in 1787, Catherine the Great commissioned the standardisation of Kurdish grammar), is naturally playing the Kurdish card to punish Erdogan's Turkey. Michael Reynolds continues:

> Success in achieving self-determination rarely comes without assistance from an outside power. Russia has been a champion of Kurdish causes longer than any other external actor, and today is uniquely positioned to facilitate further movement toward an independent Kurdistan. If the thought of Putin as Kurdistan's godfather keeps Turkish President Erdoğan and Prime Minister Ahmet Davutoğlu up at night, it should. As admirers of Sultan Abdülhamid II, they should know that Russian arms and diplomacy secured Bulgarian, Romanian and Serbian independence in 1878. Perhaps Kurdistan awaits its own liberator tsar.[17]

And though it would not be in Russia's interest to actively encourage the creation of an independent Kurdistan, Russia could have used the Kurdish card if Turkey had continued its anti-Russian behaviour in the Middle East. However, due to various factors, including Russian sanctions against Turkey, tensions between Turkey and its Western allies, and the failed *coup d'état* attempt of 15 July 2016 by Turkish military against President Erdogan led to dramatic changes in Turkey's foreign policy. Erdogan's half-apology for downing the Russian bomber led to the 9 August Putin–Erdogan meeting in St Petersburg and gradual normalisation of relations between the two countries. And who could have thought then that, at the end of January 2017, Russia and Turkey, together with Iran, would sponsor a meeting in the Kazakh capital Astana between the government of Syria and main opposition forces, with the exception of those considered terrorists by the world community?

In the immediate aftermath of the downing of the Russian military plane, most of the reactions in the West were genuine and logical. Indeed, the very next morning the French daily *Le Figaro* carried an editorial headlined 'La Turquie a cessé d'être notre alliée' ('Turkey has ceased to be our ally').[18] However, such outside-the-box thinking did not last long. Another French newspaper, *L'Obs*, a day before the Turkish attack, when it was already becoming clear that President Hollande's frantic efforts to create a broad coalition were running into the mire, entitled its article 'La France renonce à une "coalition unique" contre Daech' ('France gives up the idea of a "unified coalition" against ISIL').[19] Furthermore, the Secretary General of NATO, as well as President Obama, both claimed that, as a NATO member, Turkey had the absolute right to defend its airspace. Moreover, the European Union also became a hostage to Turkey. French military and security expert Hadrien Desuin, in an interview on 28 November 2015 to *Mediapart* entitled 'The West has been mistaken about Turkey',[20] speaks of Erdogan's authoritarianism and his relations with the jihadists of ISIS and al-Nusra, and claims that Erdogan's decision to join the fight against ISIS only served as a pretext to bomb the Kurds. Answering the question of why Western leaders had not reacted to Erdogan's dealings with ISIS, Mr Desuin responds that 'the French public opinion is not informed about these things because the media tries to play down such awkward questions' (a subtle example of propaganda). If nothing else, then at least the Turkish behaviour during the battle between ISIS and the Kurds over the Syrian town of Kobane should have opened everybody's eyes to Erdogan's duplicity. A couple of days later, the same expert in *Le Figaro*, in an article entitled 'How Turkey is Cheating Europe in the Poker Game',[21] writes about the deal between the EU and Turkey of 29 November. According to this deal, in exchange for 3 billion euros and the acceleration of EU membership negotiations for Turkey,

Turkey promised to hold back refugee flows into Europe. Mr Desuin submits that 'the refugees and migrants have become bargaining chips' while Europe, in allowing Ankara to blackmail it, is jettisoning its values and principles. A new deal between the European Union and Turkey was signed on 18 March 2016, according to which Turkey would be allocated, in addition to the earlier promised 3 billion euros, 3 billion more, and a visa-free regime for Turkish nationals travelling to the EU starting from June 2016, as well as other benefits in exchange for the promise to take back those refugees that already left for Greece from Turkey after 20 March, and take measures to curb new refugee flows to Europe via Turkey. Amnesty International's UK director, Kate Allen, condemned the deal in the strongest of words: 'This is a dark day for the Refugee Convention, a dark day for Europe and a dark day for humanity'.[22]

Too much discussion about values, especially their shared or universal nature, should always leave one wary as to the true intentions of those who do the talking. As far back as in the 1920s, German philosopher and legal theorist Carl Schmitt incisively wrote:

> When a state fights its political enemy in the name of humanity, it is not a war for the sake of humanity, but a war wherein a particular state seeks to usurp a universal concept against its military opponent [...] The concept of humanity is an especially useful ideological instrument of imperialist expansion, and in its ethical humanitarian form it is a specific vehicle of economic imperialism. Here one can be reminded of a somewhat modified expression of Proudhon's: 'whoever invokes humanity wants to cheat'.[23]

This warning from almost a century ago is especially apt today, since it is not only the Turkey of Recep Tayyip Erdogan that sees itself as a bastion for Europe against the barbarians at the gates, but President Poroshenko of Ukraine also pretends to play the same role. In his interview on 4 December 2015 to *Le Figaro*, without any irony, without blinking an eye, he claimed that 'today, in Ukraine, we are fighting to defend European values – liberty and democracy – and also for the security of the continent'.[24] Poor Europe!

If one were to remove ideological blinders, it would not be difficult to see what is hidden behind Erdogan's and Poroshenko's words regarding European values. Yet there is too much Russophobia in the mainstream of Western media, impairing objectivity. So, the 30 November 2015 edition of *Foreign Affairs* – one of the most (if not *the* most) prestigious American foreign policy publications – released an article by journalist Gregory Feifer: 'Putin's Game of Chicken and How the West can Win'. It was not about winning the 'war on terror' or containing and reversing climate change, but about winning the 'war against Russia'. A lot in the article is about Turkish–Russian relations, and if anybody who is not familiar with the facts were to read it they may be left with the impression that it was Russia who had downed a Turkish aircraft and not the other way round. As the journalist concludes:

> Even in this fight [the fight against jihadists in Syria], cooperation with Russia would be a losing proposition. It would also send the wrong message to Russians by indicating that Putin's behaviour works [so, this is what worries him]. So far, he has compounded the killing and suffering in Syria because it contravenes Western interests and values [again values, but this time even worse – the killings in Syria happen because Russia contravenes Western values], fuelling the threat of terrorism and Europe's migration crisis.

I quote him verbatim and at length, only because otherwise the reader would probably not believe me. But what is worse in all this is that Mr Feifer, I am almost certain, sincerely believes in what he wrote. And this can only be explained by Russophobia, whatever its roots in this certain case. Therefore, the strength of Guy Mettan's argument, even on the point on which I initially had doubts, is once again proven. And yet alongside other such outbursts of Russophobia, there are increasingly more and more sober voices to be heard in the West, from those who see the way forward in a cooperative effort between the responsible actors on all sides, to the vexation of those politicians who carry Russophobic cards up their sleeves, and who start behaving irrationally whenever any signs of cooperation become detectable. It would also anger and discredit those who built their careers on spreading Russophobia in the media. Now is not the time to let phobias triumph over reason; too much is at stake. Therefore, one must welcome rational and sound voices, like that of François Fillon, who, responding to an interviewer's question as to whether European sanctions against Russia should be lifted stated: 'It is necessary to put an end to the senseless and dangerous cold war between Europe and Russia'.[25] Similarly, at the beginning of 2016, 20 former high-level French diplomats, including foreign ministers such as Hervé de Charette, Roland Dumas and Hubert Védrine, as well as prominent intellectuals (Régis Debray, Renaud Girard, etc.), forming Le Club des Vingt (The Club of Twenty), wrote that 'by becoming the best student in the Atlantic classroom and rivalling there even the servile Great Britain [...] France has lost its independence'.[26] They conclude: 'The European continent without the new Russia would not be complete; a strong Franco-Russian relationship is a must for the sake of European balance. A Paris–Berlin–Moscow axis would be an ideal guarantee of peace in Europe and even beyond in order to avoid a risk of the emergence of the bi-polar (Sino-American) world'.[27]

The French philosopher Alain Badiou, in an essay published after the November 2015 terrorist attacks in Paris,[28] draws our attention to the double standards in the rightful indignation of the Western world in response to the attacks. Badiou quotes President Obama, who (justly) defined the attacks as crimes not only against Paris and France but also against all of humanity. However, Obama had never used the same approximate language, as the French philosopher reminds us, when similar atrocities had been committed in Nigeria, India, Iraq or Pakistan, to say nothing of the downing of the Russian civilian aircraft by ISIS in October 2015 over the Sinai Peninsula, where 224 Russians lost their lives. This, Badiou observes, 'means that Obama wants to remind us that for him the humanity is first of all the good old West. It is possible to say: humanity = the West'.

Similar double standards can be seen in the reactions of some in the Western media to the terrorist attacks, by Islamists of mainly Chechen origin, in Russia in the 1990s and at the beginning of the 2000s. Take for instance the October 2002 *Nord-Ost* theatre hostage crisis in Moscow, where Chechen Islamist separatists took 850 spectators hostage and of whom 130 died, or the September 2004 Beslan (North Ossetia) school siege where Islamists took 1,100, mostly children, hostage and of whom 385 died. Here the Western media, as well as everyone among the political elites, did not use the language of 'attacks against humanity', and offer unconditional support to Russia, but chose instead to concentrate their criticism on the Russian authorities who, in their opinion, had, through their undemocratic policies, brought the disaster on themselves, and who, moreover, had handled the crises incompetently.

Similar double standards appear naturally, almost instinctively, when the Western media covers events in China. Terror attacks against China either are not viewed as terror attacks at all, or it is the policies of the authorities that have brought those attacks on in the first place, as though they were almost inevitable. After the 13 November 2015 terror attacks in Paris, there was an understandable worldwide expression of sympathy with both Paris and with France. China and the Chinese, both the people and the authorities, were no exception. Yet, there was to be, with an air of inevitability, a complication concerning the evaluation of the Chinese reaction from some in the Western media. Ursula Gauthier, the French *L'Obs* Beijing correspondent, published an article entitled 'After the attacks, Chinese solidarity is not without hidden agenda'.[29] In the article the French journalist criticised the approach of the Chinese Security Minister, who had qualified attacks by Uighur militants in Baicheng (Xinjiang province), where about 50 Han Chinese were killed, as terrorist attacks. She wrote that 'though bloody, the attacks in Baicheng are in no way similar to the 13 November attacks'. This was a 'localised rage', she wrote, that was caused by policies of 'pitiless repression' by the Chinese authorities against the Uighurs in the province. Even if the Baicheng bloodshed may have had concrete and local trigger mechanisms, and agreeing that all terror attacks differ in many respects, such a 'downgrading' of the attacks against the Chinese people is insensitive and insulting. The situation in Xinjiang is much too complicated to be characterised as 'pitiless repression' ('*répression impitoyable*'). Moreover, voicing doubts as to the sincerity of the solidarity of the Chinese people and their leaders while graciously accepting the condolences of President Obama is rather thoughtless. Such approaches and mind-sets are politically short-sighted and counter-productive. They express what Alain Badiou defined as an attitude 'almost enshrined in our subconscious that leads us to believe that a death in the West is something terrible and that a thousand deaths in Africa, Asia or in the Middle East, even in Russia, is not a big deal'.[30] Terrorism must be qualified as such no matter the targets. Otherwise we are on the familiar but shaky ground of one man's terrorist being another man's freedom-fighter.

Western Advances, Russia's Responses

In the geopolitical struggle between Washington and Moscow, as well as between Washington and Beijing, Washington's primary policy is one of containment (or roll-back), and if some states which border Russia are not currently American allies, then Washington does everything possible to make them such. The regime changes in Georgia and Ukraine, notwithstanding the existing domestic discontents, are textbook examples of such policy. In these cases, Washington has used both its superior economic resources as well as its soft power to steer the change from a relatively neutral regime (it would go against common sense to argue that Eduard Shevardnadze was either anti-American or pro-Russian[31], and even Yanukovych in Ukraine was more pro-corruption than pro-Russian, and in any case tried to seduce both Russia and the West) into a pro-American one. There is often no need to take by force what one can afford to buy. As Renaud Girard writes: 'The United States has understood that it is not always necessary to shed blood in order to build an empire. Pinching others using American laws and economic warfare will often suffice'.[32] However, there are, as always, those who stand in the way of empire-building, and in this case and in Europe this is Russia. French author and banker Arnaud Leclercq observes:

> The two superpowers of the second half of the twentieth century remain natural antagonists simply due to their situations, their sizes and respective resources. The ideological conflict that opposed the West to Marxism-Leninism has gone away but the

> weight of geography and the heritage of history remain the main factors determining the will of the United States to diminish the power of a country of continental size whose resources would allow it to contest the American hegemony.[33]

Naturally, Russia responds to the attempts of containment in their various forms. In the case of Georgia, when the pro-American regime of Saakashvili attempted to regain South Ossetia by force, Russia didn't annex South Ossetia and Abkhazia, but used what may be called the 'Kosovo version' – it helped the secessionists to create, on the territory they controlled, a formally independent, but *de facto* dependent on Russia, entity. This is the strategy widely adopted against states that do not behave. In the case of Kosovo, it was Serbia which was not behaving in accordance with American scenarios,[34] while in the case of Abkhazia and South Ossetia, it was Georgia which was not behaving as Russia had wanted.

In the West, it is often emphasised that the annexation of the Crimea has been the first grab of foreign territory since World War II (at least in Europe), and that this makes this act something exceptional, a more aggravated violation of international law than other breaches, whether they had been committed either by Russia or by Western countries. For example, Daniel Treisman writes that 'Russian President Putin's seizure of the Crimean Peninsula from Ukraine in early 2014 was the most consequential decision of his 16 years in power. By annexing a neighbouring country's territory by force, Putin overturned in a single stroke the assumptions on which the post-Cold War European order has rested'.[35] But was it? What about Kosovo? Was it not separated by force from Serbia? It may not have been annexed by anybody, but these are legal niceties, about which more is written below. In terms of geopolitics the cases of Kosovo and the Crimea are quite similar. The fact that neither the Kosovars nor the

Crimeans wanted to stay in Serbia and Ukraine, respectively, also adds to their similarity. It may be true that this is the first recent annexation of the territory of another state in Europe, carried out by the threat of use of military force (in the case of Kosovo, it was actual use of force by NATO, which makes an even more aggravated violation), but is it really so exceptional when looked at in the light of ongoing geopolitical processes? Here I am not referring to historical justifications of Russia's take-over of the Crimea, nor of the desire of the majority of Crimeans to revert to the Russian fold, as was clearly expressed in the referendum of March 2014. I am talking about the geopolitical concerns of Russia. Justifying its annexation (most Russians refer to it as reunification) of the Crimea, Russia has presented a set of emotionally charged arguments: historical (the peninsular became part of the Russian Empire in 1783, and until Khrushchev's 1954 transfer of it to Ukraine had always been a part of Russia), ethnic (the majority of the population are ethnic Russians) and religious (the christening of Prince Vladimir in 988 took place in Chersonese in the Crimea) factors, and as though an afterthought – military-strategic considerations. However, in my opinion, though President Putin, other Russian leaders and the Russian media have stressed the emotional and historical aspects of the 'reunification', the proximate and most significant reason behind this act was geopolitical. The emotional angle, with its historical, ethnic and justice-based components, made it easier to justify in the eyes of most Russians that which was felt necessary to do for strategic reasons. When explaining the main reason for the annexing of Crimea (or returning it to the motherland) by Russia, I would compare the act with the attempt of the Soviet Union to install missiles with nuclear warheads in Cuba in 1962, or rather with the American responses to it. As a recent excellent study of US–Cuban relations by Nigel White generalises: '[t]he Cuban missile crisis of 1962, like so many elements of Cuba's relationship with the US, seemed to be conducted outside of the parameters of international law.'[36] Dean Acheson – a distinguished American diplomat and lawyer, the Secretary of State from 1949 to 1953 – when commenting on the 1962 crisis, said: 'The power, position and prestige of the United States had been challenged by another state; and law simply does not deal with such questions of ultimate power – power that comes close to sources of sovereignty.'[37] A frank admission. Today, Russian politicians and diplomats could have used the same language in justification of their behaviour vis-à-vis Ukraine. And they would not be wrong. As President Putin of Russia said on 18 March 2014, '[Y]ou know, I cannot imagine that we will visit NATO marines based in Sebastopol. Though most of them are good guys, we prefer to invite them to visit us in Sebastopol'.[38] For me, though the earlier historical, ethnical and religious reasons were touted as real justifications, this somewhat jokingly made statement was the real explanation for the geopolitical necessity of the annexation (or re-unification). The Kremlin believed, and not without reason, that if Ukraine were to join the American-led military alliance, the American navy would soon have had a base in Sebastopol. For the Americans to better understand the significance of the matter for Russia, it would be necessary to compare the scenario of having an American navy in the Crimea with the scenario of the Russians or the Chinese, separately or together, establishing a naval base at Guantanamo Bay.

As it has become increasingly clear that Washington and Moscow hold differing views on the future world order (unipolar versus multipolar), Russia could hardly have risked having a NATO naval base in the Crimea. The comparison between the Russian annexation of the Crimea and the 1962 Cuban missile crisis goes further. In 1962, Moscow did not breach any principles or rules of international law when it began, with the consent of the Cuban government, which had come to power in 1959 (importantly, without any assistance from the Kremlin), to deploy nuclear missiles on Cuba. However, Moscow's policies via Cuba vis-à-vis the United States were certainly going to disturb the existing balance of power between the two Cold War adversaries. Had Moscow instigated and/or militarily assisted a pro-communist regime-change in Habana, and then sent intermediate-range missiles with nuclear warheads to Cuba, the Soviet Union would have certainly been in flagrant breach of international law. However, from the point of view of geopolitical realities, as seen from Washington, such legal niceties were irrelevant. Lawful or not, Soviet missiles with nuclear warheads 90 miles from Florida would have been an unacceptable security risk for Washington.

Geopolitical expansions can take different forms: 1) expansion by way of annexing the territories of other states into one's own territory (or as a result of helping a region or people to realise an act of self-determination in the form of a secession that otherwise would have been impossible), 2) expansion by way of regime change, where independent or hostile governments are switched with friendly and/or subordinate ones (ideological expansion accompanied or followed by military-strategic expansion). If in Europe, the Crimean and Kosovan cases may be somewhat unique, the instigation by the West of regime-change in Georgia and Ukraine with the intention of eventually including them in NATO, Russia's helping hand in South Ossetia and Abkhazia and its recognition of the independence of these territories all belong to the second category.

The case of Kosovo, which is often portrayed as a model for successful humanitarian action, was in reality one of the first, if not the very first, significant steps on the path towards the triumph of geopolitics over international law. Unprincipled references to the principles of self-determination and respect for territorial integrity have continued and intensified ever since. Let us take only parts of the conflicts in the former Yugoslavia. We see that the world community is doing almost everything to hold Bosnia-Herzegovina together, though both the Croats and especially the Serbs want to leave an entity that is held together mostly by external efforts. At the same time, many states, including most members of the European Union, supported Kosovo's secession from Serbia. Even if one were to accept, together with Richard Goldstone, that NATO's use of force against Serbia over Kosovo was 'illegal but legitimate'[39], this does not explain or justify the 'manipulative administration' of Kosovo by international organisations (the UN and EU), which created conditions for this Serb province's secession and later for the recognition of its declared independence. The Advisory Opinion delivered by the International Court of Justice on 22 July 2010, in stating that Kosovo's declaration of independence 'did not violate general international law'[40] (also quoted by President Putin in his speech to both Houses of the Russian Parliament on 18 March 2014 in justification of the annexation of Crimea), though formally correct, is anodyne in content, and potentially explosive in its consequences. If I were to declare my house with its small plot of land in Tallinn independent from Estonia, I would not be in breach of any norms of general international law, since international law, general or particular, simply does not deal with such matters. However, if third states were to recognise my extravagant declaration and start giving me various forms of assistance and encouragement in my eccentric endeavour, their behaviour would certainly violate general international law; this would be a clear-cut interference in the internal affairs of my country. So was the recognition of the independence of Kosovo. The declaration of independence by Kosovo in itself may not have violated international law, but the fact that it became possible only as a result of

NATO's bombardment of Serbia in violation of international law adds credence to the declaration of independence being of doubtful legitimacy, and recognition of its declared independence by third states being a clear act of interference in Serbia's internal affairs.

In international law, the Roman legal maxim *ex injuria jus non oritur* (unjust acts cannot create law) is not as absolute as it is in most national legal systems. Therefore, the unlawful recognition of Kosovo by many states, and the later recognition of South Ossetia and Abkhazia by Russia as well as several others (the number of recognisers in these two cases does not impinge on their qualification as to legality or illegality; it reflects current geopolitical realities) are steps in the sense of another Roman maxim – *ex factis jus oritur* (the law arises from the facts). In any case, such practices have undermined some existing norms of international law, including such fundamental principles as non-interference in internal affairs and the non-use of force.

Moreover, even if we were to argue that, since Serbia in 1999 under President Milošević was not a democracy, and therefore the Kosovars could not realise their right to self-determination within the confines of Serbia, this was certainly not the case in 2008 when the Kosovars declared their independence, a declaration that was immediately recognised by most Western countries. On 15 February 2008, just two days before the Kosovars made their declaration, President Boris Tadić of Serbia, who had been democratically re-elected to his second term in office, was sworn in. Although Serbia had become a democracy, it still had some characteristics that many in the West did not like. Although there were no justifications, legal or moral, whatsoever under international law for the recognition of Kosovan independence, the explanations for such broad recognitions were exclusively political, or rather geopolitical. Serbia historically led an independent foreign policy and, significantly from the point of view of geopolitics, had long been allied and close to Russia; therefore, a weaker and smaller Serbia was to the benefit of some of the dominant Western powers. Perhaps because France too had in history been allied with Serbia more often than some of Serbia's immediate neighbours, there was more criticism from France than from other Western countries of both NATO's war against Serbia as well as the recognition of Kosovo's independence. To mention only two relatively recently published studies by French journalist Pierre Péan – *Kosovo: une guerre 'juste' pour créer un Etat mafieux*[41] (*Kosovo: A 'Just' War to Create a Mafia State*) and by French intelligence officer Jacques Hogard, who had participated in the NATO operation against Serbia, *L'Europe est morte à Pristina: guerre au Kosovo*[42] (*Europe Died in Pristina: The War in Kosovo*). These books reveal and document the double standards used to justify the 1999 NATO war against Serbia and the subsequent recognition of Kosovo's independence. Pierre Péan writes, for example, that Washington had been planning the construction of the military base Bondsteel (built by an affiliate of Halliburton – the American company whose Chairman and CEO at that time was future US Vice President Dick Cheney) in Kosovo long before NATO's bombs started landing in Serbia. In his opinion, 'this confirms the view that the Americans preferred war to peace'.[43] Péan quotes the former Foreign Minister of France, Hubert Védrine, who participated in the Rambouillet negotiations on Kosovo:

> Robin Cook [British Foreign Secretary at that time] and I were looking for a political solution, while Tony Blair was for a war. Madeleine Albright [US Secretary of State at that time] was from the very beginning the most eager to go to war, equating Milosevic with Hitler [...] As to Igor Ivanov [Foreign Minister of Russia at that time] he constantly repeated: 'I am here to

> prevent a war', though he detested Milosevic. Joshka Fischer [Foreign Minister of Germany at that time] was constantly torn between us – Cook and me – and Madeleine Albright, who was accusing the German Foreign Minister, when he was leaning towards finding a political solution, of being a leftist.[44]

A confrontational approach based on the idea of liberal expansion and the containment of those who resist continues to be the dominant approach in the West. An article by Danish international relations professor Sten Rynning is indicative in that respect.[45] To summarise: as Russia is not, at least in the foreseeable future, amenable to liberal change, it cannot be included (as France was included after the Napoleonic Wars) in a European concert, and must therefore be confronted by both NATO and the EU. Such a confrontational approach, spontaneous and almost instinctive, was also expressed by President Obama's former Security Advisor General James L. Jones during the Second Abu Dhabi Strategic Debate (1–2 November 2015), though in that case it concerned neither China nor Russia but Iran, with whom Washington, together with five other powers, had just signed a nuclear deal.[46] When asked by a participant from the United Arab Emirates how the Gulf countries could increase their security vis-à-vis new challenges (the number one challenge being, in the opinion of those Sunni monarchies, not ISIS terrorists but Iran and the whole Shiʿa world; the US having ceased, in their eyes, to be a reliable ally after concluding a nuclear deal with Iran), General Jones' immediate response was: you should think of creating something like NATO for the Gulf region. This is a confrontational mind-set that sees the world in Manichean terms where we, on the right side of history, face them, who are not only different and therefore wrong, but do not even seek to want to become like us. A Stratfor article, published already after Donald Trump had moved into the Oval Office on 20 January 2017, pointing out that as 'one of the United States' greatest geopolitical imperatives is to prevent the rise of regional hegemons with the ability to challenge Washington', argues:

> No matter who is in the White House, Washington's imperative to contain regional hegemons will continue to be a mainstay of its foreign policy. With Europe becoming increasingly divided since the Brexit referendum, Russia has another chance to recover from its strategic setbacks and regain influence in the Eurasian region in the coming year.[47]

However, this has to be seen. The dual containment of both China and Russia as well as the impossibility of American withdrawal from all of its involvements in other parts of the world (first of all in the Middle East) will be a burden that even the United States may not be able to carry. And there are more and more cooler heads in Washington who have started to recognise this new reality.

An alliance-centred, confrontational and tribal stance is not only dangerous by itself, creating and perpetuating conflicts, it is also an obstacle to cooperation in areas of common concern. So, the existence and enlargement of NATO – a relic of the Cold War – not only poisons relations between the West and Russia, but it also makes it much more difficult, if not impossible, to cooperate and coordinate on topics of global importance such as the fight against Islamist terrorism. As I will discuss below, instead of a confrontational approach to global, as well regional, politics, the world, and certain geographical regions specifically, needs cooperative, that is, concert-based, approaches – a modified nineteenth-century Concert of Europe.

This dual-track Washington policy – a world ruled from one centre, and the homogenisation of the world through, *inter alia*, the heterogenisation of individual societies – turns out to be counter-productive. Even if Washington's global dominance may be accepted by some, either willingly or unenthusiastically (seen as inevitable), many societies are more reluctant, or simply unable, to conform to a single societal model. By projecting its values and way of life Washington intends to create more reliable allies, effectively subordinates, who accept American leadership unquestioningly. Such a policy is inherently controversial and hits several obstacles. The first, and relatively minor, is that even societies that belong to the Euro-Atlantic community have their own histories, interests and even values that do not always and neatly correlate to those of the Americans. Moreover, by dominating its own allies and treating them as subordinates, Washington undermines its own power, shortens its dominance. As an example, by not listening to its NATO allies – France and Germany – in 2003, who counselled the United States against invading Iraq, Washington made a mistake of fateful consequences. This invasion of Iraq has not only considerably contributed to the current turmoil in the Middle East, terror threats in Europe and uncontrollable migration flows, its legacy is constantly nibbling away at American dominance and reputation globally. In his most recent book, the then Foreign Minister of France, Dominique de Villepin, observes that 'by supporting at the beginning of 2003 the mechanism of inspections in Iraq in accordance of Resolution 1441, we refused to follow the logic of neoconservatives of the Bush administration who hoped by liberating Iraq to trigger a virtuous cycle that would lead to the realisation of their crazy idea of creating a grand Middle East both peaceful and democratic'.[48]

The Americans and their closest allies (subordinates) in Europe constantly complain that Russia is trying to 'drive a wedge' between Europe and the USA, while there are others in Europe who claim that it is actually Washington who is seeking to break up Europe. In January 2003, Donald Rumsfeld, the then US Secretary of Defence, referred to France and Germany, who were against the invasion of Iraq, as 'the Old Europe', in distinction to 'the New Europe' aligned with the United States. How this alliance functioned is well illustrated in the following diplomatic-episode-turned-embarrassment. In the run-up to the 2003 American invasion of Iraq, the leaders of the CEE (Central and Eastern European) countries addressed a letter to President George W. Bush where they, contrary to France and Germany, wholeheartedly supported the American policy regarding Iraq. It later became known that the letter was originally written by the State Department in Washington and sent to the CEE leaders for signature. The Estonian Ambassador to NATO, Harri Tiido, in response to a question of the then Prime Minister Siim Kallas (how should one react to such an offer – or rather, order?), answered: 'If we don't sign, a big hammer will hit us now. If we sign and it becomes known, small hammers may hit us later'.[49] Instead of being destroyed right away, Estonia, like the other CEE countries, chose its moment of shame.

However, the second and bigger challenge to the policy of global homogenisation is that there are societies that are not only unwilling, but also unable to follow Washington's prescriptions. They either collapse under external pressure, becoming failed states, or face internal turmoil and even civil wars (Iraq, Afghanistan, Libya), or start actively counter-balancing (China, Russia). By now it should be clear that neither China nor Russia can be integrated into an international system under conditions determined and dictated by Western alliances and prescribed from Washington. There are other significant emerging powers who, on many issues, would prefer to retain or even increase their independence in taking foreign policy decisions. The terms and conditions of their integration into a multipolar international system have to be negotiated, taking into account the specific positions of all the significant responsible players.

If such a re-negotiation of the rules of the game, be they in the form of legally binding norms, 'soft law' documents or other political arrangements and understandings, does not take place, serious conflictual situations will be inevitable.

Washington's Competing Nightmares: A Sino-Russian Strategic Partnership or de Gaulle's Europe

An article by two American authors – Mathew Burrows and Robert A. Manning – aptly entitled 'Kissinger's Nightmare: How an Inverted US-China-Russia May Be Game-Changer'[50] expressed serious concerns about Washington's double containment policy vis-à-vis China in Asia and Russia in Europe, involuntarily driving these two powerful actors into an anti-American partnership, if not an outright alliance. This is what Henry Kissinger, while in office in the White House and the State Department, was successfully avoiding at all costs. Today, while aiming to weaken and surround Russia through its military allies, Washington is simultaneously intensifying the anti-Chinese component of its pivot to Asia. As a result, it would indeed be strange if Moscow and Beijing weren't to converge on many important issues that would not be to Washington's liking, although their formal anti-American alliance, be it political or military, seems far-fetched, at least at present. And yet, there exists another scenario which may trump even Kissinger's nightmare. This is the prospect of a Europe that stretches from Lisbon to Vladivostok, or, to use General de Gaulle's version, from the Atlantic to the Urals. This was what Gorbachev and Yeltsin spoke of, and this was even one of President Putin's preferred policies until it became clear, specifically after the continuing NATO expansions, that in a post-Chirac-Shröder Europe, the foreign policies of European countries had become almost totally subordinate to American interests. However, in Europe, and especially in France, de Gaulle's dream is still alive; it is a vision of the world, or at least of the continent, where cooperation and compromise prevail over confrontation, where there is no place for sanctions and mutual threats, and where the current Russophobic propaganda war in the West and anti-Western propaganda war in Russia, both of which exceed even the Cold War period's primitivism and offence to human intelligence, would not be a reality. And this dream is in no way anti-American. If I were to act as some American politicians and diplomats do, who love to tell other nations what is good and what is not, I would say that Washington is in dire need of allies who would behave as Jacques Chirac's Foreign Minister, Dominique de Villepin, did at the UN Security Council in February 2003, when he warned the United States against the illegal and presumptuous invasion of Iraq. He turned out to be even more prescient than he could ever have imagined, those 14 years ago.

In his book, entitled *Pour une Europe de l'Atlantique à l'Oural* (*For a Europe from the Atlantic to the Urals*),[51] Gaël-Georges Moullec analyses French foreign policy under President de Gaulle. As the author observes, 'the politics that General de Gaulle had vis-à-vis the Soviet Union was based on the complex interplay of two aspirations: his desire to have an independent and strong France and his perception of Russia [NB, Russia not the USSR] as the timeless Saint Russia'.[52] It is not easy to deny that during the Cold War NATO played a counter-balancing and crucial role in guaranteeing the security of Washington's European allies vis-à-vis Moscow's missionary efforts. However, in the post-Cold War world, NATO has become not only an anti-Russian, but an anti-European organisation, in the sense that by means of the Atlantic Alliance Washington has deprived Europe of any independent foreign policy decision-making power, particularly on matters of European and international security. Moreover, as military might and political levelheadedness are often at odds, and what may be enjoyable for Uncle Sam may not necessarily satisfy Marianne or Germania, such an outsourcing of European security may be dangerous for the Old Continent. Therefore, it is natural that many in Europe, especially in Rumsfeld's 'Old Europe', consider the current tension between Russia and the West as one of the greatest follies of the century, and it is mainly due to the policies of Western political elites. Renaud Girard wrote that 'we definitely lack a serious policy on Russia' and 'it is urgent that France become closer to Russia' (*'que la France se rapproche de la Russie'*).[53]

Let us take, as an example, today's Middle East. One of the main factors that has made the resolution of the conflict in Syria particularly difficult is that Turkey is a NATO member. Turkey's relationship with the West has many similarities and parallels with the above-mentioned American nightmare scenarios – the first pushing Russia closer towards Asia, into an alliance with China, and the second allowing Europe and Russia to ally, making both stronger and more independent, both scenarios rivalling Washington's global dominance. In the case of Turkey, Washington's choice is between support of its NATO ally in whatever it does, because it is an important asset in the policy of containing Russia, or forcing Ankara to stop its almost genocidal behaviour vis-à-vis the Kurds, not only in Turkey but also in Syria, as well as compelling Erdogan to cease the support of Islamist jihadists. In February 2016, Washington and its NATO allies in the UN Security Council rejected a draft resolution presented by Russia demanding the halt of the cross-border shelling of Kurds in Syria from Turkey, though President Obama over a phone call with Erdogan had earlier urged Turkey to 'show reciprocal restraint'.[54] Amazingly, these are the same Kurds who had been fighting ISIS, and who, moreover, had been trained by American instructors. It would be hard to imagine a more illogical situation. However, as long as Washington believes that the containment and roll-back of Russia is its primary foreign policy aim (in parallel with the containment of China), it cannot have a principled policy on Syria or anywhere else. Moreover, in 2017 this NATO member seems to be more allied to Russia than to the US, at least in matters Syrian. Such a shift, in itself, is laudable so far as it is contributing to the fight against terrorism in the Middle East. It has to be noted, however, that the American people in general are much less amenable to the anti-Russian propaganda than the political and intellectual elites, who, in a kind of collective psychosis, have started to believe that which they preach. If Obama's United States Secretary of Defence Ashton Carter had declared at the end of 2015 that though terrorist elements like ISIS are entirely opposed to American values, 'other challenges are more complicated, and given their size and capabilities, potentially more damaging', singling out two: 'Russia's provocations and China's rise'[55], most Americans had differing thoughts on the matter. One of the Gallup polls showed that the majority of Americans believe that it is international terrorism that is the greatest threat to their country – Russian military power is in 12th place, after the spread of infectious diseases, the military power of North Korea, global warming and other threats.[56] Such inversed perceived priorities are not, of course, limited to the United States and deserve their own special study: why are people in general more reasonable than political elites and the many experts affiliated to them? A perfect example of Western hypocrisy can be found in an article published in *Le Monde* just before the 2016 Easter holidays, 'Les possibles conséquences de la reprise de Palmyre par le régime syrien'[57]

('The possible consequences of the return of Palmyra by the Syrian regime'). Here, the authors, Louis Imbert and Madjid Zerrouky, seem to be at a loss as to how to react to the advances of government troops into Palmyra, which for months had been occupied by ISIS terrorists, who had already began destroying priceless ancient historical monuments, which belonged not only to Syria itself but to all of mankind. On the one hand, to have left the world heritage site in the hands of ISIS seemed fatal to its existence; on the other, it also seemed off-script, from their point of view, that these were the troops of the 'regime' which kicked ISIS out, and what made the matter even worse, they were supported by the Russians and Iranians. Moreover, such a victory would give the 'regime' the opportunity to reconquer other territories from ISIS. I despaired that it appeared that there are those who would prefer to see the world go down the drain rather than be saved by Russians or Iranians. This is an example of hypocrisy among experts which is sadly not unique. However, at the end of the article I came across some very profound comments from some of the readers, one of which I especially liked. A reader, calling himself Ayatollah Gros Minet, writes: 'I like neither the mullahs nor al-Assad nor Putin, but I have to admit that when the regular army of Syria, supported by the Iranians and by the Russian air force, fights ISIS and prevails, we have to congratulate them. I am waiting for toasts from the European leaders at least for the Russians and Iranians' (*Le Monde*, 25 March 2016). My day was saved, and faith in common sense restored when I read that the Director-General of UNESCO, Irina Bokova (not a Russian, despite the Russian-sounding name), condemning the cultural cleansing in the Middle East, also welcomed the Syrian army's advance to Palmyra.[58] And the lack of cooperation between Washington and Moscow was one of the reasons allowing ISIS to recapture Palmyra at the end of 2016 liberated anew in 2017.

NATO's post-Cold War inappropriateness and untimeliness is even more visible in Europe. The continuation of this major Cold War institution, whose very *raison d'être* had been the containment of an enemy who has since disappeared, could be considered, slightly paraphrasing President Putin (who had called the dissolution of the USSR 'the greatest geopolitical tragedy of the 20th century', with which I disagree but which I understand), *the greatest geopolitical nonsense of the twenty-first century.* The latest RAND corporation report, 'Reinforcing Deterrence on NATO's Eastern Flank'[59] opens with this categorical statement: 'Russia's recent aggression against Ukraine has disrupted nearly a generation of relative peace and stability between Moscow and its Western neighbours and raised concerns about its larger intentions'. Let us leave aside the authors' absolute certainty that Russia has committed an act of aggression against Ukraine. Like practically any unqualified opinion on complicated issues and sophisticated juridical concepts (e.g., the definition of aggression, interference in internal affairs, the right of peoples to self-determination), it is conditioned not by any concern for facts or law but by an almost religious belief informed by aggressive brainwashing. The report may indeed be correct in its calculation that it would take 'Russian forces 60 hours to reach the outskirts of the Estonian and/or Latvian capitals of Tallinn and Riga'; though in my layman's assessment it may take much less time. On this information, the Report recommends, notwithstanding the very dear cost, to add to the NATO forces present in the region 'seven brigades, including three heavy armored brigades – adequately supported by airpower, land based fires, and other enablers on the ground' to avoid the rapid overrun of the Baltic states. Maybe it is not the job of the RAND Corporation or NATO to think in non-confrontational and non-military terms, but for me as an Estonian, and having the audacity to say a thinking and critically minded Estonian (and as John Lennon sang, 'I'm not the only one'), such a uni-dimensional mindset, such inability to think 'outside the box', is simply frightening. Even if a NATO–Russia military conflict, as played out by RAND scenarios or as depicted in the BBC's documentary *World War Three: Inside the War Room* of February 2016, could be contained in its relatively early stages, and Washington and Moscow were spared, my country – Estonia – would certainly be destroyed. Instead of raising tension and ratcheting up propaganda, it would be in the interest of all involved to preserve and venerate cooperative thinking. One could start with the question formulated in the title of Doug Bandow's article in *The National Interest* – 'Why on Earth Would Russia Attack the Baltics?'[60] Why indeed? And are there any signs at all that signal Russia's intentions to expand in the Baltics or anywhere else? Russia has indeed used military force against the two former Soviet republics – in 2008 against Georgia when the government ('regime') of Saakashvili invaded Georgia's break-away territory of South Ossetia, as well as in 2014 when its troops in the Crimea threatened to use force in case the Ukrainian military were to prevent the population of the peninsula from voting. The outcome of the referendum was foreseeable, taking into account the ethnic composition of the population as well as its previous voting, as expressed in the referendum of 20 January 1991.[61] Yes, this was interference in the internal affairs of Ukraine, but not an act of aggression, and the fact that the United States and other NATO countries had earlier blatantly interfered in the affairs of Ukraine by supporting both covertly and overtly the opponents of the government of President Yanukovych may serve as a mitigating circumstance for the Russian interference. As Renaud Girard writes regarding the referendum of 17 March 2014 in the Crimea: 'Even if the conditions in which the referendum was carried out were not ideal, let us stop lying: no Russian soldier was seen dragging voters to polling stations and the jubilation of the Crimeans after the polling in the main square of Simferopol was genuine'.[62] Since then, Russia has provided assistance, including military, to those insurgents in Eastern Ukraine who rebelled against the government (or 'regime', if one prefers), which had come to power as a result of a *coup d'état*.

One of the, if not *the* main, explanations for these two uses of Russian military in Europe is that they are defensive responses to NATO's expansion. One may, of course, argue that though NATO may have invaded Kosovo in 1999 and Libya in 2011 (the latter, though mandated by the UN Security Council's Resolution 1973, also became illegal when NATO began exceeding its mandate considerably), and had used and is still using military force contrary to international law, it has not annexed any territories in Europe or elsewhere. In this context, it is of interest to note that Moscow did not annex either South Ossetia or Abkhazia; instead it used what could be called *NATO's model of expansion*. The Crimean case is exceptional, and Russia's behaviour vis-à-vis Eastern Ukraine shows that the Kremlin has no intention of either annexing any parts of Eastern Ukraine itself, or even aiding rebels there to the extent that they would be able to create their own statehood.

Russia had no choice but to respond militarily to Georgia's invasion of South Ossetia, but, in my opinion, the Kremlin was wrong in recognising the independence of South Ossetia and Abkhazia. Not only was such a recognition contrary to international law (as was Kosovo's recognition, which may have served as a precedent), it was also a politically short-sighted, hasty and strategically counter-productive move. A friendly Georgia, post a single-mindedly anti-Russian Saakashvili, would have been a much more important security guarantee for Russia than these two small break-away territories. In today's world, states' expansion through annexation of territory is an outdated mode of operation. Although not a new method, one of recent fashion is the extension of military alliances that often take place after foreign-assisted regime changes. Both forms of expansion are dangerous and illegal in the light of international law.

NATO's enlargement to the east, as well as the establishment of formal links between NATO and the European Union – a policy that Richard Sakwa calls the '"militarisation" of the EU'[63], the fact that all the most recent EU member states have also become NATO members and that under the Lisbon (the Reform) Treaty of 13 December 2007 accession countries are required to align their defence and security policies with those of NATO, shows that the Berlin Wall, instead of being demolished, has only been moved further east. And if in 1961 it was Moscow that built a wall in Berlin, in the literal as well as in figurative senses of the word, since the end of the Cold War it has been Washington who has restored it and moved it eastward. In the opinion of one of the finest American experts on Russia, Stephen Cohen, this has created a new Cold War situation which

> has all of the potential to be even more dangerous than the preceding forty-year Cold War, for several reasons. First of all, think about it. The epicenter of the earlier Cold War was in Berlin, not close to Russia. There was a vast buffer zone between Russia and the West in Eastern Europe. Today, the epicenter is in Ukraine, literally on Russia's borders. It was the Ukrainian conflict that set this off, and politically Ukraine remains a ticking time bomb. Today's confrontation is not only on Russia's borders, but it's in the heart of Russian-Ukrainian 'Slavic civilization.'[64]

In May 2016, Anders Fogh Rasmussen, the former NATO Secretary General, calling for an increase in the military spending of member states and for a more permanent presence of NATO forces in member states bordering Russia, stated that Russia believes that 'countries bordering Russia can either choose to join Russia's so-called sphere of interest or risk military occupation if they opt for stronger ties with NATO and the EU – as seen in Georgia, Moldova, and Ukraine'.[65] Leaving aside Rasmussen's unfounded claims about Russian military occupation, it is amazing that the former NATO Secretary General so offhandedly brushes away the issue of Russia's 'sphere of interest', calling it 'so-called'. It is only natural that Russia, like any country – big or small – shows a keen interest in the doings of their neighbours' houses, and especially in whether they align with a hostile military organisation or not.

In 1998, George Kennan, the father of the containment policy vis-à-vis the Soviet Union, warned against moving NATO closer to Russian borders:

> I think it is the beginning of a new cold war. I think the Russians will gradually react quite adversely and it will affect their policies. I think it is a tragic mistake. There was no reason for this whatsoever. No one was threatening anybody else. This expansion would make the Founding Fathers of this country turn over in their graves. We have signed up to protect a whole series of countries, even though we have neither the resources nor the intention to do so in any serious way. [NATO expansion] was simply a light-hearted action by a Senate that has no real interest in foreign affairs.[66]

As French economist Hervé Juvin observes, the main purpose of NATO and EU enlargements was 'to separate the European Union from Russia and make impossible the unification of Eurasia, what would be the Anglo-American nightmare'.[67] Arnaud Leclercq writes that, after the withdrawal from Eastern Europe and the dissolution of the Warsaw Pact,

> Russia expected that the West would recognise her European nature and establish with her relations of partnership while confirming her legitimate interests in maintaining a zone of influence that would correspond to her history and current interests. However, this was not to be the case and soon Russia saw NATO expanding to the East and the Americans increasing their presence in the countries of the 'New Europe' to the point of starting to build the infamous missile shield in the Old Continent to protect from the most implausible Iranian threat.[68]

'In the end, NATO's existence became justified', writes Richard Sakwa, 'by the need to manage the security threats provoked by its enlargement'.[69]

Michael Mandelbaum, in his most recent book, *Mission Failure: America and the World in the Post-Cold War Era*, observes that due to the humanitarian messianism of the Democrats and neoconservative ideology of the Republicans, American foreign policy ever since George H.W. Bush has gone from failure to failure. He blames Bill Clinton for waking up the Russian bear by recklessly expanding NATO to Russia's borders, George W. Bush for creating the chaos in Iraq, from whence ISIS emerged, and Barack Obama for allowing himself to be dragged into a war against Libya (ostensibly by Nicolas Sarkozy) with disastrous consequences.[70] 'The expansion of NATO', writes Mandelbaum, 'over their [Russian] objections taught Russians two lessons that it was not remotely in the American interest for them to learn: that American promises were not to be trusted; and that the West would take advantage of a weak and accommodating Russia'.[71] And he blames the Clinton administration 'for turning Russian foreign policy from a pro-American to an anti-American orientation'.[72] Whether more due to inertia and thoughtlessness (if nature abhors a vacuum, so does geopolitics; the gap left by the withdrawal of the USSR and then Russia was instantly filled by NATO) or a concerted effort to keep Russia down and out,

Washington's policy vis-à-vis Russia has indeed erected a new wall in Europe. Professor Bertrand Badie of Sciences Po Paris writes that the Clinton administration's foreign policy looked very much like a symbolic continuation of the Cold War:

> the first post-bi-polar world American President didn't hesitate to nominate in January 1997 Madeleine Albright as Secretary of State – a person who incarnated the very spirit of the Cold War by her background and family history. The daughter of a Czech diplomate having left the country just after the coup in Prague, and who had worked in the *Center for Strategic Studies* as one of the specialists on the USSR.[73]

The appointment of Cold War warriors to the top posts in the post-Cold War period was certainly not the wisest move. For reference, when, at the end of the 1980s, Professor Lori Damrosch of Columbia University and I led a group of American and Soviet international lawyers to work on a joint project to gain rapprochement between the US and Soviet approaches to international law, we, being then young and enthusiastic, chose only scholars who had not been tainted by the Cold War mentality.

The attempts by the West to tear Ukraine away from Russia and anchor it to the West have been especially painful for Russia and somewhat unnecessary and complicated for Europe, if we were to discount the geopolitical rationales which serve largely American interests. For quite a few 'pro-Europeans' in Ukraine, those European values that they proclaim to adhere to are not necessarily those that are inherently associated with the West, such as liberty, pluralism and tolerance, but those that today's Europe has by and large outlived or is struggling against, though not always successfully (xenophobia, intolerance and a readiness to resort to violence). Richard Sakwa writes:

> The enlargement of Wider Europe to the post-Soviet area and Ukraine meant pushing back Russian influence and limiting its geopolitical pretensions. In other words, for Svoboda [Svoboda – meaning Freedom – is one of the extreme nationalistic political parties in Ukraine] and others of that ilk the EU came to be associated not with normative values of human rights and good governance, and, above all, with the overcoming of the logic of conflict, but with the projection of Western European geopolitics, reinforced by the power of the Euro-Atlantic security community. The nationalists favour the EU not for its principles but because it embodies a set of interests that increasingly run counter to those of Russia.[74]

French historian Emmanuel Todd is of the opinion that

> The emergence of extreme right movements with Nazi colourings in the Ukrainian provinces of Galicia, Volhynia and Ruthenia would be surprising only for those who believe that liberation releases only the best in the people. However, for those who have observed the emergence of the Basque, the Irish, the Flemish or the Quebec nationalisms, this should not have been a surprise. We have to understand that Polish or Western Ukrainian Russophobia, even if it expresses itself in terms of the past, is a manifestation of the present crisis that has little to do with Russia's power.[75]

Ukraine is a country which, by Robert Cooper's classification[76], shares quite a few characteristics of a pre-modern state that is aspiring to become a modern one. This makes its attempt to join the post-modern European world somewhat schizophrenic. For example, the Ukrainian authorities are responding to centrifugal tendencies in a way that most modern or pre-modern states usually do – by resorting to military force. Instead of guiding this fractured society to choose the ways of compromise and de-escalation (though 'de-escalation' has often been hypocritically and/or naïvely misplaced), the main foreign actors (Washington, Brussels and Moscow) have put their strategic and economic interests above the wellbeing of the Ukrainians. The immensity of Ukrainian internal problems combined with the unfavourable external environment has made the building of Ukrainian nationhood an especially arduous task.

Although the current Ukrainian crisis, including the loss of the Crimea, civil war in its East and Russian involvement on the side of the 'separatists' began with the decision of President Yanukovych not to sign the Association Agreement with the European Union, the geopolitical competition over Ukraine is not so much between the EU and Russia, as between NATO and Russia, and the elephant in the room is Washington. From the Russian perspective, NATO looms behind the European Union, including behind the latter's Eastern Neighbourhood Policy (ENP). This is also an obstacle to closer EU–Russia relations. While the EU is a post-modern entity by definition and also, using Robert Kagan's metaphorical description, from Venus[77], NATO as a military alliance is by that analogy from Mars. Russia too, similar to NATO and the US, is from Mars, and acts in a Hobbesian geopolitical world with its zones of interest and influence. The West, represented by these two organisations – the EU and NATO – uses the good cop, bad cop tactic against Russia. While NATO keeps Russia at arm's length, containing it and pushing it back, the EU implores post-modern behaviour from Russia. The European Union would like to have the best of both worlds – a Russia acting as if it were from Venus, while sub-contracting to NATO the task of keeping Russia at arm's length. The first Secretary General of NATO, Lord Ismay, is credited with having been the first person to define the purposes of the alliance: 'to keep the Russians out, the Americans in, and the Germans down', a saying that during the Cold War period became a common way of describing what the North Atlantic alliance was all about. Now things have changed, but only by a third. Germany has been up, well and in for some time now, but the two other elements of NATO's *raison d'être* are still firmly in place.

It is interesting to note that though Washington is also using the politics of containment vis-à-vis Beijing (towards Russia it has been more of a roll-back policy), the Americans are less aggressive in their containment of China. This may be due to several factors. First, the Soviet Union, with its nuclear arsenal which matched their own, had been the main adversary for decades, while relations with China during the Cold War were even used to counter-balance the Soviet Union. Secondly, the United States has become economically and financially interdependent with China to such an extent that undermining Beijing's authority by instigating anything remotely similar to the 'Arab Spring' or the Colour Revolutions in China would have devastating consequences for the United States.

Terrorism – A Global Threat or the Small Fish of Geopolitics?

I started writing these lines shortly after terror acts were committed in European capitals – Paris and Brussels most recently, when all doubts had been extinguished as to the cause of the disintegration of the Russian civilian aircraft that had taken off from Sharm el-Sheik in Egypt in October 2015, when people had been murdered by terrorists in Bamako and in other places in Africa and Asia. It seemed that the world, at least that part of it that likes to call itself civilised, was finally facing a global threat, which in distinction to another, probably even more fundamental global threat – that of global warming – was 'instant, overwhelming, and leaving no choice of means, and no moment for deliberation', to use the words of the famous *Caroline* case,[78] which every international lawyer knows by heart. Such a threat should unite us all to fight it, whatever and notwithstanding our differences. As President François Hollande of France said when opening the Paris climate conference, the fight against global warming and terrorism 'are two big global challenges we have to face up to, because we have to leave to our children more than a world freed of terror, we also owe them a planet protected from catastrophes'.[79] During the previous decades, not only our natural habitats, but also our socio-political lives have both radically deteriorated in many societies. On the day of the Paris climate conference, *Le Monde* stated:

> If the attacks of 9/11 against the United States could have been seen as a thunderbolt coming out of the blue, the attacks of 13 November in Paris, on the contrary, took place in the atmosphere already darkened by the multitude of crises. During those fifteen years not only geopolitical tensions in the world had exacerbated, but Europe and particularly France were already facing challenges one worse than the other. At the end of 2015 all the lights were already in red.[80]

It should have been obvious that there was no need to wait for an extra-terrestrial invasion in order to admit that we were all in the same boat. As obvious as such a conclusion is for any reasonable mind, especially for a mind that has not lost its Pollyannaish innocence, this is much less obvious for experienced thinkers, for those who are familiar with the intricacies of international politics. My innocence in that respect was first severely broken some decades ago when a disastrous earthquake hit a small mountainous nation in what was still the Soviet Union, killing tens of thousands of people. This nation had long had (and still has) conflictual relations with its bigger neighbour (neighbours), relations that at the time were undergoing one of those intermittent periods of aggravation. As I was personally involved in the attempts to de-escalate the tension, I sincerely, though as it turned out naïvely, hoped that in the face of such tragedy people would put aside, if not forget, their historical grievances and humiliations, especially as many were more imagined than real anyway. However, this was not to be the case. Instead of condolences for the victims and their families and practical assistance, which poured in from all over the world, the neighbours sent messages celebrating the occasion as well-deserved, and as they put it, punishment. Unfortunately, for far too many it is not at all natural to rise above tribal instincts, even in the face of calamities that threaten to engulf all of us, be it global warming or the current terrorist wave, neither of which are showing signs of slowing down.

Olivier Roy, one of the rare connoisseurs of Islam in Europe, in answering a question posed by the French journal *L'Obs* regarding how to better fight Daech (the preferred French name for Islamic State or ISIS or ISIL), observed: 'the fighting against Daech is especially complicated by the fact that most regional actors have no interest in the disappearance of this organisation'.[81] The Shiʿas in power in Bagdad have no interest in fighting the Sunni extremists in Sunni territory; Turkey is much more involved in fighting its own Kurds than the jihadists of the Islamic State because the latter's defeat would benefit Kurds in Syria as well as Bashar al-Assad; for the Saudis the priority is Shiʿa Iran as well as all Shiʿas before the Sunni extremists of ISIS (the same is true of all the Sunni-led Gulf monarchies), and Israel is happy for Hezbollah to fight the Arabs instead of them. All of these regional powers have their bigger and more important fish to fry before ISIS. Moreover, several have actively contributed to the emergence of ISIS and other terrorist groups. But what about the really big fish? Do all global players feel the threat of militant Islamism equally?

Of course, one may have believed that after the 13 November 2015 carnage on the streets of Paris, threat perceptions should have changed everywhere. In Europe that could well have been the case, though it is hard to be equally optimistic about the United States. The main reason is not that America is much further from the source of the current turmoil, better protected by the world's oceans as well as by its post-9/11 domestic security protocols (I am referencing the relative effectiveness of American domestic security measures; internationally, on the contrary, the American-led 'war on terror' has made the world as a whole, including the United States, much less safe than it had been before). The main reason why Washington, though naturally recognising the terror threat, concerned by it and sometimes showing a readiness to fight it, nevertheless does not really consider it an existential threat, is because the political elite in the United States (but not the American people, as seen from the Gallup poll referred to above) also has its own bigger fish to fry.

Less than a week before one of the most terrible terror attacks carried out by ISIS in Paris, the then US Secretary of Defence Ashton Carter, as we commented above, at the Reagan National Defence Forum in California, declared: 'Terror elements like ISIL, of course, stand entirely opposed to our values. But other challenges are more complicated, and given their size and capabilities, potentially more damaging'.[82] And he singled out two overwhelming challenges: 'Russia's provocations and China's rise'.[83] In March 2016, commenting on the Pentagon's 2017 draft budget, French journalist Régis Soubrouillard underlined that instead of the small fish ($5.7 billion dollars to fight Islamist terrorists) 'the Pentagon has this time turned attention to the real enemies of a different calibre, which are not completely new: either Russia as a resurgent power or China as a rising power with whom it would be necessary to engage on the long-term basis'.[84] Such an approach should not be surprising, since there is little new in such a prioritisation of security threats to the United States, with the exception, perhaps, of the unipolar 1990s. Even then there were those who prophesised conflict and prepped the American psyche for the coming clash between really serious players. So, an influential report published in 1998 by the RAND Corporation and written by Zalmay Khalilzad (who later became the US Ambassador to the United Nations, Afghanistan and also to Iraq) and Ian Lesser, conjured four scenarios for the coming century: the 'great game', the 'clash of civilisations', the 'coming anarchy' and the 'end of history'.[85] The authors considered the last two scenarios less probable than the first two; they foresaw the great-game theory as the most probable, which would pitch the West (and Washington first) against China and Russia in a new great-power game. The Islamic threat was not seen as the most serious challenge to the United States. 9/11 may have altered these priorities, but only – as it turned out – for a time. Now we face the 'great game' scenario combined with the 'coming anarchy'.

Washington has oftentimes before tried to use movements with potentially destructive repercussions in the hope of being able to ride the tiger, to channel their destructive capabilities against global rivals. In February 2016, the French newspaper *Le Monde Diplomatique* published an article appropriately entitled 'Quand les djihadistes étaient nos amis'[86] ('When jihadists were our friends'), which concentrates mostly on the French support of those who fought the Soviet forces in Afghanistan (in contrast to the American, Pakistani or Saudi support, the French contribution to the jihadists was mostly 'intellectual').

Although nothing justifies the 1979 Soviet invasion of Afghanistan, Western behaviour was sometimes even uglier since not only was it equally wrong and counter-productive to its own interests (though this only became known later and is still not fully recognised), it was also very hypocritical. When the jihadists were Western allies and freedom-fighters, the criticisms regarding the oppression of women in mujahedeen territory, an issue that later became one of the justifications for a continuing Western presence in the country, was toned down because they were 'wholly Eurocentric and would not help to understand the country'.[87] The only reference in the *Le Monde Diplomatique* article to non-French support for the jihadists is to Zbigniew Brzezinski's February 1980 address from Pakistan: 'Your cause is just. God is on your side'. Has God since changed his mind? It was also then that the young French liberal interventionist Bernard-Henri Lévy started his crusade for 'le droit d'ingérence' (the right of intervention) and who, notwithstanding all the set-backs, be they in Libya, Afghanistan or Iraq – has still not slowed in his interventionist zeal, travelling from one potential hot-spot to another (from the Balkans to Libya, from Afghanistan to Ukraine) to fan the flames of conflict. People like him on both sides of the Atlantic continue to claim after every set-back that it was not their noble and doable aims that had been misguided, it was the execution, inadequate means and inferior resources of the intervenors, as well as the inaptitude of local allies, as it always is. The United States has a long history of walking the tightrope of using Islamic extremism against its global rivals. This started against the Soviet Union in Afghanistan and is still ongoing despite the boomerang effects that culminated in the catastrophic experience of 9/11. Yet, in 1998 Zbigniew Brzezinski proudly confirmed that by giving covert support to radical Islamic forces in Afghanistan in the 1970s, President Carter and he had induced Moscow to intervene on the side of the pro-Soviet government in that country, thereby miring the Soviet Union in its own 'Vietnam'.[88] Asked as to whether he had any regrets in having supplied arms to 'freedom-fighters'-turned-terrorists, President Carter's Security Advisor responded: 'What is most important to the history of the world? The Taliban or the collapse of the Soviet empire? Some stirred-up Moslems or liberation of Central Europe and the end of the cold war?' When confronted with the statement that 'Islamic fundamentalism represents a world menace today', Brzezinski retorted: 'Nonsense'.[89]

Unfortunately, such marriages of convenience continue today. As I write these words, a fragile ceasefire holds in Syria (March–April 2016), in accordance with the *Joint Statement of the United States and the Russian Federation on Cessation of Hostilities in Syria*, which does not apply to ISIS, the al-Nusra Front or other terrorist organisations as designated by the UN Security Council (*sic*, not by Russia, Iran or the USA unilaterally). There are many influential policy-makers who will try and turn some of these terrorist organisations against their greater threat, be it Bashar al-Assad, Russia or Iran. As Geoffrey Aronson writes in Al-Jazeera English, 'Retired generals David Petraeus, father of the "Sahwa" in Iraq, and John Allen, who until November last year coordinated Washington's anti-ISIS strategy, are among some in Washington who have been prepared, however fitfully, for an alliance of convenience in Syria with al-Qaeda's local agent [i.e., al-Nusra]'.[90]

The veteran American investigative journalist Seymour M. Hersh wrote about the Washington–Riyadh contacts back in 2007 when George W. Bush was still in the White House:

> the US government consultant told me, Bandar [Prince Bandar bin Sultan was the Saudi Ambassador to Washington from 1983 to 2005 and later the director general of the Saudi

> intelligence agency] and other Saudis have assured the White House that 'they will keep a very close eye on the religious fundamentalists'. Their message to us was: 'We've created this movement, and we can control it. It's not that we don't want the Salafists to throw bombs; it's *who* they throw them at – Hezbollah, Moqtada al-Sadr, Iran, and at the Syrians, if they continue to work with Hezbollah and Iran.'[91]

The legacies of previous administrations haunted President Obama. It has been noted that President Obama himself 'never believed in the notion of moderates' within Syrian opposition, but pushed by 'hawks' among his own advisors as well as by Sunni monarchies, he also decided 'to expedite President Assad's ouster'.[92]

One of the causes of the current turmoil in the Middle East is the reawakening of the once dormant Sunni–Shi'a conflict, most prominently manifested in the struggle for dominance in the region between Iran and Saudi Arabia. The current exacerbation of this cosmic stand-off is one of the reasons for the wars in Iraq, Syria and Yemen, which, in turn, are fanning the flames in all the current as well as potential conflicts in the region. This stand-off is also one of the main obstacles to finding solutions to them. Up until now, the West had clearly chosen the Sunnis as their allies, since they have provided oil and gas, invested petro-dollars into the Western world and have bought Western-made weapons. The recent book *Nos très chers émirs* (*Our Dearest Emirs*) by French journalists Christian Chesnot and Georges Malbrunot well chronicles how the Sunni monarchies of Saudi Arabia and Qatar had contributed to the rise of Islamist terrorism in the region.[93] However, there is more to it than that. Angelo Codevilla, Professor Emeritus of Boston University and a former Foreign Service officer, observes that 'all presidents since Jimmy Carter have searched the Sunni Arab world for counterweights to Iran'.[94] Such an attitude for the United States and the West as a whole to take is understandable, but this does not make it justifiable. Taking sides in this murky Sunni–Shiʿa conflict, which very few in the West (and certainly not among the political class) understand, may provide temporary and opportunistic advantages and benefits, but it is both morally wrong and politically short-sighted. It is morally wrong because those who have been oppressed and persecuted most in the Middle East have been Shi'as, be it in Bahrain where they constitute the oppressed majority, or in Saudi Arabia, where they constitute a sizable minority. Of course, one may also say that when Iraq had a Shiʿa Prime Minister in Nouri al-Maliki, he also was little concerned about the well-being of the Sunni minority under his care, a policy that contributed to ISIS's recruitment in the Sunni heartlands of Iraq. However, this was rather an exception. The general rule is that Shiʿas are oppressed in countries where Sunnis hold power. As a longer-term strategy, such side-taking is wrought with foreseeable boomerang effects. As Angelo Codevilla explains: 'Daesh/ISIS stands on three legs, without any of which it falls: the Sunni people in former Syria and Iraq over which it rules, the Sunni states from which it receives money and supplies, and the Sunni "fan boys" (and girls) around the globe who come to join it or who strike at the infidel where they are'.[95] Moreover, French professor Gilles Kepel – one of the most knowledgeable experts on Islam in the West – has shown that since 2005, when Mustafa Setmariam Nasar, alias Abu Musab al-Suri – a jihadist 'theoretician' – published his *Call for a Global Islamic Resistance*,[96] the main thrust of the movement's efforts, the so-called third wave of jihadism (the first being against the Soviets in Afghanistan in the 1980s, the second being the emergence and terror of al-Qaeda), has been carried out in European countries by dissatisfied young immigrants with the aim of unleashing a civil war in the West.[97] And though in my book I concentrate on ideologies that form both an intellectual background and justification for the geopolitical rivalries of great powers, the ideologies of Wahhabism and Salafism which form the 'scholarly' or ideological background of jihadism are of Sunni origin, emanating primarily from Saudi Arabia, and have been actively, even aggressively, promoted and sponsored by the Gulf monarchies (the United Arab Emirates being a clear exception).[98] As I wrote a decade ago, taking my experience of working for the United Nations in Central Asia as well as having visited the region regularly on other occasions, 'one may well understand the concerns of Central Asian experts and politicians when Arab and Pakistani missionaries in the 1990s started to import "genuine" Islam into Central Asia, "spoilt" by imposed Soviet atheism but also by Sufism and elements of traditional religions'.[99] And though it is true that even the absolute majority of the followers of Wahhabism and Salafism never resort to terrorism, it would be also wrong to deny the ideological impact of such conservative interpretations of Islam, which are rigid and extremely hostile to any other views and visions – be they religious or secular.

On the morning of 22 March 2016, just hours before the terrorist attacks in Brussels, in his interview to *Le Figaro*, Gilles Kepel had stated: 'It is very important today to think about the link between jihadism and Salafism since during dozens of years the Salafist narrative has acquired hegemonic dimensions among the French Muslims'.[100] It is not only necessary to use effective military or law enforcement measures to fight terrorism, but also to openly recognise and counter ideologies that nourish and encourage extremist behaviour. To do that, there is no need to become an Islamophobe. At the same time, the danger of being accused of Islamophobia, a tactic that is used not only by Salafists themselves but unfortunately also by some human rights organisations, should not prevent rational thinking and talking. It is one of those situations when it is impossible to at the same time be accurate and remain polite, to think rationally and be politically correct, and try to please everybody at once. Political correctness and doublespeak, which is if not a Soviet invention then at least a perfection, has today engulfed the West. After the terror attacks of 22 March 2016 in Brussels – the capital of Belgium as well as of Europe – Alain Destexhe, a senator from Belgium, admitted that 'we have for too long lived in denial. The political correctness has aestheticized the debate'.[101] Too much is at stake for us to continue in the same vein. The 22 May 2017 attack at Manchester Arena only confirms that Islamic terrorism remains a universal threat.

Robert F. Kennedy Jr, the son of the late US Attorney General Robert Kennedy and nephew of President John F. Kennedy, has revealed that one of the proximate causes of the war in Syria was not at all the 'Arab Spring' coming to Damascus and being brutally suppressed by President Bashar al-Assad (though there was obviously that too), but the rejection by the President of Syria of a Qatari proposal to construct a $10 billion, 1,500-kilometre-long gas pipeline through Saudi Arabia, Jordan, Syria and Turkey.[102] Such a pipeline would have hugely benefited the Sunni states, while running counter to the interests of the traditional supporters of Syria – Iran and Russia. 'The idea of fomenting a Sunni–Shiite civil war', writes Robert F. Kennedy Jr, 'to weaken the Syrian and Iranian regimes in order to maintain control of the region's petrochemical supplies was not a novel notion in the Pentagon's lexicon. A damning 2008 Pentagon-funded RAND report proposed a precise blueprint for what was about to happen. That report observed that control of the Persian Gulf oil and gas deposits will remain, for the US, "a strategic priority" that "will interact strongly with that of prosecuting the long war"'. RAND recommended using '"covert action, information operations, unconventional warfare"' to enforce a '"divide and rule" strategy'. 'The United States and its local allies could use the nationalist jihadists to launch a proxy campaign' and 'US leaders could also choose to capitalize on the sustained Shia–Sunni conflict trajectory by taking the side of the conservative Sunni regimes against Shiite empowerment movements in the Muslim world [...] possibly supporting authoritative Sunni governments against a continuingly hostile Iran.'[103] And Robert F. Kennedy Jr concludes his study:

> Despite the prevailing media portrait of a moderate Arab uprising against the tyrant Assad, US intelligence planners knew from the outset that their pipeline proxies were radical jihadists who would probably carve themselves a brand new Islamic caliphate from the Sunni regions of Syria and Iraq. Two years before ISIL throat cutters stepped on the world stage, a seven-page August 12, 2012, study by the US Defence Intelligence Agency, obtained by the right-wing group Judicial Watch, warned that thanks to the ongoing support by US/Sunni Coalition for radical Sunni Jihadists, 'the Salafist, the Muslim Brotherhood and AQI (now ISIS), are the major forces driving the insurgency in Syria.' Using US and Gulf state funding, these groups had turned the peaceful protests against Bashar al-Assad toward 'a clear sectarian (Shiite vs. Sunni) direction.' The paper notes that the conflict had become a sectarian civil war supported by Sunni 'religious and political powers'.[104]

The 5+1 nuclear deal with Iran, while being a step in the right direction on its own, may also lead to a more balanced approach to the Sunni–Shiʿa conflict by the West. In that respect, Russia's approach has also been more sensible in comparison with the West's. Allying with Iran in order to fight ISIS and supporting Bashar al-Assad (in the situation as it stands now, Assad's army is one of the few ground forces able, with Russian air support, to fight ISIS), Russia is at the same time bending over backwards in an attempt to not alienate the Sunni states of the region. Additionally, there are around 20 million Muslims in Russia (15 per cent of the population), of whom almost 95 per cent are Sunnis. The drastic temporary deterioration of relations with Turkey was wholly of Turkish making, and the shooting down of the Russian aircraft revealed what should have been obvious earlier – Erdogan's hypocrisy both within his country and outside had become too great, even in a world where everybody is dirty.

The inevitable answer to the question of whether it is ISIS or Russia and China that are the biggest threat to the West depends much less on what Russia or China are or do, or even on the fate of ISIS, than on the United States, its political elites, their understanding of the world and the tendencies of its development. Of course, both Russia and China, like other so-called emerging powers, have and will in the future have more and more say in world politics; they are in no way passive recipients of Washington's policies. And much will depend on Europe too. And yet, much more depends on the US. Not only because it has been, and for the time being remains, the most powerful nation in the world, the decline of its relative power notwithstanding. The main reason why so much (too much) in the world depends on what the United States does is that too many people in that country, especially among its political, economic and military elites, have that impossible dream for the whole world.

Chapter 4

The Future of International Law

The Separation of Powers and the Balance of Power as Foundations of the Rule of Law

As we observed earlier in the book in reference to Nico Krisch, it is international law, alongside the educational systems and the mass media, which is all-too-often used not as an impartial system of principles and norms, but as an ideological tool, which, though necessarily setting some limitations on a dominant power (or powers), also tends to 'legitimise', if not legalise, dominance. Moreover, international law is applied, interpreted and reinterpreted in the context of the ongoing propaganda war, as was analysed previously, and reflects and services differing visions of current tendencies and both their desirable and unwelcome outcomes. How, in such a situation, to make international law and its interpretation and application less ideological and more impartial? How to prevent that potential for the domination of international law to attain normalisation?

Every political system, and the international system is no exception, faces the problem of power. Without effective power there is anarchy and chaos, while the concentration of power suppresses individual as well as collective liberties. Within societies organised as states, that is, relatively hierarchical societies, one of the most effective remedies against the excessive concentration of power is the principle of the separation of powers into the legislative, executive and judicial branches, and their balance. International society is a horizontal, or relatively anarchical, system[1] where power is much more dispersed in comparison with societies organised as states. However, there is no absolute anarchy even in international society, otherwise there would be a *bellum omnium contra omnes*. Although the latter has existed at times in many places, politically organised societies have usually found some *modus vivendi* by curbing anarchy and inserting at least relative order into their relations. One may imagine all societal systems as being arranged along a spectrum between A (anarchy) and H (hierarchy). If most societies organised as states are closer to the H end of the spectrum, though never, of course, achieving it (the DPRK in North Korea may come closest), most international systems are closer to A, never of course achieving it as otherwise there would not be any society to speak of. In different international societies, as the late British diplomat and international relations theorist Adam Watson has convincingly shown,[2] the element of anarchy may vary quite significantly: 'There is a notional range of ways of organising a system of states, from absolute anarchy or multiple independences to total centralisation or empire'.[3]

Ordering anarchy in various international systems, both in regional and in today's global international systems, has taken different institutional forms, from imperial dominance to institutions such as the nineteenth-century Concert of Europe, the European Union or the United Nations with its Security Council. Empire is a form of international governance where an imperial centre rules over imperial peripheries. Here, dominance and order go hand-in-hand. Although the time of formal empires seems to be over, and anarchophilia[4] inspires international law through the principle of self-determination, dominance for the sake of order has never completely disappeared. The composition of the UN Security Council with its five permanent members out of 15 and their right of veto are some of the formal institutional examples of attempts to use shared dominance in order to curb anarchy. The nineteenth-century Concert of Europe was an even more successful, though less formal, attempt to order anarchy through the collective dominance of five European powers (Great Britain, the Austro-Hungarian Empire, the Russian Empire, Prussia and France – the latter being admitted later, after initial reluctance, as a full member), formed after the 1815 Vienna Congress.

However, just as in societies organised as states, power in international society also has the tendency to concentrate increasingly in one or more centres. Adam Watson, after studying various international systems over the past 2,500 years, observed: 'Powers that find themselves able to lay down the law in a system in practice do so'.[5] The phenomenon of power concentration, be it in economics (the tendency toward monopolisation absent regulation) or in politics, seems to be a general rule of societal life. Even in academia we can see that some universities, think tanks and laboratories are successful in imposing their schools of thought, while effectively supressing and marginalising dissenting views and opinions. In international society too, the necessity of a concentration of power for the sake of order tends to lead to its super-concentration. Guy Mettan observes that 'a power when becoming hegemonic, as Great Britain was after the Napoleonic wars, has a tendency to establish permanent supremacy, trying to destroy any rivalry until there is somebody who would bring it to its senses'.[6] And he emphasises:

> Any power without counter-power has a tendency to become absolute whether this takes place within a state or outside, if there is no other power (powers) who would be able restrain it; law in itself is not the sufficient guarantee against such tendencies. A candidate for a dictatorship can always change the constitution in his favour if there is nobody strong enough to challenge him and a power that is dominant internationally is able to 'interpret' or re-write international law in accordance with its own interest if there is no other power able to resist. And law becomes simply a façade that is called to conceal the pure relations of power.[7]

Any balance of power presumes, by definition, the existence of more than one power, just as a separation of powers domestically presumes the existence of at least legislative, executive and judicial branches between whom a certain balance should exist. With one single dominant centre of power there is either a totalitarian state (domestically) or an imperial system (internationally). If the multipolarity in the international system, ultimately, is essentially a necessity due to the sheer scale of the world, then its social, cultural and developmental diversity becomes a necessary, though not sufficient, condition for the existence of effective international law. As Lassa Oppenheim wrote in the first edition (1905) of his famous treatise on international law, 'Law of Nations can exist only if there is equilibrium, a balance of power, between the members of the Family of Nations'.[8] International law as such (in distinction, for example, to the imperial legal systems or current EU law) cannot exist in a societal system with one dominant centre. International law as a more or less coherent system of rules and principles, that is, as a legal system, started developing after the Westphalian peace of 1648, which had concluded the devastating Thirty Years' War in Europe. Before that period in Europe, there had existed a political system of multi-layered authority, where the Papacy, the Emperor of the Holy Roman Empire and a multitude of kings, counts, earls and dukes competed for a place under the Sun.[9] Hedley Bull, more than a quarter of a century ago, insightfully observed, having in mind the development of European institutions and the European regional system, that it might seem 'fanciful to contemplate a return to the medieval world, but it is not fanciful to imagine that there might develop a modern and secular counterpart of it that embodies its central characteristic: a system of overlapping authority and multiple loyalty'.[10]

The Westphalian international society that emerged in the aftermath of the Thirty Years' War was a regional international society, which in the end managed to extend itself, as well as its characteristics and principles, to the rest of the world. Adam Watson writes: 'The European society of states evolved out of the struggle between the forces trending towards a hegemonial order and those which succeeded in pushing the new Europe towards the independences end of our spectrum [...] The Westphalian settlement was the charter of a Europe permanently organised on an antihegemonial principle'.[11]

Only with the emergence of relatively equal centralised nation-states did modern international law (then often called the 'international law of civilised nations', i.e., European international law) take shape, with its concepts of sovereignty and domestic affairs. Of course, not all states were equal, and there was a constant struggle for dominance and attempts to either ignore international law, re-interpret it in accordance with one's interest or instrumentalise it for one's own purposes.[12] However, with the exception of the relatively brief period of Napoleonic Europe, no power was able to dominate the whole continent. And it was exactly for that reason that, after Napoleon Bonaparte had disturbed the existing power balance to its very roots and established an almost continental-wide empire, the victorious powers then consciously and conscientiously created a continental international system, which became known as the European Concert, and guaranteed the longest peaceful period the European continent had ever known.

Therefore, the comment by John Kerry, the then US Secretary of State, in March 2014 on Russia's policy vis-à-vis Ukraine, shows surprising historical ignorance. He said: 'You just don't in the 21st century behave in 19th century fashion by invading another country on completely trumped up pretext.'[13] The problem with this quote is not only that in both the twentieth and twenty-first centuries it has been Washington that has more often than anybody else invaded countries on trumped up pretexts, but also that Russia's annexation of the Crimea, beside the various historical, ethnic and even religious explanations and justifications, was intended to counter the unfavourable change to the balance of power which had already become threatening for Russia. The nineteenth-century Europe of the post-Napoleonic Wars had been so exceptionally peaceful that in 1910 English politician and writer Norman Angell wrote a book entitled *The Great Illusion*, in which he argued that a war between industrial countries had become practically impossible.

President Nixon and his national security advisor and Secretary of State Henry Kissinger have both showed considerably better knowledge of history than John Kerry. Richard Nixon, in 1971, speaking with the editors of *Time* and referring to the nineteenth-century European Concert, stated:

> We must remember the only time in the history of the world that we have had any extended period of peace is when there has been balance of power. It is when one nation becomes infinitely more powerful in relation to its potential competitor that the danger of war arises. So I believe in a world in which the United

> States is powerful. I think it will be a safer world and a better world if we have a strong, healthy United States, Europe, Soviet Union, China, Japan, each balancing the other, not playing one against the other, an even balance.[14]

And though Kissinger's diplomacy and Nixon's visit to China in 1972 served, *inter alia*, the purpose of balancing against the Soviet Union, the realism of the Nixon–Kissinger tandem is in stark contrast with the Wilsonian (or Lenin's, for that matter) utopian messianic idea of the betterment of the world, in the process of which societies are destroyed and thousands, if not millions, are killed. Kissinger warns us that a stable balance of power remains as crucial now as it was in the era of Westphalia, by emphasising that today,

> To achieve a genuine world order, its components, while maintaining their own values, need to acquire a second culture that is global, structural and juridical – a concept of order that transcends the perspective and ideals of any region or nation. At this moment of history this would be a modernization of the Westphalian system informed by contemporary realities.[15]

International law, especially in its most sensitive and politically loaded areas, does not work well in a world with unipolar tendencies, since in such a world international law (itself a result of bargain and compromise) and its interpretation is dictated from a unipolar centre, which is contrary to the very nature of international law. Until the beginning of the 1990s, international law had evolved as a balance-of-power normative system, though the bipolar system was not international law's best environment. The Cold War balance of power was almost exclusively a competitive balance where both poles not only constantly tried to outplay each other strategically, but also believed in the worldwide triumph of their respective social, economic and political systems. This is even though the period of détente (1969–79) was marked with bi-lateral and multilateral agreements (the latter were sometimes initiated by the two superpowers and then sent to allies on a FYA basis – for your attention), especially in the field of disarmament, as well as with informal rules of the game and political understandings. Although such a system, with only two dominant actors – which, moreover, believed in and strove for absolute dominance – was not the most stable, in such a situation this relative power equality, a constraint on each other's arrogance, had a soothing impact, even if it were the realities of Mutually Assured Destruction (MAD) more than international law that had the strongest pacifying effect. Therefore, Martti Koskenniemi's ironic remark that

> to apply Schmitt's description of the new Nomos [law] to the behaviour of the Western Powers in Kosovo and Iraq, the 50-year interlude may be explained by the Cold War having prevented a full-scale moralization of international politics. Ironically, then, for a century, the Soviet Union may have taken the role of the Schmittian *Katechon* – restrainer of the coming of the Antichrist.[16]

Of course, Moscow did not play the role of an idealistic restrainer to Washington's arrogance, but one of the effects, or side-effects if you will, of the relative balance of power between Moscow and Washington was certainly that it put limits on the use of force in international relations, and not only between the two superpowers; it had restraining effects beyond.

Even in such circumstances, far from ideal for the development of international law, it nevertheless progressed in many fields, and played a role that should not be underestimated. And although central principles of international law such as non-interference in internal affairs and the non-use of force (I would compare these principles to domestic law norms guaranteeing the right to privacy and personal security, and the right to life respectively) were sometimes breached, the balancing system played a positive role in the development and observance of international law. When today some liberal imperialists claim that the UN-authorised intervention in Libya in 2011 has not led to the expected results because it was carried out in the wrong way (in their view not because it went beyond the Security Council's authorisation but because not enough force was used) and lament that intervention in Syria was prevented by the exercise of veto power by Russia and China, they show complete ignorance of the real world. Any intervention in Syria, taking account of its location, size, ethnic and religious patterns and the interests of regional and global players, would have been a significantly more explosive matter than the destruction of Libya. Renaud Girard, writing about the problems and causes of the failure of the 'Arab Spring' and the almost inevitable choice in some Arab countries between military dictatorships and militant Islamists, like in Egypt, nevertheless singles out Syria. He emphasises: 'In Syria, the reality is that there is the civil war between the army of the regime and rebels, who in their majority are Islamists. The third way [i.e., between the authoritarian regime and Islamists] exists only as a minute candle at the end of an immense tunnel – as a dream supported by the Westerners'.[17]

The post-Cold War unipolar moment also led to attempts to transform existing law into a unipolar normative system controlled from the single centre, where there should be no room for counter-balancing. For a while, it seemed that international law would indeed evolve in that direction. The widespread use of military force for humanitarian purposes, both authorised by the UN Security Council (therefore lawful, though not necessarily legitimate) or bypassing the Council (illegal, but for some legitimate), the rapid evolution of international criminal law and jurisdictions, as well as high expectations that this could change the world, downgrading the role of state sovereignty and the principle of non-interference, were among the signs of such a tendency. But from the onset of the twenty-first century, not only have the 'usual suspects' of China and Russia begun counter-balancing, but other regional powers have also begun to force multipolar elements in the system to take shape. However, such an emerging trend was not to Washington's liking, and through its containment and roll-back policies, either unilaterally or through NATO and even the EU, it targeted Russia and China in an attempt to perpetuate the unilateral moment of the 1990s. The normative effect of these developments has been that while in most sensitive areas the existing norms became undermined, new ones have not been able to crystallise. Consequently, today we live in an atmosphere of increased normative uncertainty.

More effective international law, at least in the world as it is today and not in any utopian imaginations, can be based on three interrelated phenomena: multipolarity, balance-of-power and concert of powers. If the first two may naturally emerge due to the uneven development of societies over relatively extended periods and their relative (or sometimes absolute) rise and decline, the third phenomenon needs to be built by way of cooperative efforts and has to be accepted by participants as legitimate. Using language familiar to international lawyers, there should be *opinio juris sive necessitatis* of the balance of power, and not only a *de facto* existing situation of balance. Hugh White, an Australian author, writing on the need of Washington to accommodate a rising China in Asia (neither confronting China nor withdrawing from Asia) observes: 'Balance of power is what emerges naturally [...] By contrast, a concert is an agreement to minimise the risk of war that is inherent in the balance of power system. A concert of power does not happen naturally. It has to be carefully built and maintained, and this is not easy'.[18] Henry Kissinger observes in the same vein: 'The challenge in Asia is the opposite of Europe's. Westphalian balance-of-power principles prevail unrelated to an agreed concept of legitimacy'.[19] What is needed, in his opinion, for South and South-East Asia is a regional concert based on the balance of power among the main actors. Moreover, such a system is urgently needed at the global level, and today we do not have, primarily due to NATO expansion, such an agreed-upon balance, even in Europe.

What are the realistically possible alternatives to the principle of balance of powers in international politics? The whole history of international relations shows that where there is no balance of powers, it is either anarchy or empire that reigns supreme. Of course, international relations in their long history have seen all three models – anarchy, empire and balance of power – and elements of their various combinations or modifications can even be seen today. Clearly, the principle of balance of power is not an ideal form of international relations. The principle of the sovereign equality of states may suffer, though this principle may also benefit particularly small nations, which usually do not have much say at the table of power balancing. As Travers Twiss, a prominent British jurist and one-time professor of international law at King's College, London, wrote, 'the concept of a general balance designed by treaty-systems would guarantee particularly the existence of the sovereignty of less powerful nations against the more Powerful States'.[20] In a more anarchical system, smaller countries, which instinctively, though sometimes counter-productively, may be more anarchophilic than more powerful states, would be constantly threatened by their stronger neighbours (e.g., in the present-day Middle East), while in a more imperial system (e.g., the American and Soviet informal empires during the Cold War) smaller nations have very little say. In a balance-of-power system, smaller states may find support from other powers if one of them starts imposing upon its smaller and weaker neighbours. And it is necessary to bear in mind that we are talking here about a civilised, consciously built and accepted balance-of-power system, that is, about a concert of powers, and not a spontaneously emerging or existing system where some powers try to break the balance[21] in an attempt to obtain absolute security, thereby threatening not only security of others, but also security in general, including their own security. Such competition leads to a system of alliances competing for absolute or relative security, not to a civilised balance-of-power system. The two American authors from the Atlantic Council, Mathew Burrows and Robert A. Manning, express concerns that the United States, by containing and attempting to roll back Russia and China simultaneously are thereby pushing them into an anti-American alliance. Considering that 'turning the clock back to a Western-centric – albeit more inclusive, integrated world order – seems increasingly remote', they outline three possible new world order scenarios. The first two scenarios, though more plausible than the third, are wrought with conflicts and possible chaos, at least in several regions if not worldwide. The authors believe that:

> A less likely but altogether better outcome for everyone would be the establishment of a new global concert. This would require US and China to move beyond current strategic competition and actually define a 'new model of major power relations'. Lowering tensions with the US and West could give China space to move forward with market reforms in an effort to avoid getting stuck in the middle income trap. Russia, while pursuing its interests in Asia, would opt eventually for moving closer towards Europe politically and economically in order to work out a modus

> vivendi with NATO. A German-led Europe would reciprocate with shaping a new inclusive security architecture that takes into account Russian interests in its neighbourhood.[22]

It has sometimes been discussed as to whether the balance-of-powers principle is a legal or political principle. It is foremost a political principle, which can, however, have legal implications, and as such it may become a political underpinning of international law. Moreover, if elements of the balance are enshrined in legal documents, like they were, for instance, confirmed in the Utrecht (1713) and Vienna (1815) peace treaties or in the United Nations Charter (1945), the political principle of the balance of powers becomes underpinned by norms of international law. Therefore, it would be rather futile to argue as to whether the balance-of-power principle is more political or legal. Foremost, it is certainly a political principle and arrangement which should be underpinned by legal norms to be stable and predictable.

International societies, because of their essentially interstate nature, are also considerably more politicised than most domestic societies. In a sense, of course, domestic law is also a political phenomenon; it is formed in the cauldron of domestic politics. However, most of its principles and norms govern relations that are not political by nature and interpretation, and the application of domestic law is (or at least should be) free from direct political influences. States, however, as well as interstate relations (i.e., the main object of legal regulation in international society), are political phenomena *par excellence*. This feature has a significant impact on international law. International law is in many ways a much more politicised phenomenon than domestic legal systems, and it is usually interpreted and applied not by impartial and independent courts or other quasi-judicial bodies (the exception rather than the rule in international society) but by states themselves, or by international political bodies like the UN Security Council. As Dame Rosalyn Higgins has written, 'there is, of course, a very substantial difference between the use, the employment, of international law by the Security Council, on the one hand, and by a purely judicial body such as the International Court of Justice, on the other'.[23]

And though international judicial bodies, differently from the Security Council which is guided mainly, if not exclusively, by political considerations, are supposed to apply law impartially without being influenced by any extra-legal concerns, there is no doubt that in many cases and before different courts and tribunals, extra-legal factors influence judicial decision-making; if not directly, then at least as background (where you stand depends on where you sit, or for that matter where you have been brought up and educated). But for lack of space, I would refer to different studies concerning the practices of international criminal tribunals showing that the approaches of judges may well have depended on their backgrounds and origins. But for a few brief examples, it has been observed that the judges of the International Criminal Tribunal for the former Yugoslavia (ICTY) from NATO countries had sentenced Serbian defendants more harshly than did other judges.[24] Then, there was the scandalous dismissal from the ICTY of the Danish judge Frederik Harhoff, who had criticised controversial acquittals in the *Gotovina* and *Perišić* cases and the biased attitude of some of his colleagues.[25] It has also been observed that though

> judges at the ICC [International Criminal Court] and other ICTs [international criminal tribunals] strive to be independent and impartial, [...] they cannot be expected to act as representatives of the international community and its values in cases where they will be under psychological and economic pressure to rule in accordance with domestic interests.[26]

As these anecdotal cases testify, in international relations, politics and other extra-legal factors and considerations have an inescapable influence even over judicial decision-making.

International relations are, by their very nature, highly political relations (since their main actors – states – are political entities *par excellence*) where the role of criminal justice is rather limited. The establishment of the *ad hoc* tribunals (ICTY and ICTR – International Criminal Tribunal for Rwanda) and the elaboration of the Rome Statute that provided for the creation of the ICC are parts of the attempts, together with the advancement of the concept of R2P, to create a world law instead of international law. The effectiveness of the *ad hoc* tribunals has been rather controversial (most defendants before the ICTY are considered as heroes among their own people and receive a red-carpet treatment at home when released from prisons). The ICC is in crisis, and attempts to react to accusations that only Africans are prosecuted by the ICC may lead to new unexpected challenges to the Court's jurisdiction. Although there may be a modest place for international criminal jurisdiction, one may conclude that the enthusiasm of the 1990s as to the role of criminal justice in international relations was temporary, contingent and unjustified.

The international community, and especially the most powerful and responsible states, should take various steps to consolidate and legitimise a worldwide multipolar balance-of-power world. Some of these steps may be the following:

- As a realist, I would not advocate the immediate dissolution of NATO, yet the world should come to the conclusion that any system of permanent military alliances is a threat to peace. The alliance mentality has to be broken. Alliances are always against somebody, starting from the Peloponnesian League (led by Sparta) against the Delian League (led by Athens) at the time of the Peloponnesian War, to the Catholic League and the Protestant Union in the Thirty Years' War, to NATO against the Warsaw Pact in the period of the Cold War. Alliances or coalitions may be justified to meet concrete threats or when facing aggression, like Operation Desert Storm in 1991 to force Saddam Hussein out of Kuwait and restore peace and security in the region. This Operation was lawful both as an exercise of the right to self-defence (collective) and as a measure of collective security authorised by the UN Security Council. Permanent military alliances, in order to justify their existence, are almost forced to exaggerate, if not invent, threats they face from their designated (or designed) enemies; they have to demonise their greatest enemy, thereby poisoning relations between states and peoples, making cooperation and compromises very difficult, if not impossible, to achieve. The continuation of the existence of NATO, as a military alliance, when its opponent – the Warsaw Pact – had disappeared and even its leading actor – the Soviet Union – had collapsed, to say nothing of NATO's enlargement, is the biggest mistake at the turn of the twenty-first century. Talk that the post-Cold War NATO is not against anybody is childish prattle. Military alliances, in contradistinction to collective security systems, always exist to face concrete threats, whether real or imagined. Some timid and prudish attempts to find a new role for NATO at the beginning of the 1990s have been subsumed by the extension of the Alliance to the retracted frontiers of its erstwhile enemy.

- It would be necessary – instead of undermining and weakening the principle of respect for the sovereign equality of states, non-interference in their internal affairs and the non-use of military force – to strengthen these principles, to make them central to a new international order. Therefore, in the following sections we will study in some detail the current state of international law governing the use of military force in international relations.

- It is necessary to strengthen and reform the United Nations Security Council so that it should work as the principal organ of the balance-of-power world in matters of international security. The following sections will go into some detail on that respect too.

International Law and the Use of Force

One of the most important but also one of the most controversial areas of international law is the legal regulation of the use of military force. The nature, content and effectiveness of this domain of international law expresses, much more clearly than any of its other branches, the very nature of international law. One of the most prominent twentieth-century international lawyers, Louis Henkin, wrote: 'Almost all nations observe almost all principles of international law and almost all of their obligations almost all of the time.'[27] This observation is true – almost all nations, almost all of the time, also observe the principle prohibiting the use of force and the threat of force in international relations. However, the use of military force between states belongs to what one may call 'low probability-high consequence events', and therefore every use of military force, even if relatively minor, has almost incomparable negative consequences in terms of human lives lost, properties and livelihoods destroyed, refugee flows created and all kinds of miseries increased. Therefore, a greater observance and respect for the principle of the non-use of force in international relations remains one of the most important tasks of international law and international lawyers.

Earlier, when analysing the geopolitical situation in the world, we already discussed some new developments, which the post-Cold War world that coincided with the unipolar moment of uncontested American hegemony had introduced to the law concerning the use of military force. In this section we will concentrate on two developments in this domain – the use of force in self-defence against terror attacks, and the use of force to protect people either from their own governments or from anarchy and lawlessness during civil wars. Although neither of them are a completely new phenomenon, from the 1990s onwards these problems have come to the fore, as opposed to the Cold War period's danger of a clash of superpowers. In order to grasp the essence of the current debate in these areas of international law and politics it would be helpful to start with a brief overview of the evolution of the restriction and proscription of, use of military force in international relations.

From the Right to War to the Prohibition to Use Military Force

Thucydides' *History of the Peloponnesian War* demonstrates a complete absence of any legal (or even legal-moral-religious) restrictions on the recourse to war in the ancient world. As Thucydides writes, 'the Athenians and the Peloponnesians began the war after the thirty-year truce' since 'Sparta was forced into it because of her apprehensions over the growing power of Athens.'[28] Such an explanation for going to war sounds not only familiar but eerily contemporary. There had been a change in the balance of power in Ancient Greece favouring Athens, which caused Sparta to ally with smaller Greek city-states, forming the Peloponnesian League to militarily counter the Delian League, as led by Athens. But, differently from today's or even from yesterday's world, Greek city-states did not need any justifications for their recourse to arms. Athenians believed it to be 'an eternal law that the strong can rule the weak', as 'justice never kept anyone who was handed the chance to get something by force from getting more.'[29] Athenian ambassadors explained to the Melians (Melos – a small island in the Aegean Sea) that 'those who have power use it, while the weak make compromises. Given what we believe about the gods and know about men, we think that both are always forced to dominate everyone they can. We didn't lay down this law, it was there – and we weren't first to make use of it. Each of us must exercise what power he really thinks he can.'[30] The most significant difference, which testifies to the progress made by mankind, is that today a threatening change in a balance of power is not in and of itself a good enough cause to go to war. Other justifications have to be found.

Adam Watson writes that 'warfare was not considered reprehensible in the ancient world. Indeed, the ability to decide when to go to war was the hallmark of independence, for a king or city corporation'.[31] The words 'emperor' and 'empire' did sound proud indeed. For the Romans any war, if duly declared, would then be 'just' as well as 'pious'.[32] Starting from St Augustine of Hippo (354–430), through Thomas Aquinas (1225–74) to Spanish theologians-philosophers-lawyers Francisco de Vitoria (1483–1546) and Francisco Suarez (1548–1617), different just war theories tried to limit the recourse to war (just war should have just cause, right authority, right intention and be the last resort). After Emmerich de Vattel (1714–67), positivism gradually started to prevail in international law, and the differentiation between just and unjust wars based on religious laws or the laws of nature (human nature or the nature of the state) lost its importance. As Vattel, whose book – *Le Droit des gens* – was on the desk of every diplomat for a century or more[33], wrote, 'it belongs to each nation to judge whether her situation will admit of pacific measures, before she has recourse to arms'.[34] Although this was not a return to the naked power politics of Ancient Greece, it was only thinly veiled power politics where any offence, real or perceived, may have sufficed to justify the use of military force. Even under the international law of 'civilised nations', states could legitimately use military force for a wide range of purposes. The right to resort to arms was an important attribute of state sovereignty. In the nineteenth century the only limitation on the use of force by a state was the requirement that there should have been a previous violation of practically any right of that state. Any violation, and the offended state was the only judge in its own case, could give rightful cause to use military force to restore justice and punish the offender. Ian Brownlie writes that:

> The right of war, as an aspect of sovereignty, which existed in the period before 1914, subject to the doctrine that war was a means of last resort in the enforcement of legal rights, was very rarely asserted either by statesmen or works of authority without some stereotyped plea to a right of self-preservation, and of self-defence, or to necessity or protection of vital interests, or merely alleged injury to rights or national honour and dignity.[35]

For example, in 1914, during the Vera Cruz incident, which was triggered by the arrest by Mexican authorities of several crew members from the USS *Dolphin*, the United States used military force against Mexico when Mexican authorities refused to honour the US flag with a 21-gun salute as an official apology.[36] Similarly, Great Britain and Germany used gunboats to force Venezuela to pay its debts to nationals of these states.[37]

Although the idea of a world without wars has already existed for hundreds of years,[38] the first attempts at legal limitations on the use of force are no more than a century old. The 1907 Hague Peace Conference adopted the Convention Respecting the Limitation of Employment of Force for the Recovery of

Contract Debts, which provided that there should be no recourse to armed force unless the debtor state should refuse submission to arbitration, or should fail to carry out the arbitration award (the Convention never entered into force).[39] The so-called Bryan Treaties that the United States concluded with various states in 1913–14 established a 'cooling off' period during which it was prohibited to use military force.[40] The Covenant of the League of Nations purported to put some further brakes on the right of states to use military force.[41] Finally, the Kellogg–Briand Pact of 1928 outlawed 'war as an instrument of national policy'.[42] However, it was not so much shortcomings in these legal documents as much as political realities that led to World War II, after which the members of the victorious coalition created the United Nations, whose main task was meant to be to put an end not only to wars but also to any unilateral use of military force.

The current UN Charter paradigm concerning the use of force can be called normative positivism, since it is based on the consent of states and not upon what states (or at least the most powerful of them) always do in practice. It is normative since it is not premised on the actual practices of states. It is positivist since it does not make distinctions between just, unjust, more justified and less justified causes for the use of military force.

The UN Charter Paradigm on the Use of Force

Article 2(4) of the UN Charter reads: 'All Members shall refrain in their international relations from the threat or use of force against the territorial integrity or political independence of any state, or in any other manner inconsistent with the Purposes of the United Nations'. This means that not only is the use of military force prohibited, but so is the threat to use such force. The Charter makes only two express exceptions to this prohibition: the use of military force in self-defence if an armed attack occurs (Article 51), and as a collective security measure authorised by the UN Security Council in cases of threats to international peace and security (Articles 39 and 42). However, notwithstanding, or maybe because of, its brevity, Article 2(4) has raised some heated discussions and doubts. First, as the article does not clarify what kind of force is prohibited, some authors and even states have tried to read economic and political pressure into the definition of force as prohibited by Article 2(4). However, it is clear from the *travaux préparatoires* of the UN Charter, as well as from the interpretations given by the majority of states to the content of this article, that its prohibition covers only the use, or threat of use, of military force. This, of course, does not mean that economic or political pressure is always lawful under international law; it only means that Article 2(4) does not cover such pressure. Secondly, as Article 2(4) singles out for special protection the above-mentioned three factors (territorial integrity, the political independence of states and uses of force otherwise inconsistent with the purposes of the United Nations), certain, especially some American, authors have tried to argue that if the use of force does not breach any of them (e.g., the use of force for the sake of the protection of human rights or the promotion of democracy), such a use of force may be lawful. We will discuss some of these controversial issues later in this chapter, but here it suffices to say that such arguments express a minority view and are not accepted by most states. Although no state has overtly referred to such interpretations of Article 2(4) as a defence when using military force in violation of international law (e.g., NATO against Serbia over Kosovo in 1999, or Russia in annexing the Crimea in 2014), it is probable that some states may have believed that their behaviour did not breach either the letter or the spirit of Article 2(4). There have also been an increasing number of scholarly writings about the need for (or dangers of) the revival of medieval 'just war' doctrines and their adaptation to the realities of the twenty-first century.[43] Bertrand Badie, for example, observes that today 'France is at war almost everywhere, fighting not just enemies but simply "criminals" in "just wars" – the doctrine that had already fallen into desuetude but has now become resuscitated'.[44] Recourses to 'just war' theories have, of course, various causes and reasons, but usually the most ardent adherents of these theories have been those who have believed in the exclusivity of their social, political and economic models, who have been sure that their cause, in comparison with different causes, is so impartial, so just and so unbiased that it justifies resorting to military force. In addition, of course, one must have enough power in order to believe that one is able to prevail in a 'just war'. For the weak, 'just war' doctrines are of little practical use, if only as justifications of their acts of desperation.

The prohibition of the use of force is one of the few imperative (*jus cogens*) norms of international law, from which states cannot derogate even with mutual consent. Although it may be surprising, it is nevertheless true that the prohibition of the use of force in international relations became a legally binding norm relatively recently. As a legal principle it started its evolution after World War I and matured as a result of World War II; it was enshrined in the United Nations Charter and its importance has not diminished since, notwithstanding its overly frequent breaches. As the International Court of Justice put it in the *Nicaragua* case:

> If a State acts in a way *prima facie* incompatible with a recognized rule, but defends its conduct by appealing to exceptions or

> justifications contained within the rule itself, then whether or not the State's conduct is in fact justifiable on that basis, the significance of that attitude is to confirm rather than to weaken the rule.[45]

Frederic Kirgis, commenting on the relationship between practice and *opinio juris* in the *Nicaragua* case, proposes the rule of sliding scale:

> On the sliding scale, very frequent, consistent state practice establishes customary rule without much (or any) affirmative showing of an *opinio juris* so long as it is not negated by evidence of non-normative intent. As the frequency and consistency of the practice decline in any series of cases, stronger showing of an *opinio juris* is required. At the other end of the scale a clearly demonstrated *opinio juris* establishes a customary rule without much (or any) affirmative showing that governments are consistently behaving in accordance with the asserted rule.[46]

Oscar Schachter, like Kirgis, concludes that 'issues of proof of custom involve an inverse (and, some might say, dialectical) relation between evidence of State practice and of *opinio juris*. The cases show that a strong finding of *opinio juris generalis* tends to reduce the required proof of State practice',[47] and, 'conversely, a record of widespread and consistent practice revealing a pattern of claim and response has given rise to inferences of *opinio juris*, without any further evidence'.[48] However, Schachter goes further than Kirgis in his explanation of this phenomenon. He emphasises the differences between the rules which, for instance, determine territorial limits, relate to the right of passage and deal with the modalities of treaty relations on the one hand, and the rules against aggression, the rules outlawing genocide, the killing of PoWs, torture and large-scale racial discrimination, on the other. He is right that, for example, 'the rules against aggression and on self-defence are not just another set of international rules'.[49] The special status of some rules has been expressed by characterising such rules as *jus cogens* (no derogations allowed) or *erga omnes* (rights and obligations owned towards every other state or the world community as a whole). And Schachter concludes that 'it is that difference in their normative claim, reflected in the *opinio juris*, that underlies decisions to recognize their continued customary law status even if State practice in regard to them is not uniform or consistent'.[50]

We may conclude that the relationship between the objective and subjective elements of practice varies in different areas of international relations. Legal norms (usually these are general principles) which govern relatively invariable (structural) relations can be changed or annulled only together with a radical change of the structure of an international society. Value-loaded norms can survive notwithstanding contrary 'actual' practice because of the strong support of *opinio juris generalis*, while value-neutral norms need much more consistent 'actual' practice for their formation as well as survival. The more consistent and general the practice, the lower the necessity to look for the subjective element confirming the acceptance of such practice as legally binding. And on the contrary, strong *opinio juris generalis* is able to compensate the lack of consistency in 'actual' practice.

In international society, there are different categories of relations: variable and relatively invariable relations; relations based on values where compromises may be rare and difficult to make; and relations based mainly on interests, which often differ (like, for example, the interests of states with long coastlines and those of landlocked states), but where compromises (sometimes as package deals) are not only necessary, but quite possible. International law does not develop and function in the same way in these different areas. Some basic principles of international law reflect the relatively invariable structure of international society. The principle of the sovereign equality of states certainly belongs to this category. *Pacta sunt servanda* (agreements must be kept) and the principles of the non-use of force and the non-interference in the internal affairs of states may also come close to this category, though not every part of their content is so invariable. The principles reflecting the relatively invariable structure of international society can be violated but their violation, even if frequent, cannot abolish them without undermining, or even bringing down, the very foundations of existing international order. Such principles may, of course, change over time, but they can cease to exist only when the basic characteristics of the existing international system change (such a change took place, for example, when the medieval feudal multi-layered European system was replaced by the Westphalian international system).

Although some international lawyers have claimed that, due to the inefficiency of the UN collective security system, the Charter prohibition of the use of force has become redundant,[51] no state has made such a claim. While justifying their own transgressions states are usually 'appealing to exceptions or justifications within the rule', and when condemning the use of force by others, they confirm their own adherence to the principle.

The Right to Self-defence

Article 51 of the UN Charter provides:

> Nothing in the present Charter shall impair the inherent right of individual or collective self-defence if an armed attack occurs against a Member of the United Nations, until the Security Council has taken measures necessary to maintain international peace and security. Measures taken by Members in the exercise of this right of self-defence shall be immediately

> reported to the Security Council and shall not in any way affect the authority and responsibility of the Security Council under the present Charter to take at any time such action as it deems necessary in order to maintain or restore international peace and security.

The right to self-defence is the only right in the UN Charter that is called 'inherent'. On the one hand, such a reference to the inherent, inalienable, even natural character of this right shows its importance. Indeed, if states were not able to lawfully protect themselves against armed attacks, their very right to existence would be questionable. One the other hand, this formulation has led to some heated discussions, and opened doors to wide interpretations and even abuses.

Article 51 requests that states which use military force in self-defence report all the measures taken in the exercise of this right to the Security Council. The Council then decides what measures to take 'in order to maintain or restore international peace and security'. If the Council, say, authorises economic sanctions against an aggressor as a measure necessary to restore peace and security, does this mean that the victim state alone or together with its allies is barred from using military force in self-defence? Such an ambiguous legal situation existed in the period between the Iraqi invasion of Kuwait on 1 August and 29 November 1990, when the Security Council adopted Resolution 678 authorising the 'use of all necessary means' (a euphemism implying the right to use military force) to liberate Kuwait and implement all the relevant Security Council resolutions. Could Kuwait and its allies start using military force in self-defence before the deadline given by the Council to Iraq to withdraw from Kuwait (15 January 1991)? Such an ambiguous legal situation also caused the dispute over the character of Operation Desert Storm, which led to the liberation of Kuwait. Was it an operation of collective self-defence or an operation of collective security? In my opinion it had characteristics of both.

Moreover, the Security Council may find that a state that is allegedly using force in self-defence is wrong in its assessment of its actions, that instead of lawfully using force in self-defence, it is in breach of the prohibition to use force. The possibility of facing such a situation means that states are not the final arbiters on matters of lawfulness regarding the use of force even in self-defence and therefore the right to self-defence may not be so inalienable after all.

However, the term 'inherent' in the context of self-defence has caused even more heated academic discussions and much more serious practical consequences in respect of so-called anticipatory self-defence, which is sometimes also called pre-emptive or even preventive self-defence. In short, the problem is the following: is it necessary for a victim of an armed attack to wait until, figuratively speaking, the bombs and missiles of the attacker begin to explode, or is it legally justifiable to take counter-measures involving military force at some earlier point, for example, intercepting missiles or bombers before they reach their targets?

In the positivist era of international law, the right of anticipatory self-defence was grounded on the formula put forward by the American Secretary of State Daniel Webster in the *Caroline* incident of 1837. In that case, the British authorities situated in Canada – at that time a British colony – destroyed the US steamboat *Caroline* while she was anchored on the American side of the Niagara river, the reason being that the *Caroline* was used to supply rebels against the British rule in Canada with medicaments, ammunition and other goods. The United States disagreed with the British government as to the legality of the action. Secretary of State Daniel Webster wrote to Mr Fox, the British Minister to Washington, that it had to be demonstrated that it was necessary to use force in self-defence against an attack that was 'instant, overwhelming, and leaving no choice of means, and no moment for deliberation' and that the act 'justified by the necessity of self-defence must be limited by that necessity, and kept clearly within it'.[52] It seems to be possible to generalise all these criteria by the terms of necessity, immediacy and proportionality. Every use of force, even in self-defence, in order to be lawful, has to be necessary (e.g., it is possible that a limited military incursion by the forces of state A into the territory of state B remained without adequate immediate response; in such a case state B is not entitled to respond *ex post facto* militarily against state A; this would breach both the requirements of necessity and immediacy), exercised within a reasonable time period and *proportionate to the situation that calls for the use of force*. Here, clarification may be necessary. Sometimes it is assumed that there should be proportionality between the scale of an armed attack and the scale of the defensive response. It may well be the case, but not always. For example, in order to expel Iraq from the occupied Kuwait in 1991, the coalition needed significantly more massive force than Saddam Hussein had needed in August 1990 to occupy Kuwait. The requirement of proportionality of the response of the coalition relates to the task of liberating Kuwait, which, taking account of the strength of the Iraqi army, necessitated massive use of air and land power by the coalition.

Analysing self-defence modalities, Yoram Dinstein distinguishes between 'on the spot reaction', 'defensive armed reprisals', responses to an 'accumulation of events' and 'war of self-defence', all different modalities of the use of force that can be resorted to depending on the character of the armed attack that has triggered the right to use force in self-defence.[53] The legality of these various modalities of self-defence is dependent on the character of the armed attack.

Thus, while the *Caroline* incident evidences that the occurrence of an armed attack is not necessary to justify the exercise of self-defence, it qualified the right of pre-emptive action with several rather strict conditions in order to be legally accepted. According to this formula, pre-emptive action is only lawful when the danger is imminent in a way that leaves the defending state no time for deliberation or to choose an alternative course of action. This implies that the danger can be identified credibly, specifically and with a high degree of certainty.[54]

The Israeli use of force in 1967 in the Six-Day War against Egypt and other Arab states seems to be an example of an anticipatory use of force in self-defence as per the terms of the *Caroline* case, customary international law and, it is possible to argue, of Article 51 of the UN Charter, since the Charter has to be interpreted in the context of existing customary international law. The withdrawal of UN peacekeepers (UNEF) at the request of President Gamal Abdel Nasser of Egypt, the mobilisation and movements of Egyptian and other Arab armed forces and, last but not least, the blockade of the Straits of Tiran for Israeli navigation, seem to indicate, with high probability, that an attack on Israel would have been imminent. Israel, in the UN, referred to the blockade of the Straits of Tiran as an act of war, and therefore didn't raise the defence of anticipatory self-defence. However, it seems that if Israel were relying on this fact alone, its response may have breached the requirement of proportionality. The Israeli response, surely, was much more massive than, say, an on-the-spot reaction in the Straits of Tiran would have been and can be justified as an act of anticipatory self-defence.

Developments related to the 'war on terror' have given support to the two – hitherto somewhat controversial – interpretations of self-defence: it is now more widely accepted that there is room for anticipatory self-defence as well as for what Oscar Schachter, Yoram Dinstein and some others have called *defensive reprisals*, that is, reprisals whose main purpose is not to punish (so-called *punitive reprisals* are certainly prohibited by international law). Or rather, in responses to terrorist attacks these two wider interpretations of the lawful use of force go hand-in-hand. Effective responses to typical terrorist pin-prick attacks have to be carried out in most cases either *ex post facto* or in anticipation of new probable attacks from the same source. That is why such responses can be characterised both as defensive reprisals or acts of anticipatory self-defence.

Often, military responses to terrorist attacks have to draw a fine balance between these two controversial modalities of the use of military force in self-defence – the Scylla of anticipatory self-defence and the Charybdis of reprisals. As Gregory Travalio writes, 'if the anticipated action by terrorists is not sufficiently imminent, the right to use force is not available for purposes of deterrence. On the other hand, if past terrorist actions by a group are too remote in time, the response by force is likely to be characterized as an illegal reprisal'.[55] Because terrorist warfare usually consists of a series of relatively small-scale attacks that often need to be dealt with by measures that combine some elements of retaliation (since a response comes after the attack) and anticipation (since a response comes in anticipation of new attacks), the exercise of the right to self-defence against terrorist attacks requires at least some (sometimes quite considerable) practical use of the concepts of a anticipatory self-defence and defensive reprisals.

However, there is a different interpretation of the right to self-defence, which is sometimes called the 'Bush doctrine' or 'preventive self-defence'. In response to its perception of a fundamentally changed international situation in the wake of the 9/11 attacks against the United States, in 2002 the USA adopted a new National Security Strategy that stated: 'While the US will constantly strive to enlist the support of the international community, we will not hesitate to act alone if necessary, to exercise our right of self-defence by acting pre-emptively against such terrorists, to prevent them from doing harm against our people and our country'.[56] What the 'Bush Doctrine' implies is that the traditional conditions of anticipatory self-defence and the requirement of a clear demonstration of the threatening intentions of the adversary are no longer tenable, since an attack by terrorists using weapons of mass destruction could be launched at any time, anywhere, without warning. Rather than wait for that to happen, or waiting for the last moment that would reduce the chance of forestalling such an attack, states have the right to use force preventively to eliminate such a threat in its early stage. Thus, the strategy would be better described as 'preventive' rather than 'pre-emptive' self-defence, because the aim is to prevent the materialisation of generalised threats, rather than to avert an identified, foreseeable and imminent threat.[57]

Michael Reisman has defined preventive self-defence as

> a claim of authority to use, unilaterally and without international authorization, high levels of violence in order to arrest a development that is not yet operational and hence is not yet directly threatening, but which, if permitted to mature, could be neutralized only at a high, possibly unacceptable, cost. It is not hard to imagine circumstances in which PSD [preventive self-defence] might appear justified. Yet if universalized, the claim, by increasing the expectation and likelihood of violence, could undermine minimum order.[58]

German scholar Michael Bothe believes that to adapt the right to self-defence to these new perceived threats is unacceptable, would lead to vagueness and would increase the risk of abuse. He argues:

> If we want to maintain international law as a restraint on the use of military force, we should very carefully watch any attempt on the part of opinion leaders to argue that military force is anything other than an evil that has to be avoided. The lessons of history are telling. If we revert to such broad concepts, such as the just war concept, to justify military force we are stepping on a slippery slope, one which would make us slide back into the nineteenth century when war was not illegal.[59]

This seems to be the dominant position within international legal scholarship. To clarify the differences between anticipatory self-defence, which under certain strict conditions is arguably lawful, and preventive self-defence, which is contrary to existing international law, it is possible to compare two uses of military force both involving Israel: the Six-Day War of June 1967 (discussed shortly above), which many international lawyers have considered to be within the frame of legitimate self-defence, and the 7 June 1981 Israeli attack on the Osirak nuclear centre in Iraq which, in the eyes of most international lawyers, as well as those of the UN Security Council, was a clear breach of international law. In its Resolution 487 of 19 June 1981 the Security Council strongly condemned 'the military attack by Israel in violation of the Charter of the United Nations and the norms of international conduct'.[60]

The concept of self-defence is inherently linked to the concept of an armed attack. The mere possession or attempted acquisition of nuclear weapons or other weapon systems cannot be equated with an armed attack, notwithstanding how wide an interpretation we give to the concept of 'armed attack'. The proliferation of weapons of mass destruction (WMD) and self-defence are phenomena from different legal domains or branches of international law. The proliferation of nuclear weapons may be considered a threat to international peace and security.

When we talk about possible use of force against nuclear proliferation we are not in the domain of self-defence; we are in the domain of arms control, or in the domain of threats to international, including regional, peace and security, and this is a matter for the UN Security Council to decide. Such use of military force is not only beyond the pale of international law but it is also dangerous in political and military terms. Andrea Armstrong and Michael Reisman have observed that Washington's claims of the preemptive (what I would prefer to call preventive) use of military force have copycat or mimetic effects. They correctly write that

> although the doctrine of the United States [the Bush doctrine] not unreasonably aims at enhancing its own security against an adversary apparently impervious to deterrence, wider adoption of a legal policy of preemptive self-defense may actually undermine international security. States simply appropriate the language of preemption to fit their individual security concerns and the strategies they craft to maintain their security – essentially becoming 'free riders' in the international legal system.[61]

Moreover, an empirical study carried out by Tai-Heng Cheng and Eduardas Valaitis shows that the US's large-scale use of force in the 'war on terror' has not observably reduced aggregate attacks against the United States and has likely increased hostility against it.[62] This means that not only has the United States become less secure as a result of the wide use of military force abroad in its 'war on terror' but also the existing legal restrictions on the recourse to military force have become undermined. Jean-Yves Le Drian, the former French Minister of Defence and current Foreign Minister, adds a practioner's touch to the matter, arguing that we should not accept

> the notion of preventive war – the notion lacking juridical precision, which was introduced a dozen of years ago by the American administration then in office and whose destabilising effects we feel today [...] It is clear that the obsession with absolute security, leading to interventions in anticipation and resting on the idea of preventive war, has had serious consequences.[63]

The use of military force in self-defence against terrorist attacks shows also that the drawn dividing line, as in the example of the International Court of Justice in the *Nicaragua* case between armed attacks and 'less grave forms' of the use of force,[64] is no longer tenable, if it ever was. Yoram Dinstein, referring to J.L. Hargrove and J.I. Kunz, has rightly emphasised that 'in reality, there is no cause to remove small-scale armed attacks from the spectrum of armed attacks. Article 51 in no way limits itself to large, direct or important armed attacks.'[65] The same criticism also applies to Article 3(g) of the Definition of Aggression, which emphasises that actions by armed bands, groups, irregulars or mercenaries 'sent by or on behalf of a state', which carry out acts of armed force against another state 'of such gravity as to amount to an actual armed attack conducted by regular forces' could be considered as acts of aggression.[66] Why only attacks of such gravity? Why this difference? It falls on the requirement of proportionality between a legitimate purpose for the use of force, and the character and scale of force necessary to achieve that purpose, to hopefully assure that relatively minor incidents involving the use of military force do not escalate (sometimes unintentionally) into whole-scale wars.

Finally, the necessity of using military force against terrorist attacks has raised the issue of the place of non-state actors in international relations generally, and particularly in the law regulating the use of military force in international relations.

Until 9/11, the issue had been rather mute. Article 51, determining that 'Nothing in the present Charter shall impair the inherent right of individual or collective self-defence if an armed attack occurs *against a Member of the United Nations* [emphasis added]', does not, however, say anything about who may or should be the author of such attacks in order to invoke the right to use military force in self-defence. When, in the aftermath of World War II, the UN Charter was drafted, it was understood, even without explicit statement, that it must be another *state* that is the author of an armed attack. However, even before 9/11, it had become clear that some non-state actors had acquired the capabilities to use military force against states that in their scale and *modus operandi* amounted to armed attacks as per the terms of the UN Charter and customary international law. 'It is by now', as the former Legal Advisor of the British Foreign Office Daniel Bethlehem writes, 'reasonably clear and accepted that states have a right of self-defense against attacks by non-state actors – as reflected, for example, in UN Security Council Resolutions 1368 and 1373 of 2001, adopted following the 9/11 attacks in the United States'.[67]

However, as non-state terrorist organisations operate from and have their bases on the territories of states, the issue of the role of such states arises both in terms of their responsibility for the behaviour of non-state actors and the right of victim states and their allies (or the world community as a whole) to take coercive measures against such states. Of course, in the first place, it is the responsibility of all states to see to it that their territories are not used by non-state actors, or by third states for that matter, to attack other states. A failure to do so may be due either to the fact that they are unwilling or unable to do so. Sometimes there may even be a combination of both of these factors. Such may have been the situation, for example, in Afghanistan in 2001 when the Taliban government was not only unwilling but also unable to take all necessary measures to stop al-Qaeda from attacking the United States.

In 2012, in the *American Journal of International Law*, Daniel Bethlehem published an article where he enumerated 16 principles relevant to the scope of a state's right of self-defence against an imminent or actual armed attack by non-state actors. In my opinion, principles 9–11 concerning the position of states, the territories of which are used by non-state actors for the purposes of armed activities against third states, correspond indeed to the law governing the use of military force, as well as rules of state responsibility, and are not at all controversial. They are as follows:

> 9) States are required to take all reasonable steps to ensure that their territory is not used by nonstate actors for purposes of armed activities – including planning, threatening, perpetrating, or providing material support for armed attacks – against other states and their interests.
>
> 10) Subject to the following paragraphs, a state may not take armed action in self-defense against a nonstate actor in the territory or within the jurisdiction of another state ('the third state') without the consent of that state. The requirement for consent does not operate in circumstances in which there is an applicable resolution of the UN Security Council authorizing the use of armed force under Chapter VII of the Charter or other relevant and applicable legal provision of similar effect. Where consent is required, all reasonable good faith efforts must be made to obtain consent.
>
> 11) The requirement for consent does not operate in circumstances in which there is a reasonable and objective basis for concluding that the third state is colluding with the nonstate actor or is otherwise unwilling to effectively restrain the armed activities of the nonstate actor such as to

> leave the state that has a necessity to act in self-defense with no other reasonably available effective means to address an imminent or actual armed attack. In the case of a colluding or a harboring state, the extent of the responsibility of that state for aiding or assisting the nonstate actor in its armed activities may be relevant to considerations of the necessity to act in self-defense and the proportionality of such action, including against the colluding or harboring state.[68]

There is, however, a problem with principle 12, which allows the use of military force on the territory of a state where non-state actors are operating *without* the consent of that state if that state is unable (though willing) to prevent these non-state actors from committing armed attacks against third states. First of all, this does not correspond to state practice, meagre though it may be. For example, after 9/11, the United States did not rush to bomb Afghanistan, but demanded that the Taliban, which moreover was recognised as the legitimate government of Afghanistan only by three states – Pakistan, Saudi Arabia and the United Arab Emirates (UAE):

> Deliver to United States authorities all the leaders of Al-Qa'ida who hide in your land. Release all foreign diplomats, including American citizens, you have unjustly imprisoned. Protect foreign journalists, diplomats, and aid workers in your country. Close immediately and permanently every terrorist training camp in Afghanistan, and hand over every terrorist and every person in their support structure to appropriate authorities. Give the United States full access to terrorist training camps, so we can make sure they are no longer operating.[69]

Only when the Taliban rejected this ultimatum did Washington launch Operation Enduring Freedom. The rejection of these demands by the Taliban government made the Taliban an accomplice of al-Qaeda; it demonstrated the Taliban's unwillingness to put an end to al-Qaeda's terrorist activities from within the territory of Afghanistan.

If a state is unwilling to take effective measures to prevent its territory from being used by non-state actors that attack third states, it becomes a harbouring or accomplice state, that is, a state that in itself is in breach of the prohibition to use military force. Therefore, it has to bear consequences for its illegal behaviour. However, this is not the case with a state that is unable to prevent its territory from being used by non-state actors against a third state. For example, a substantial part of the territory of Syria was occupied by ISIS – a terrorist entity that had emerged and spread from the territory of Iraq, and that was operating not only on the territory of these two countries but which also attacked other states, including those in Europe. However, the coalition led by the United States did not seek the consent of the government of Syria, and did not even inform the latter before using airpower against ISIS on Syrian territory. And though the coalition did not use force against governmental forces (this would have been an armed attack under Article 51 of the UN Charter), but against ISIS, the fact of not even seeking the consent of the government of Syria amounts, at least, to interference in the internal affairs of Syria.

Of course, one may say that in the eyes of the Washington-led coalition, the government in Damascus had lost its legitimacy. Moreover, they had all earlier recognised the National Coalition for Syrian Revolutionary and Opposition Forces as the sole representative of the Syrian people. This, however, is pure geopolitics thinly covered by moralising preaching that has nothing to do with international law. Above we already dealt with the dubious case of the use of chemical weapons during the civil war in Syria, which was attributed to the forces of President Bashar al-Assad immediately and without any serious proof by Western politicians and media. The world was lucky that, due to Russian diplomatic efforts, Western intervention against Syria was avoided and Syria's chemical weapons arsenal destroyed. Renaud Girard is right that 'if the Russians would not have intervened and Damascus would have fallen, a genocide against the Alawites would have been unleashed and the Christians would have been expelled, while their churches would have been in flames'. And he blames French diplomacy of naïvely believing in the myth of 'the moderate opposition'. Although there were such people, they were not in Syria, but 'in hotels of London or Geneva'.[70]

Unilateral – that is, not authorised by the UN Security Council – support for opposition forces, labelling them as democratic movements or freedom-fighters, the demonisation of incumbent governments (calling them 'regimes' instead) and threats to use or the actual use of direct or indirect military force is a very slippery slope. The case of Syria shows that such policies may instead give support to terrorist groups. Moreover, as the propaganda machine rolls forward, it becomes almost impossible to put the whole machine in reverse gear – backpedalling, even if necessary, is not an easy option, as no state is ever prepared to admit: sorry, we were wrong.

Although the war in Syria, as we have shown above, was to a great extent caused and is more so sustained by geopolitical reasons and the ambitions of regional as well as global actors, there are also some important legal considerations as to the role of outside powers and their military in this armed conflict.

After the two terrible terrorist attacks claimed by and attributed to ISIS against the Russian passenger jet over the Sinai peninsula on 31 October 2015 and the Paris attacks of 13 November 2015, the UN Security Council of 20 November 2015 unanimously adopted Resolution 2249 (2015), that

> [C]alls upon Member States that have the capacity to do so to take all necessary measures, in compliance with international law, in particular with the United Nations Charter, as well as international human rights, refugee and humanitarian law, on the territory under the control of ISIL also known as Da'esh, in Syria and Iraq, to redouble and coordinate their efforts to prevent and suppress terrorist acts committed specifically by ISIL also known as Da'esh as well as ANF, and all other individuals, groups, undertakings, and entities associated with al-Qaeda, and other terrorist groups, as designated by the United Nations Security Council, and as may further be agreed by the International Syria Support Group (ISSG) and endorsed by the UN Security Council, pursuant to the statement of the International Syria Support Group (ISSG) of 14 November, and to eradicate the safe haven they have established over significant parts of Iraq and Syria.[71]

Resolution 2249 (2015), though reaffirming 'that terrorism in all forms and manifestations *constitutes one of the most serious threats to international peace and security* [emphasis added] and that any acts of terrorism are criminal and unjustifiable regardless of their motivations, whenever and by whomsoever committed', lacks some traditional attributes of resolutions that have been used to undertake military measures against states or non-state actors in the past. It does not refer to Chapter VII of the UN Charter, nor does it 'authorise' the use of 'all necessary means', as the Council had done on numerous occasions before (e.g., RES. 678 (1990) on Iraq or RES. 1973 (2011) on Libya) but, as shown above, only calls on member states

> to redouble and coordinate their efforts to prevent and suppress terrorist acts committed specifically by ISIL also known as Da'esh as well as ANF, and all other individuals, groups, undertakings, and entities associated with al-Qaeda, and other

> terrorist groups, as designated by the United Nations Security Council, and as may further be agreed by the International Syria Support Group (ISSG) and endorsed by the UN Security Council.

This Resolution has been defined by some as an exercise in 'constructive ambiguity'[72], while others believe that Resolution 2249 does not give any new legal authority for using force.[73]

The Resolution of the Security Council of 20 November 2015 was the first resolution of the UN Security Council regarding Syria where the permanent members could agree upon measures to be taken against various terrorist groups, quite a few of which had hitherto been under the protective umbrella of their powerful sponsors. As a result of many compromises, it indeed contains some convoluted and sometimes even obscure language that does not follow usual patterns. Moreover, the wars against terrorist groups, including by the coalition led by the United States, as well as by Russia and Iran, were already taking place and it was certainly the fact of Russia stepping in that had provided the impetus for the peace process, if it could be so called. That is why the Resolution confirmed the right of those states which had already been involved in military attacks against ISIS and other terrorist groups as designated by the Security Council, to continue doing so. Authorising something ongoing lacks logic. Moreover, it has to be also said that the term 'calls upon' in the Resolution is in no way weaker than the term 'authorises'. I read it as active encouragement to undertake all necessary measures to defeat designated terrorist groups, while the term 'authorises' is weaker since it makes something, which would otherwise have been illegal, lawful without explicitly urging states to do anything. In that respect, the Resolution gave both political and legal support to the Russian position, since earlier both the United States as well as France had demanded that Russia hit only ISIS. This was certainly not acceptable for Russia, since the Kremlin's strategy was from the outset based on acting in concert with the ground troops of the governmental forces. This was also the only way to have any sustainable success in the fight against the terrorist groups, including ISIS. Besides, for military strategic reasons it could have indeed been necessary to hit other groups that were fighting governmental forces first and distracting them from attacking ISIS. Moreover, attacking ISIS only from the air, without the ground troops which would have defeated the terrorists on the terrain and made their reappearance impossible, would have been an almost certainly futile exercise (only the Kurdish forces in Syria had fought in concert with American airpower; from whence came success).

Therefore, I believe that Resolution 2249 had both a political and legal impact by authoritatively confirming not only the right but also the obligation (at least political) of all states that were capable of contributing to the defeat of the designated terrorist groups in Syria to take all necessary measures in order to achieve this end.

It should be noted that the American-led coalition on the one hand, and the Russian Federation on the other, had different, though partly overlapping, legal grounds for using military force in Syria. If the Western powers had used the arguments of self-defence, both individual and especially collective, Russia additionally had the consent (invitation) of the government of Syria. The American-led coalition's use of force in Iraq is based on the Iraqi government's letter of 22 September 2014 to the President of the Security Council, in which the government had sought for international assistance against ISIS/Daesh. In this letter, the Iraqi Foreign Minister noted that ISIS posed a direct threat to Iraq and had established a safe haven outside of Iraq's borders; he requested for the US to strike ISIS.[74]

Hence, the right of the American-led coalition to use force against ISIS in Iraq arose from the request of Iraq and the right to collective self-defence. Moreover, since France was attacked and other Western states threatened by ISIS, it is possible to argue that they also used their right to individual self-defence.

It has to be noted, however, that by using military force against ISIS on Syrian territory without any consultation with or the consent of the government in Damascus, the coalition was, at least until the adoption of Security Council Resolution 2249, violating the sovereignty of Syria – notwithstanding that military force was used on territories not controlled by the government of Syria and not against the armed forces of Syria. Professor Peter Hilpold is right in observing:

> A last brief consideration has also to be made as to the question whether the fragile nature of the Syrian state broadens the scope for any possible intervention. This question has to be answered in the negative. Syria has an internationally recognized government and even if government troops have withdrawn from many regions and are embattled, in others state sovereignty is still in place and foreign intervention is prohibited without authorization by the government or the UN Security Council. In an *argumentum de minore ad maius* it should be remembered that the use of force is even prohibited against de facto regimes or failed states.[75]

Russia, acting upon an invitation from the government of Syria, was also acting in collective self-defence together with the government of Syria, as ISIS, besides downing the Russian aeroplane on 31 October 2015, had already for some time been a clear and present danger for Russia. Hundreds of young Russian men and also some women were fighting for ISIS in Syria and Iraq, establishing links with terrorist groups in Russia. Therefore, Russia was also acting in individual self-defence. Due to the request and consent of the government of Syria, Russia's attacks did not need to be limited to ISIS.

Collective Security and the Use of Force

Although the UN Security Council has not always worked as it should, it is not the time nor is there reason to weaken the Council further. On the contrary, the Security Council is one of the only existing bodies that reflects, though imperfectly and somewhat outdatedly, the balance of power in the world. Strengthening the Council should not be accomplished by means of abolishing the right to veto, or bypassing the Council in cases of threats to international peace and security, but through the enlargement of its membership and increasing cooperation, particularly between the permanent members of the Council. As long as permanent members see each other more as global competitors and rivals and less as responsible partners (though not necessarily friends), allies or like-minded peoples, who may have different interests and values but who are ready to compromise and bracket their differences to find solutions to the challenges facing humankind, the Council will not function effectively. The abolition of the veto power may even lead to new military conflicts or aggravate existing ones. Imagine what would happen if the Council were to authorise the use of 'all necessary means' against one of the veto-holding powers or their close allies. Therefore, it seems adequate that we also shortly analyse the potential and shortcomings of this collective security mechanism.

Article 39 of the UN Charter provides: 'The Security Council shall determine the existence of any threat to the peace, breach of the peace, or act of aggression and shall make recommendations, or decide what measures shall be taken in accordance with Articles 41 and 42, to maintain or restore international peace and security'. Further, Article 42 stipulates:

> Should the Security Council consider that measures provided for in Article 41 (i.e., measures not involving use of military force) would be inadequate or have proved to be inadequate, it may take such action by air, sea, or land forces as may be necessary to maintain or restore international peace and security. Such action may include demonstrations, blockade, and other operations by air, sea, or land forces of Members of the United Nations.

These articles of the UN Charter, and more widely Chapter VII as a whole, provide for the possibility of the use of military force for the purposes of collective security. Such uses of force have to be decided or authorised by the UN Security Council. For example, in its Resolution 678 of 29 November 1990, the Security Council authorised 'Member States co-operating with the Government of Kuwait, unless Iraq on or before 15 January 1991 fully implements, as set forth in paragraph 1 above, the above-mentioned resolutions, *to use all necessary means* [emphasis added] to uphold and implement Resolution 660 (1990) and all subsequent relevant resolutions and to restore international peace and security in the area'. It is important to note that here the Security Council did not decide or order the 'use of all necessary means'; instead it authorised states individually and collectively to do that. The reason for such a nuance is that the initial intention of the drafters of the UN Charter to create United Nations armed forces, as provided in Article 43 of the Charter, was never realised in practice. Instead, special operations, involving relatively lightly armed UN military personnel, were invented, whose main task has been to help maintain peace, serving mostly as buffers between conflicting states or factions within the same state, though gradually such operations have become more muscled; they are no longer acting only as passive buffer zones.[76] These operations are called UN peace-keeping operations, and forces participating in them are called peace-keepers. Later, some regional organisations, like the European Union, African Union and the Commonwealth of Independent States (CIS), also resorted to peace-keeping operations. However, where there is no peace to keep but the situation constitutes a threat to international peace and security, the United Nations may have to authorise states either individually or collectively to use all necessary means, including military force, in order to maintain or restore international peace and security.

Chapter VIII of the UN Charter foresees the creation of regional organisations of collective security, and provides for the use of enforcement actions by such organisations. However, Article 53 stipulates that 'no enforcement action shall be taken under regional arrangements or by regional agencies without the authorization of the Security Council'. Notwithstanding this clause in the UN Charter, some regional organisations have taken such actions without the Security Council's authorisation (e.g., the ECOWAS – the Economic Community of Western African States – at the beginning of the 1990s in Liberia and Sierra Leone). Moreover, the ECOWAS and the African Union changed their respective constitutive documents in order to provide for such enforcement actions without the Security Council's authorisation.[77] In January 2017, the ECOWAS decided to intervene in Gambia where the incumbent president Yahya Jammeh, who had ruled the country for 23 years, having lost the December 2016 elections, refused to concede power. Operation Restore Democracy was put under way by the ECOWAS and military forces from Senegal and Ghana entered Gambia. On 19 January, the UN Security Council passed Resolution 2337 (2017) where the Council 'Expresses its full support to the ECOWAS in its commitment to ensure, by political means first, the respect of the will of the people of the Gambia as expressed in the results of 1st December elections'. As Jammeh left the country there was no need for actual use of military force. Moreover, the army chief of Gambia had pledged not to use force against the ECOWAS troops. Here we see that it was rather the regional organisation ECOWAS that was in the driving seat, while the UN Security Council provided, more or less *ex post facto*, legitimising cover. The African Union (AU) has formally claimed for itself the right to intervene in member states in instances of gross human rights violations. In accordance with Art. 4 (h) Constitutive Act of the AU, the organisation may intervene in a member state pursuant to a decision of the Assembly of Heads of State and Government in respect of grave circumstances, namely: war crimes, genocide and crimes against humanity. In accordance with Art. 7 (1) Constitutive Act of the African Union, the Assembly may take such a decision on the basis of a 2/3 majority. Aside from arguing that the AU would be claiming a 'right of emergency' for itself, it is also arguable that Art. 4 (h) constitutes a collective, *ex ante* form of *intervention by invitation*. Since the member states of the AU have given their express consent to military intervention under certain conditions, the use of force would fall outside the scope of the prohibition in Art. 2 (4) UN Charter and not be in violation of the UN Charter. However, this argument raises, in turn, the question whether such an invitation can be extended for an open-ended period of time, or whether it has to be limited to a particular conflict.[78]

The Use of Force for Humanitarian Purposes

In the 1990s, after the collapse of the bipolar world, with its imposed discipline and relative stability, there was an increase in internal conflicts in different parts of the world. Somalia, and then even more terribly Rwanda, and also Haiti and the former Yugoslavia in the Balkans, have been the most prominent examples. Such conflicts involved massive human rights violations (even acts of genocide) that often escalated into prolonged humanitarian crises. Some of these tragedies spilled over and constituted threats to regional peace and security, while others, though limited to a single state, like the military coup and its effects in Haiti in 1991, created refugee flows and disturbed public opinion abroad, especially in the nearby United States. As a result, the UN Security Council started adopting so-called Chapter VII resolutions (on Somalia, Haiti, the former Yugoslavia, etc.) whereby the Council, having found that certain situations involving massive human rights violations constituted threats to international peace and security, decided to send peace-keepers whose mandate, among other tasks (maintaining or restoring peace, helping find political solutions to the conflict, etc.), included wide-ranging humanitarian components. As such, operations were authorised by the UN Security Council and constituted a form of maintenance or restoration of peace and security. There have not been any serious doubts raised as to their legality or legitimacy, though such practice rather creatively enlarged the competences of the Security Council, extending it to humanitarian crises that had traditionally been beyond its remit.

However, there remains a much more controversial question of the unilateral, that is, not authorised by the UN Security Council, use of military force for humanitarian purposes – or as it has been usually called, 'humanitarian intervention' or R2P (responsibility to protect). Historically, eminent authors such as Hugo Grotius and Emmerich Vattel had supported the idea that in certain extreme circumstances states could lawfully use military force to protect nationals of other states from their own governments (however, one should not forget that at that time the use of military force was not prohibited, and was even considered an attribute of state sovereignty). In the nineteenth century, some European powers indeed intervened in the Ottoman Empire in support of the Christians in the Balkans and the Middle East.[79] However, when the conditions for the lawful use of military force became increasingly restricted, and especially after the adoption of the UN Charter with its Article 2(4) prohibiting the use and threat of force, it also became more and more difficult to justify the use of military force for humanitarian purposes.

Today, in most circumstances, the use of military force for humanitarian purposes is not only counter-productive, but in the absence of the Security Council's authorisation it is also unlawful. As a general proposition, such a conclusion is predicated on, in my opinion, political realities, existing legal norms and, maybe most importantly, sound morality, notwithstanding an allegedly noble aim for the use of force – the protection of human rights in cases of their massive violation. The important point to be made is that any use of military force, even one that would genuinely be carried out for the sake of saving human lives, contains in itself the significant potential for even greater loss of life, the infliction of grievous bodily harm on a massive scale, the loss of property and the infringement of other values, including those which are protected as fundamental human rights.

Of course, the same may be said about the use of force in exercising one's inherent right to self-defence 'if an armed attack occurs', as confirmed in Article 51 of the UN Charter. However, wars of self-defence (though this right is also abused) are by their very nature wars of necessity – they are never wars of choice, if we discount surrendering as an acceptable moral choice (in which case there is no use of force in self-defence).

Yet, the use of force by state A with humanitarian purposes against state B, in a case where B does not in any way threaten A's security, can never be a war of necessity in the same sense (both physical and moral) as wars of self-defence are (though a humanitarian crisis in neighbouring country C may constitute a security threat for A due, for instance, to refugee flows, but this is a different issue to be addressed separately). However, one may ask: can there not be any circumstances in which the use of force by state A in the territory of and against state B, in the case of a severe humanitarian crisis in the latter, even if the crisis does not constitute security threats to A, may be considered a 'war of necessity' – if not in the physical sense (in that respect there is always a choice: intervene militarily or not) as wars of self-defence are, but in a moral sense, which wars of self-defence also are? I believe that in certain circumstances it would be possible to give a positive answer to this question. In situations where the use of military force is the only means of preventing or stopping massive human rights violations such as genocide or crimes against humanity, an absolute proscription against using force would make it impossible to enforce a prohibition of human rights violations. In such a case these prohibitions cannot be considered valid human rights norms, since one of the conditions of validity for legal norms is their enforceability, at least in principle, if not always in practice. In that sense the use of military force in certain extreme circumstances may have the characteristics of a 'war of necessity' – a war of moral necessity. For example, both the world community of states and individual states that had the necessary capacities to first prevent and then stop genocide in Rwanda (this would have clearly been a lesser evil than allowing the foreseeable and preventable genocide to happen and, once started, not stopping it) failed in their duty both collectively and individually. Theirs was a moral surrender similar to the behaviour of those nations which surrender without even trying to resist.

Moral justification for the use of military force for the sake of the protection of human rights in a foreign country can be best based on ideas developed by British political and legal philosopher Lord Raymond Plant. As human rights are real only to the extent of their enforceability (at least in principle, though not always in practice, but this is another, though no less important matter which belongs more to the realm of practical politics and law than moral philosophy), their unenforceability, even in principle, deprives them of their quality as human rights. Lord Plant writes:

> Our responsibility for the rights of others is therefore not confined to *non-interference* in those rights, but also has to involve responsibility for doing what we can to secure those *enforceability* conditions, just because these are part of having a right and therefore must be involved in what respecting rights means. This seems to me to be the best way of linking a concern for rights and the possibility of intervention in a particular country, which may not be securing the enforcement conditions.[80]

If there are circumstances when the use of military force is the only means of protecting rights, and the resort to such an extreme measure, which in itself is fraught with the danger of massive violations of most fundamental human rights, is proportionate to the seriousness of the human rights violations (genocide, crimes against humanity and systemic massive violations of international humanitarian law), then the use of military force may be morally justified as a necessary condition of these rights being rights. The most important general guiding principle in such a situation should be that *extreme human suffering, which one attempts to stop or prevent, has to be significantly and foreseeably higher than the human suffering that inevitably results from the use of force to end the suffering.* And the objective should always be to stop or prevent extreme human suffering and not to effect regime change or promote democracy, though this may occur as an inevitable or even necessary corollary of the intervention.

From these arguments of moral philosophy, it is possible to move to the legal justification of the use of military force for the sake of the protection of human rights.

The UN Security Council's authorisation would make interventions on humanitarian grounds both lawful under international law and legitimate in the eyes of most people, and even though they may, in principle, do more harm than good, in such cases there is less chance that hasty decisions, dictated by narrow self-interest and facilitated by an ignorance of the risks that any military operation involves, are made. However, in extreme circumstances, I believe, there may not only be a moral-philosophical, but also a legal justification for intervention on humanitarian grounds, even without the Security Council's authorisation. It is necessary to emphasise, first, the importance of the words 'in extreme circumstances' since any use of military force, as we have just discussed, inevitably leads to a serious loss of life. It always creates circumstances conducive to massive violations of the right to life – the most basic human right, without which the enjoyment of all other rights becomes meaningless and impossible. Nevertheless, there may be circumstances when the use of military force may be justified not only on moral, but also on legal, grounds.

First, let us deal with a preliminary point. It is often said that if there were a right to use military force for the sake of human rights, states would constantly abuse it. This may well be the case, and in some military interventions allegedly carried out for humanitarian purposes, such justifications have been used to conceal other aims, or at least other aims have been paramount. However, so far states have more often referred to the right to self-defence when using force abusively, rather than referring to humanitarian concerns. Moreover, the fact that the use of military force with the purported aim of protecting human rights in cases of their gross and massive violation is sometimes abused, should not in itself serve as an absolute obstacle on the road to human rights protection even by means of force, if other means have proven to be, or would clearly be, inadequate, and it is also one of those rare situations when the use of force foreseeably does less harm than the abstention from the use of force would do. Almost every right, almost every good, may be open to abuse. As the former President of the International Court of Justice Dame Rosalyn Higgins has written, 'we must face the reality that we live in a decentralised international legal order, where claims may be made either in good faith or abusively'.[81] The fact that claims over some goods or rights are made abusively should not mean that these goods or rights thereby become any less valuable.

Now, here is the main, in my opinion, argument in favour of both the legality and legitimacy of the use of force for humanitarian purposes in extreme circumstances of human suffering. There is no doubt, as we have discussed above, that the principle of the prohibition of the use of force is one of the fundamental principles of international law. The United Nations International Law Commission, in its various reports dealing with the issue of peremptory norms in international law (*jus cogens* norms), from which states cannot deviate or derogate even with the consent of other states, has always given as an example of such norms the norm prohibiting the use of military force.[82] As we discussed above, this norm has not lost and should not lose its fundamental importance, notwithstanding its all-too-frequent violation. On the contrary, its significance is only enhanced by such breaches; the reason being that if a norm protects something that people continue to value highly (peace in this case) then violations of such a norm indicate that it is necessary to strengthen the norm instead of discarding it. In legal terms, we may say that, in such cases, strong *opinio juris* compensates for a less-than-perfect observance of the norm in practice. However, the prohibition of the use of force is not the only fundamental principle of international law. The principle of respect for and protection of human rights acquired, during the second half of the previous century, the same status. In its *Draft Articles on Responsibility of States*, the International Law Commission emphasises not only the importance of the non-use of force principle as a peremptory norm of international law, but also the same character of certain human rights norms, such as the prohibition of genocide, slavery and torture.[83]

In cases of gross and massive violation of such fundamental human rights as the right to life, which are always accompanied by egregious violations of many other rights, the prohibition of the use of military force may yield to the obligation to respect and protect human rights. In such cases we have two equally important and weighty principles of international law that cannot be observed at the same time and in the same context; one has to give way. Such a potential for collision is enshrined in the very nature of the principles of international law. As one of the greatest twentieth-century international lawyers, Oscar Schachter, wrote, 'principles, in contrast [to rules], lack the element of definiteness, they are "open-textured", leaving room for various interpretations'.[84] And he emphasises that sometimes 'particular situations are covered by more than one principle [...] They point to different legal conclusions. Indeed, it has often been observed that principles like proverbs can be paired off into opposites'.[85] In particular situations, the prohibition against committing acts of genocide or crimes against humanity, and even more importantly, the obligation to prevent such acts being committed,[86] may outweigh the prohibition against the use of military force. In such extreme and rare situations, the use of force for humanitarian purposes, even without (though of course it would be better with) the Security Council's authorisation, may be both legitimate and lawful. Such legitimisation takes place *ex post facto* and may acquire different forms. Let us consider some examples.

There have been three significant, rather large-scale and successful foreign invasions that have put an end to massive human rights violations, which may have been characterised either as genocide, crimes against humanity or war crimes (though interestingly and understandably, none of the invading states referred to humanitarian concerns as the only or main reason or justification for their actions). The overthrow of the regimes of Idi Amin in Uganda in 1979, the ousting of Pol Pot in the same year in so-called Democratic Kampuchea, and the Indian 1971–2 military intervention in Eastern Pakistan all put an end to massive crimes against civilian populations, and all ended with the removal of the regimes that had committed those atrocities (in the case of the Indian intervention it led to the breakup of Pakistan and the creation of a new state in Eastern Pakistan – Bangladesh). None of these interventions were sanctioned by the United Nations, and the intervening states preferred to refer more to the right of self-defence as the justification than to 'purely humanitarian concerns'.[87] Naturally, in all these cases, besides the humanitarian issues, there were other concerns and interests present, if not dominant, but none of these military operations could be qualified as actions of self-defence. There is something significant in the fact that all three of these large-scale, successful foreign military interventions, which were responses to genuine humanitarian catastrophes (even if not justified wholly by references to them) and which put an end to those catastrophes, were carried out by non-Western nations. One of the reasons for their success in the sense of the sustainability of the main objective of their interventions (the end of mass atrocities and not democracy-building) may have been in that after overthrowing bloody dictators (Idi Amin and Pol Pot) and putting an end to Islamabad's repressions in Eastern Pakistan, the intervening states did not attempt to put in place pro-Western or Western-sounding and Western-looking governments, and did not carry out nation-building exercises with the aim of 'widening the circle of liberal democracies' in the world.

In favour of the legitimacy, and at the end of the day also of the legality, of these interventions speaks the fact that, though there was some criticism from at least certain states and circles at the time of the interventions, in two out of the three cases – the Indian and Tanzanian interventions – their results were relatively quickly accepted by the world community. So, Bangladesh – a state that emerged as a result of the Indian intervention, which took place in 1971–2 – became a member of the United Nations as soon as 1974, being approved for UN membership by its Security Council and the General Assembly. Compare this with the continuing non-recognition of the so-called Turkish Republic of Northern Cyprus, which was created as a result of the Turkish invasion of Cyprus in 1974. Neither the United Nations nor the Organisation of African Unity (the predecessor of the current AU) condemned the Tanzanian military invasion of Uganda, and most states soon recognised the new government in Kampala. The reaction to the Vietnamese intervention in Kampuchea was different due to the geopolitics of the region, where the interests of three permanent members of the Security Council – China, the Soviet Union and the United States – clashed. It is of interest to note that, in 1999, Mr A. P. Van Walsum, the Dutch Representative to the United Nations, referred to the Vietnamese intervention in Cambodia in 1979 that had helped to put an end to Pol Pot's genocide. He expressed regret that at that time his own country, by its behaviour in the UN, had allowed the genocidal Khmer Rouge to occupy the Cambodian seat in the General Assembly for more than a decade.[88] Although this statement was somewhat ingenious and self-serving, as it was made, *inter alia*, to justify the Dutch support for the military intervention against Serbia over Kosovo, it nevertheless has some evidential value. As to the role and approach of the United States to the issue at the time, the attitude of Robert Rosenstock, an international lawyer and the then legal advisor of the US Mission to the United Nations, is revealing. Debbie Sharnak writes:

> The Carter Administration confronted the difficult choice of whether to vote to seat the Khmer Rouge's genocidal regime; support Samrin's communist, Vietnamese-installed government; or, to abstain from voting altogether. *After weighing geopolitical concerns about human rights costs against national interests in a Cold War context* [emphasis added], Carter's representative to the Credentials Committee, Robert Rosenstock, cast the vote in favor of seating the Khmer Rouge. As he rose from the table, someone grabbed his hand to congratulate him. Rosenstock looked up to find to his horror that he was shaking hands with Pol Pot's foreign minister, Ieng Sary. 'I felt like washing my hands', Rosenstock reported. Rosenstock's reaction to this episode, a mixture of disgust and resignation, encapsulates well the contradiction of what this vote ultimately signified. In the act of seating the Khmer Rouge at the United Nations, Jimmy Carter, the supposed human rights president, aligned himself with an ousted genocidal regime.[89]

One could also take note of the ECOWAS's unauthorised intervention in Liberia, which instead of being condemned, was *ex post facto* ratified by the Security Council.[90] In February 1998, the ECOWAS, once again without the prior authorisation of the Security Council, intervened in the civil war and humanitarian crisis in Sierra Leone.[91] These developments seem to indicate that in extreme circumstances of humanitarian crises, the world community is ready to legitimise non-authorised (by the Security Council) use of military force for humanitarian purposes. However, these cases have been exceptions rather than a rule. And though it has been possible, as we showed above, to build moral and even legal justifications for such interventions, successful (i.e., those doing more good than harm) interventions on humanitarian grounds have been so exceptional, that the more recent developments in the field, instead of giving support for the use of military force to protect human rights, have shown that the world community is not ready to accept military interventions on humanitarian grounds, if not authorised by the UN Security Council. And the most important reason for this is not theoretical or normative, but pragmatic – military interventions for humanitarian purposes have not, in most cases, worked. They have done more harm than good.

The twenty-first century started with an attempt to reformulate and rephrase the concept of humanitarian intervention in terms of responsibility to protect (R2P). First, the International Commission on Intervention and State Sovereignty elaborated this idea in its report in 2001's *The Responsibility to Protect*.[92] Then the idea was developed by the High Level Panel on Threats, Challenges and Change in its report *A More Secure World: Our Shared Responsibility*[93] in 2004. Then came the report of the United Nations Secretary General in *Larger Freedom: Towards Development, Security and Human Rights for All*[94], and finally, the concept found its expression in the UN General Assembly's *2005 Outcome Document*.[95]

First, it is necessary to underline that none of these documents creates legally binding rights and obligations. Secondly, though using different terminology and emphasising different aspects of the problem, in substance they did not add much to what was already known. Neither did they clarify the most controversial issues on which discussions had been, and continue to be, held. For example, there was not, and there still is not, any doubt that every state is responsible for the protection of the rights of its citizens (this obligation stems from numerous universal and regional human rights documents, as well as from customary norms of international law), and that if a state commits acts of genocide, war crimes, ethnic cleansing or crimes against humanity it bears responsibility for these acts under international law. Moreover, those individuals who are personally responsible for such acts, be they heads of states or governments or the highest-ranking military officers, bear criminal liability under international law. What is not clear, and what none of these documents clarifies, is the question: is it lawful for individual states or international organisations to use military force in order to protect the nationals of foreign countries in the territory of a foreign country, if the government of that country commits acts of genocide, crimes against humanity, ethnic cleansing or war crimes against its own people or is unable or unwilling to protect its people in cases of such crimes committed on its territory by any other party?

It was the Commission on State Sovereignty and Intervention that in 2001 attempted to go furthest in allowing the use of military force in certain circumstances, even without the Security Council's authorisation. The Commission developed five criteria of legitimacy for intervention (just cause, right intention, last resort, proportionality of means and reasonable prospect of success[96]), applicable both to the Security Council and states. In these criteria we see a kind of revival of the old idea of 'just wars' that was prevalent when natural law concepts reigned in international legal literature, before positivist approaches started to prevail and the use of military force became outlawed in international law. The furthest the Commission went on the road towards legitimising the use of military force without the Security Council's authorisation is in the following two paragraphs:

> 6.39 The first message is that if the Security Council fails to discharge its responsibility in conscience-shocking situations crying out for action, then it is unrealistic to expect that concerned states will rule out other means and forms of action to meet the gravity and urgency of these situations. If collective organizations will not authorize collective intervention against regimes that flout the most elementary norms of legitimate governmental behaviour, then the pressures for intervention by ad hoc coalitions or individual states will surely intensify. And there is a risk then that such interventions, without the discipline and constraints of UN authorization, will not be conducted for the right reasons or with the right commitment to the necessary precautionary principles.
>
> 6.40 The second message is that if, following the failure of the Council to act, a military intervention is undertaken by an ad hoc coalition or individual state which does fully observe and respect all the criteria we have identified, and if that intervention is carried through successfully – and is seen by world public opinion to have been carried through successfully – then this may have enduringly serious consequences for the stature and credibility of the UN itself.[97]

These propositions are not, and are not meant to be, legally binding norms, but rather warnings to the Security Council that if it does not act, others may react and the Council may lose its exceptional position and authority under international law.

Addressing the UN Human Rights Commission in April 1999, the then Secretary General of the United Nations, Kofi Annan, emphasised: 'Emerging slowly, but I believe surely is an international norm against the violent repression of minorities that will and must take precedence over concerns of State sovereignty'.[98] Later, when speaking of Kosovo in Stockholm, he said: 'There is emerging international law that countries cannot hide behind sovereignty and abuse people without expecting the rest of the world to do something about it'.[99] Speaking in The Hague on the occasion of the centennial of the first Hague Peace Conference, the Secretary General, once again, stressed the need to act through the Security Council. At the same time, he expressed his belief that 'unless the Security Council can unite around the aim of confronting massive human rights violations and crimes against humanity on the scale of Kosovo, then we will betray the very ideals that inspired the founding of the United Nations'.[100] In autumn of the same year, in his article in *The Economist*, Kofi Annan wrote that 'in cases where forceful intervention does become necessary, the Security Council – the body charged with authorising the use of force under international law – *must be able to rise to the challenge* [emphasis added]'.[101] Two days later, in his address to the General Assembly, the Secretary General warned: 'The Charter requires the Council to be defender of common interest, and unless it is seen to be so – in the era of human rights, interdependence, and globalisation – there is a danger that others could seek to take its place'.[102]

It seems to be possible to draw the following three conclusions from the statements of the former Secretary

General: (1) Although the United Nations has to be 'respectful of the sovereignty of States', in cases of massive human rights violations and crimes against humanity, humanitarian concerns must prevail over state sovereignty; (2) The role of the Security Council, and the United Nations as a whole, should be central in dealing with extreme humanitarian catastrophes threatening international peace and security; (3) However, the Security Council, and especially its permanent members, have to act responsibly and 'unite behind the principle that massive and systematic violations of human rights conducted against an entire people cannot be allowed to stand'.[103] The world community has to rely on the Security Council on issues involving the use of force, but it can do so only if the Council and its permanent members act with the utmost sense of responsibility. If the Council neglects its responsibility, other institutions may have to fill the void.

However, notwithstanding the report of the Commission on State Sovereignty and Intervention, Kofi Annan's cautious statements and other documents mentioned above that were adopted later foreclose any interventions on humanitarian grounds if unauthorised by the United Nations Security Council. Alex Bellamy's conclusion that

> as agreed by world leaders in 2005, R2P does not countenance non-consensual military force without the authorization of the Security Council and does not set out criteria for the use of force beyond the four threshold crimes [i.e., genocide, crimes against humanity, ethnic cleansing and war crimes] and the idea that the Council should assume responsibility in cases where the host state is 'manifestly failing' to protect.[104]

Therefore, Carsten Stahn is justified in calling R2P partly 'Old Wine in New Bottles'.[105]

How relying on various interpretations of R2P may backfire can be seen in the situation in which Gareth Evans found himself. Being an ardent supporter of the concept of R2P as well as a co-chair of the International Commission on Intervention and State Sovereignty, Evans – the former Foreign Minister of Australia – encountered difficulties in explaining why Russia was wrong in August 2008 when invoking the R2P concept as justification for the Kremlin's response to the Georgian attack on Tskhinvali, the capital of South Ossetia.[106] He was forced to admit that 'in the absence of UN Security Council approval, there is no legal authority for an R2P-based military intervention'. And he added: 'The 2005 General Assembly Outcome Document makes it clear that any country or group of countries seeking to apply forceful means to address an R2P situation – where another country is manifestly failing to protect its people and peaceful means are inadequate – must take that action through the Security Council'.[107] And Evans is certainly right that 'the sense of moral outrage at reports of civilians being killed and ethnically cleansed can have an unintended effect of clouding judgement as to what is the best response, which is another reason to channel action collectively through the United Nations'.[108] The point is not whether Russia correctly invoked the R2P concept (in any case, it was only secondary in the Kremlin's justifications for its military response – and as Gareth Evans correctly points out, Russia's response was 'manifestly excessive', that is, disproportionate to the Georgian attack. The point is that, depending on the political, economic and strategic interests as well as the ideological proclivities, states use various concepts in their own self-interest. Moreover, as Alex de Waal comments on Gareth Evans' and Samantha Power's enthusiastic support of the concepts of R2P and humanitarian intervention, 'in the face of "evil", the idealists tend to turn righteous and forget to ask important questions about what they want to achieve and how'.[109] More often than not, less sharp instruments than military intervention or a dogged insistence on regime change save more lives. Although, they may hurt the idealists' sense of self-righteousness, and also prevent or delay the achievement of other goals such as the 'democratisation of the wider Middle East' or securing control over energy resources.

The events, developments, mistakes, tragedies and disappointments after the high expectations of the post-Cold War period (though, no doubt, there have also been success stories, and they have to be taken into account and lessons learned from them also) testify that central principles of international law and the UN Charter, confirmed in the *Nicaragua* case by the International Court of Justice, such as the non-use of force and the non-interference in internal affairs of states, retain their relevance. And this notwithstanding (or maybe even because of) the emergence of international human rights law and the evolution of humanitarian law. This also means that the concept of responsibility to protect (R2P) has to be interpreted in the light of these and other principles of international law. The Institute of International Law (l'Institut de Droit International) studied the problems of humanitarian intervention, which now is mostly considered under the heading of R2P, for more than a decade. In 2007, the Santiago (Chile) session of the Institute adopted a resolution where the question of 'the lawfulness of military actions which have not been authorised by the United Nations but which purport to have been taken to end genocide, large-scale crimes against humanity, or large-scale war crimes' was left for further study due to the differing, often opposing, views of the members of the Institute.[110] However, in 2015 at the Tallinn session, the Institute, having meticulously studied the practice and views of various states in the period after 2007 (done by Professor Michael Reisman together with Judge Hisashi Owada and the 10th Commission), came to this conclusion:

> The Commission has concluded that state practice over the past decade has not witnessed enough clear movement away from the traditional requirement of Security Council authorisation for a putative Humanitarian Intervention; while some unilateral actions may have received a degree of informal or post hoc approval, practice indicates that the international community continues to view unilateral Humanitarian Intervention undertaken without the authorisation of the United Nations Security Council as presumptively unlawful, though sometimes subject to retroactive validation.[111]

After the high expectations of some that the world community, or those acting in its name, would be able to impartially interfere in order to prevent, or put an end to, atrocities within countries, the majority of experts have become rather pessimistic as to the ability of outside intervenors to make things better. Usually the opposite is true.[112] And the matter is not only, or even principally, that unilateral (i.e., without authorisation of the Security Council) interventions in the name of humanity are often abusive, but also that foreign military (and often non-military) interventions rarely make things better. Moreover, as Mathew Burrows and Robert A. Manning observe, 'in this increasingly post-Western world, Western policies and norms that are viewed as threats to national sovereignty are being more broadly questioned. Thus, value-based issues such as democracy promotion and the Right to Protect (R2P) tend to spark strong counteraction from not just authoritarians like China, but also many emerging democracies who worry about maintaining their national sovereignty'.[113] And it is not only that. As two 2016 published books with revealing titles – *Mission Failure: America and the World in the Post-Cold War Era* by American Michael Mandelbaum and *Pourquoi perd-on la guerre?* by Frenchman Gérard Chaliand – testify, no Western intervention in the post-Cold War era has achieved its political aims. Professor Mandelbaum writes:

> The United States did not succeed in getting China to protect human rights, or constructing smoothly functioning free markets or genuinely representative political institutions in Russia. It did not succeed in installing well-run, widely accepted governments in Somalia, Haiti, Bosnia, or Kosovo. It did not transform Afghanistan or Iraq into tolerant, effectively administered countries. It did not bring democracy to the Middle East or harmony between Israelis and Arabs.[114]

Gérard Chaliand observes that 'the balance sheet of wars waged by the major military power of the XXI century, the United States, often backed up by numerous allies, is without any doubt negative: enormous sums squandered with mediocre military results and politically disastrous consequences.'[115] However, notwithstanding such a dismal record of American interventions abroad, including the one in Iraq in 2003, General David Petraeus, while conceding that the United States has to learn its lesson of humility, nevertheless recommends 'more American interventions in today's crises, only better executed'.[116] Obviously, for him there are no lessons learnt, no humility available.

Instead of Conclusions

While re-reading my text I was wondering whether I had not been too critical of the United States and too soft on, say, China and Russia, which have recently become the main counter-balancers to the only 'hyperpower', to use the term offered by the former French Foreign Minister Hubert Védrine in 1999 for the identification of 'a country that is dominant or predominant in all categories'.[1] Maybe, yes, there is a certain bias against the hyperpower. But there are at least two good reasons against changing the tonality of my analysis. The first is the disappointment I share, probably with many others, who in the late 1980s and early 1990s believed in a world free of great power rivalries. And the power that could have contributed the most to make such a world possible sadly and dismally failed to do that. In addition to what has been written and argued above, I would like to refer to what a prominent American intellectual, Stephen Kinzer, recently wrote:

> After the collapse of the Soviet Union in 1989, the United States had an epochal opportunity to redefine the role of a world power. We could have declared victory, congratulated

> ourselves for avoiding nuclear annihilation, stepped back from global security commitments designed to contain the Soviet Union, and begun an era of rebuilding our own country. Instead we proclaimed a 'new world order' in which, as President George H. W. Bush put it, 'American leadership is indispensable' because 'we have a unique responsibility to do the hard work of freedom.' Feeling invincible and armed with absolute truths, the United States set out to subdue the rest of the world. Successive presidents pushed our power into new regions. We assumed the role of global policeman and tried to impose a 'Washington consensus' under which all countries would fall in line behind us. Our blind triumphalism led us to scorn diplomacy and compromise. For our aggressions, we have paid a heavy price in blood, treasure, and national security.[2]

The second is that the US, still – at least for a while – the most powerful actor in the world, has the biggest, though diminishing in relative terms, potential for both good and for bad. Its errors – even if done for the sake of good intentions – are, for the same reason, costlier that those of other states. The world after the end of the Cold War has not become more peaceful. Not only are there more 'low-impact-high-probability' threats such as the spread of terrorism or uncontrolled migration flows, but a 'low-probability-high-impact' crisis, in the form of a potential clash of superpowers (or of the hyperpower with its allies vis-à-vis disobedient counter-balancers), looms at the horizon – to say nothing of the 'high-probability-high impact' effect of the environmental crisis.

In an inspiring, futuristic and provocative book (*War! What Is It Good for? Conflict and the Role of Civilization from Primates to Robots*),[3] Ian Morris describes how war, notwithstanding all of the people killed and properties destroyed, has nevertheless played a positive role in the evolution of humankind. Primarily through the creation, enlargement and consolidation of states, wars have not only contributed to the technological, economic, political and social progress of humankind but also decreased net violence, notwithstanding even the violence committed in all those wars (however, Morris does not discuss the issues of moral progress and this omission is significant, as we will try to show below). Ian Morris believes that 'what has made the world so much safer is the war itself'.[4] As well as making people safe, he further suggests, 'the larger societies created by war have also – again, over the long run – made us richer'.[5] So far so good, and notwithstanding these somewhat disturbing conclusions, or maybe because of his sharp and academically detached analysis, Ian Morris is still rather persuasive. He is obviously also right in claiming that the idea, first developed in full by Norman Angell, 'that economic interconnection makes war unthinkable – was wrong, and is still wrong today'.[6] (Economic interdependence, though not making wars unthinkable, may nevertheless lessen the likelihood of military conflicts; we can see that in the fact that so far Washington has been less forceful in containing Beijing than Moscow since, with the latter, its economic cooperation is rather negligible.) And I would agree with Morris that, by creating new institutions and perfecting existing ones, humankind cannot completely get rid of war (though, once again, this also may lessen its likelihood). Therefore, Immanuel Kant was also wrong in his *Perpetual Peace*, though I believe that even in being wrong (he was wrong only in the sense that there will never be an absolute or perpetual peace, but progress on the way is still possible) he made an important intellectual contribution to the potential of a more peaceful world. So, it seems that there is not much hope in having a world without wars and all talk, including my comments in the last chapter concerning Article 2(4) of the UN Charter, prohibiting not only the use of force but even the threat of force, as well as all the other legal niceties in numerous documents, will not help prevent almost inevitable wars. However, Ian Morris nevertheless believes that the situation is not so hopeless, though differently from Angell; it is neither the economic interdependence of societies nor a world federation of democratic republics à la Immanuel Kant that will be our saviours. That is something else.

There have usually been, writes Morris, 'globocops', who have waged 'progressive' wars, wars that ultimately have decreased violence and increased prosperity for all of humankind. These have historically been ancient empires such as the Roman Empire or the British Empire. Now it is, of course, the American Empire that performs such a role. But it always so happens that the better the 'globocop' does its job, the stronger become also its global rivals. Once again, we are in a vicious circle: hegemonic power creates its own counter-balancers. At this stage of the development of weaponry and military technology as a whole, a new world war may be also the last one, the one that instead of making us richer and more peaceful, would return us to the stone age. And here too, it is difficult to disagree with Ian Morris. The only way to break this vicious circle, in his opinion, is the rapid development of information technology, artificial intelligence and, finally and especially, the emergence of a combination of natural and artificial intelligence, the merging of humans and machines, a world where trans- or post-humans live and act (I would add: and, naturally, also rule). And then gradually a Pax Technologica would replace the Pax Americana. Until then, believes Morris, the United States will have to play the inevitable, unenviable and ungrateful role of the 'globocop', whose main task would be to see to it that the transfer will go on as smoothly as possible. For the sake of fairness to Ian Morris, it has to be said that he sees many difficulties and pitfalls on this road.

This all may sound rather like a sci-fi story or social-scientific utopia, but I would not brush it away as such. Francis Fukuyama, who became famous in the 1990s for his end-of-history theory, in 2003 published another book,[7] which unfortunately, though understandably, is much less known, where he foresaw the possible creation of post-humans through DNA manipulation. Differently from Morris, Fukuyama was more alarmed by, than optimistic about, such scientific breakthroughs, and especially their social consequences. And rightly so. In that respect, let me tell a story from my young days when I was a first-year undergraduate at Moscow State University (MGU). In Marxism there is a theory of social evolution, which claims that humankind's progress follows a path that looks like a rising spiral, where at the highest levels of the spiral a society repeats some features from the lowest levels. The evolutionary road, the theory explains, goes from a primitive, classless society (primitive communism), through the slave-owning, feudal and capitalist phases, to reach, finally, socialism and communism. Of course, like a Fukuyamian end-of-history theory, this Marxist spiral theory also had its end. This was communism. Nothing new or better could be, by definition, possible. However, being then still a naïve Estonian country bumpkin, I asked our professor: doesn't this mean that after communism there should again come along a slave-owning society, only at a much higher level of development? My scientific communism professor did not appreciate my naïvety, and probably thought that I was being intentionally provocative and therefore lowered my mark a notch. She was obviously one of those Marxist 'the end of history' professors. But now, when I think of Fukuyama's worries in *Our Posthuman Future*, or the warnings of Stephen Hawking, Elon Musk and Bill Gates, or even Ian Morris' optimism about trans- and post-human 'humans', I believe that such a slave-owning future, differently from the utopian world-wide triumph of communism, at the highest possible level of evolution of humankind, is not at all impossible. Moreover, there are at least two big problems with Morris' optimism (albeit cautious). The first, which we have just mentioned, is that this would most probably lead to a world that, even if more peaceful, would indeed be a kind of slave-owning society at its highest level of development. The second problem is that there would be so much opposition to efforts that would lead to such a world, that military conflicts and revolts would be inevitable before, if ever, the world becomes trans- or post-human.

Ian Morris writes that 'right now, the United States is the indispensable nation, and it must lean forward, but as it approaches the culminating point of globocoppery, the United States will need to pull back. The *Pax Americana* will yield to a *Pax Technologica*'.[8] However, why would these trans- or post-humans, be they genetically modified or the result of a human-machine combination, pull back? Their human potentials are enhanced by machine capacities, not by principles derived from morality that have resulted from a long process of evolution and moral contractualism. And as the United States is at the forefront of technological revolution, it seems plausible (though not inevitable; these may be the Chinese or somebody else – for that read the brilliant futuristic trilogy of Ramez Naam, *Nexus*, *Crux* and *Apex*) that the resulting world system would be Pax Americana or Pax Sinica enhanced by Pax Technologica, or Pax Technologica Americana (Pax Technologica Sinica), and this would also be a slave-owning world at its highest possible level of development. However, then the spiral would possibly continue. The slaves will revolt and bring down the whole world so that the survivors, if any, could start from scratch.

Why such a pessimistic approach? As we mentioned at the beginning of these conclusions and showed throughout the book, at the end of the 1980s and the beginning of the 1990s, when the

US had the opportunity to change the world and pull back, it did exactly the opposite, and this is probably what everyone who can rule the world will do. In 1991, Washington had the best opportunity humankind has ever had to get closer to a warless world, at least as good, possibly even better, than the long peace which stretched from the Napoleonic Wars to World War I (1815–1914). Can we be sure that machine-enhanced Americans would do better? I would not bet on it. Therefore, the best, imperfect but perfectible, way forward would be a multipolar balance-of-power concert-based world, as argued above. Of course, this does not mean that the progress in the fields of nanotechnology, biotechnology, information technology and cognitive science (NBIC) will not be able to considerably benefit humankind. French philosopher Luc Ferry may well be right that the progress of science in these domains 'will, within the next forty years, change healthcare and economics to an extent comparable to the previous four thousand years'[9] and many millions may benefit from this scientific revolution in the making. However, it would be too risky to bet on the ability of such a revolution to resolve all known as well as yet-unknown social problems, including wars and human rights violations. Within the next 40 years humankind may also have more opportunities to put an end to its own existence than during the previous 4,000 years. To avoid this happening, political wisdom and a dialogue of cultures and civilisations are no less important than the advances of science. Genetically modified and technologically advanced trans-, post- or hybrid-humans would not necessarily be any wiser.

The pessimistic report prepared for the February 2017 Munich Security Conference and alarmingly entitled 'Post-Truth, Post-West, Post-Order' is full of anxieties that the world may be 'on the brink of a post-Western age, one in which non-Western actors are shaping international affairs, often in parallel or even to the detriment of precisely those multilateral frameworks that have formed the bedrock of the liberal international order since 1945'. 'Are we entering a post-order world?', questions the report. However, there is no need to be so pessimistic. Indeed, the world, and particularly liberal democracies, has certainly benefited from the liberal international order. But no order, be it international or national, is forever. And this liberal international order was not so liberal after all. Rather, it was an order where liberal states ruled the world, attempting to widen the circle of liberal societies (especially after the collapse of the USSR) while ostracising or even destroying those which could not or did not want to become liberal. An international order that we foresee rising – a multipolar, balance-of-power and concert-of-powers world – may indeed not be liberal in that sense, but it would be much more democratic to an extent and in the sense that these notions – liberal and democratic – are applicable in international relations. It would accept differences not only within societies, as liberal orders do, but also between states. In that respect, it could be even more liberal than the post-1945 international order.

Notes

All translations from the French, Russian and Estonian are the author's own, unless stated otherwise.

Introduction

1 When confronted by a significant external threat, states may balance or bandwagon. Balancing is defined as allying with others against the prevailing threat, whereas bandwagoning refers to alignment with one of the main adversaries, thereby expecting to increase one's security. Bandwagoning in international relations occurs when a state aligns with a stronger power for reasons of security or economic benefit. Bandwagoning is a strategy usually employed by weaker or smaller states. Bigger and stronger states, like China, Russia or India today, could hardly be expected to practise bandwagoning.

2 D. Deudney and G. John Ikenberry, 'The Myth of the Autocratic Revival. Why Liberal Democracy Will Prevail', *Foreign Affairs*, January–February 2009.

3 *Ibid.*

4 See, for example, T. Franck, 'The Emerging Right to Democratic Governance', *American Journal of International Law*, 1992, Vol. 86; J. Crawford, 'Democracy in International Law' (Inaugural lecture), Cambridge, 1994.

5 W. Friedmann, *The Changing Structure of International Law* (Columbia University Press, 1965).

6 M. Koskenniemi, *The Gentle Civilizer of Nations* (Cambridge University Press, 2001).

Chapter 1 Geopolitics and International Law through the Prism of Ideology

1 See R. Müllerson, 'The Tunkin Diary and Lectures: The Diary and Collected Lectures of G.I. Tunkin at the Hague Academy of International Law', ed. by William E. Butler & Vladimir G. Tunkin (The Hague Eleven Publishing, 2012), *American Journal of International Law*, 2013, Vol. 107, No. 3, pp. 710–14.

2 P.J. Saunders, 'Barack Obama is not a realist', *The National Interest*, 26 August 2014.

3 Z. Majed, 'Treve en Syrie: "C'est comme si on invitait les Syriens à s'entretuer"', *L'Obs*, 24 February 2016.

4 H. Kodami, 'Bilan des victimes: l'impossible comptage', *Libération*, 13 March 2016.

5 R. Girard, 'Syria: les rebelles tuent aussi des enfants', *Le Figaro*, 1 November 2016.

6 *Guardian*, 6 July 1996.

7 S. Kinzer, 'Where There's War There's Amanpour', *New York Times*, 9 October 1994.

8 See, for example, L. Cooper, M. Pal, 'Lectures from a Spin Doctor: A NATO strategist's position at a top British university', *Open Democracy*, 30 June 2011.

9 Council on Foreign Relations, *Terrorist Groups and Political Legitimacy* (http://www.cfr.org/terrorism/terrorist-groups-political-legitimacy/p10159).

10 *Ibid.*

11 www.publications.parliament.uk/pa/cm199899/cmhansrd/vo990118/debtext/90118-06.htm.

12 T. Ali (ed.), *Masters of the Universe? NATO's Balkan Crusade* (Verso Books, 2000), p. 163.

13 M. Tresca, 'Le Kosovo tente de controller la diffusion de l'Islam radical', *La Croix*, 16 August 2016.

14 I. Morris, *Why the West Rules – For Now: The Patterns of History and What They Reveal about the Future* (Profile Books, 2010), p. 24.
15 W.R. Mead, 'The Return of Geopolitics: The Revenge of the Revisionist Powers', *Foreign Affairs*, May/June 2014.
16 http://nationalinterest.org/blog/the-buzz/geopolitics-back%E2%80%94-global-governance-out-12868.
17 http://www.delfi.ee/archive/barack-obama-tallinn-speech-in-full-nato-will-defend-estonia-latvia-lithuania?id=69666267.
18 M. Slama, *La Guerre des Mondes: Réflections sur la croisade idéologique de Poutine contre l'Occident* (Editions de Fallois, 2016), p. 59.
19 R. Müllerson, 'Ideology, Geopolitics and International Law', *Chinese Journal of International Law*, 2016, Vol. 15, No. 1.
20 Z. Brzezinski, *The Grand Chessboard: American Primacy and Its Geostrategic Imperatives* (Basic Books, 1998), p. 46.
21 J-Y. Le Drian, *Qui est l'Ennemi?* (Les éditions du Cerf, 2016), p. 379.
22 P. Boniface, *La Géopolitique: 40 fiches thématiques et documentée pour comprendre I 'actualité* (Eyrolles, 2014), p. 533.
23 D. Moïsi, *La Geopolitique des Series ou le triomphe de la peur* (Stock, 2016), p. 498.
24 D. Deutsch, *The Fabric of Reality* (Penguin Books, 1997), pp. 91–2.
25 B. Russell, *History of Western Philosophy and its Connection with Political and Social Circumstances from the Earliest Times to the Present Day* (Allen & Unwin 1946), p. 637.
26 C. Schmitt, *The Nomos of the Earth in the International Law of the Jus Publicum Europaeum* (Telos, 2006).
27 See, R. Müllerson, 'F.F. Martens – Man of the Enlightenment: Drawing Parallels between Martens' Times and Today's Problems', *European Journal of International Law*, 2014, Vol. 25, No. 3.
28 See, for example, F.F. Martens, 'La Conférence du Congo à Berlin et la politique coloniale des états modernes', *Revue de droit international et de legislation comparé*, 1886, tome XVIII, pp. 113–56.
29 A. Jurkevics, 'Hannah Arendt reads Carl Schmitt's The Nomos of the Earth: A Dialogue on Law and Geopolitics from the Margins', *European Journal of Political Theory*, 2015, p. 10.
30 *Ibid.*, p. 1.

31 D. Chandler, 'The Revival of Carl Schmitt in International Relations: The Last Refuge of Critical Theorists?', *Millennium: Journal of International Studies*, Vol. 37, No. 1, p. 27.

32 *Ibid.*, p. 31.

33 M. Koskenniemi, 'International Law as Political Theology', *Constellations*, 2004, Vol. 11, No. 4, pp. 492–511.

34 *Ibid.*, para. 44.

35 *Ibid.*

36 See Gabriel Matzneff, *Venus et Junon* (La Table Ronde, 1999), p. 50.

37 M. Koskenniemi, *Op. cit*, para. 9.

38 *Ibid.*, para. 10.

39 P. Boniface, *La Géopolitique: 40 fiches thematiques et documentee pour comprendre l'actualite* (Eyrolles, 2014), p. 124.

40 D. Moïsi, *La Geopolitique des Series ou le triomphe de la peur* (Stock, 2016), p. 565.

41 *Ibid.*

42 Zhang Weiwei, *The China Wave: Rise of A Civilizational State* (World Century Publishing Corporation, 2012), p. 374.

43 Zhang Weiwei, *China Horizon: The Glory and Dream of a Civilizational State* (World Century Publishing Corporation, 2016), p. 1880.

44 'China's Role in the World: Is China a Responsible Stakeholder?' Statement by Thomas J. Christensen, Deputy Assistant Secretary of State for East Asia and Pacific Affairs before the US-China Economic and Security Review Commission, 3 August 2006.

45 H. White, *The China Choice: Why America should Share Power* (Black Inc., 2012, Kindle version), p. 648.

46 D. Moïsi, *Op. cit*, p. 596.

47 See, for example, David van Reybrouk, *Contre les élections* (Actes Sud Editions, 2014).

48 M. Slama, 'Il y a du Soljenitsyne dans le discours de Poutine', *Figaro Vox*, 24 May 2016.

49 A. Orakhelashvili, 'International Law and Geopolitics: One Object, Competing Legitimacies', *Netherland Yearbook of International Law*, 2008, Vol. 39, p. 155.

50 P. Boniface, *Op. cit.*, p. 526.

51 *Ibid.*, Empl. 477.

52 R. Kaplan, *The Revenge of Geography: What the Map Tells Us About the Coming Conflicts and the Battle Against Fate* (Random House, 2012), p. 183.

53 For more on that, see R. Müllerson, 'Precedents in the Mountains: On the Parallels and Uniqueness of the Cases of Kosovo, South Ossetia and Abkhazia', *Chinese Journal of International Law*, 2009, Vol. 8, No. 1.

54 http://www.oxfordlearnersdictionaries.com/definition/english/ideology.

55 M. Seliger, *Ideology and Politics* (Allen & Unwin, 1976), p. 14.

56 T. Adorno, *Ästhetische Theorie* (Frankfurt am Main: Suhrkamp Verlag, 1990), p. 345.

57 F. Lukyanov, 'They Don't Trust Each Other, They Don't Respect Each Other', *Russia in Global Affairs* (in Russian), 25 February 2016.

58 S. Karaganov, 'A New Ideological Struggle?', *Izvestia*, 21 April 2016 (http://izvestia.ru/news/610812).

59 M. Slama, 'Il y a du Soljenitsyne dans le discours de Poutine', *Figaro Vox*, 24 May 2016.

60 T. Frye, 'Why IR Theory Gets Russia Wrong, *Foreign Affairs*, 23 May 2016.

61 F. Hiatt, 'Diplomacy as anesthetic in Syria', *Washington Post*, 14 February 2016.

62 J. Bolton, 'Obama's Peace Talks Are Latest Blunder in Feckless Syria Policy', *The Algemeiner*, 3 February 2016 (http://www.algemeiner.com/2016/02/03/obamas-peace-talks-are-latest-blunder-in-feckless-syria-policy/#).

63 D. Brooks, 'Obama, Gospel and Verse', *New York Times*, 26 April 2007.

64 R. Niebuhr, *Moral Man and Immoral Society* (Continuum, 2005), p. 57.

65 *Ibid.*, p. 59.

66 E. Gellner, *Nations and Nationalism* (Basil Blackwell, 1983), p. 2.

67 L. Ferry, *La Révolution Transhumaniste: comment la technomédecine et l'uberisation du monde boulverser nos vies* (Plon, 2016), p. 222.

68 R. Niebuhr, *The Irony of American History* (University of Chicago Press, 2008, first published 1952), pp. 2–3.

69 *Ibid.*, p. 3.

70 *Ibid.*, p. 79.

71 '"Cut off head of snake" Saudis told US on Iran', Reuters, 29 November 2010 (http://www.reuters.com/article/us-wikileaks-iran-saudis-idUSTRE6AS02B20101129).

72 For those who are not basketball fans: a 'slam dunk' shot is when a player puts the ball, usually with both hands, into the basket from above. There is no way to miss.

73 J. Goldberg, 'The Obama Doctrine', *The Atlantic*, April 2006.

74 S.M. Hersh, 'The Red Line and the Rat Line', *London Review of Books*, 17 April 2014, Vol. 36, No. 8.

75 R. Parry, 'Neocons Red-Faced Over 'Red Line', *Consortiumnews*, 16 March 2016 (https://consortiumnews.com/2016/03/10/neocons-red-faced-over-red-line/).

76 C. Galactéros, 'La décision de Vladimir Poutin humilie la diplomatie français', *Figaro Vox/Tribune*, 11 October 2016.

77 *Ibid.*

78 L. Hadar, 'Trump and Obama: On Foreign Policy, Two Peas in a Pod', *The National Interest*, 10 August 2016.

79 R. Girard, 'Trump: une stratégy internationale réaliste', *Le Figaro*, 15 November 2016.

80 http://www.theatlantic.com/international/archive/2016/04/obamas-worst-mistake-libya/478461/.

81 See, for example, D. Runciman, *Political Hypocrisy: The Mask of Power, from Hobbes to Orwell and Beyond* (Princeton University Press, 2008). In his book, David Runciman shows that it is particularly politicians in liberal democracies that resort (are forced to resort) to hypocrisy in order to have the wolves sated and the sheep intact.

82 R. Girard, *Le Monde en Guerre: 50 clefs pour le comprendre* (Carnets Nords, 2016), p. 13.

83 Secretary of State Condoleezza Rice, Special Briefing on Travel to the Middle East and Europe, 21 July 2006, US Department of State (http://www.state.gov.secretary/rm/2006/69331.htm).

84 https://www.kyivpost.com/article/content/ukraine-politics/former-us-state-secretary-rice-calls-on-ukrainian-youth-to-develop-ukraine-despite-difficulties-409714.html.

85 Quoted from R. Kaplan, *The Revenge of the Geography: What the Map Tells Us About the Coming Conflicts and the Battle Against Fate* (Random House, 2013), p. 540.

86 *Ibid.*

87 *Ibid.*

88 'L'éditorial d'Alexis Brezet: reconquerir les peuples', *Figaro Vox Monde*, 27 June 2016.

Chapter 2 Processes of Homogenisation and Heterogenisation in the World

1 N. Krisch, 'International Law in Times of Hegemony: Unequal Power and the Shaping of the International Legal Order', *European Journal of International Law*, 2005, Vol. 16, No. 3, p. 375.

2 A. Badiou, 'Notre mal vient de plus loin', 3 December 2015 (http://la-bas.org/la-bas-magazine/textes-a-l-appui/alain-badiou-penser-les-meurtres-de-masse-du-13-novembre-version-texte).

3 Russia has indeed had long and close links with the rest of Europe. Therefore, President Putin was right when he stated that 'Russia is an inalienable and organic part of Greater Europe and European civilization. Our citizens think of themselves as Europeans' (www.rt.com/politics/official-word/putin-russia-changing-world-263/).

4 Zhang Weiwei, *The China Wave: Rise of a Civilizational State* (World Century Publishing Corporation, 2012), p. 104.

5 S. Karaganov, *Op. cit.*

6 See, for example, M. Eltchaninoff, *Dans la tête de Vladimir Poutine* (Actes Sud, 2015).

7 D. Trenin, *Russia and the World in the XXI Century* (E Publishing House, 2015), p. 125.

8 R. Suskind, 'Faith, Certainty and the Presidency of George W. Bush', *New York Times Magazine*, 17 October 2004.

9 C. Krauthhammer, 'The Unipolar Moment', *Foreign Affairs*, 1990/1, Vol. 70, No. 1, pp. 23–33.

10 J.F. Witt, 'The Legal Fog between War and Peace', *International Herald Tribune*, 10 June 2012.

11 For example, the *New York Times* well summarised the 1992 US Defence Department's national security document in the following words: 'The classified document makes the case for a world dominated by one superpower whose position can be perpetuated by constructive behavior and sufficient military might to deter any nation or group of nations from challenging American primacy.' The leaked document itself stated that: 'Our first objective is to prevent the re-emergence of a new rival, either on the territory of the former Soviet Union or elsewhere, that poses a threat on the order of that posed formerly by the Soviet Union. This is a dominant consideration underlying the new regional defense strategy and requires that we endeavour to prevent any hostile power from dominating a region whose resources would, under consolidated control, be sufficient to generate global power. These regions include Western Europe, East Asia, the territory of the former Soviet Union, and Southwest Asia.' ('US Strategy Plan for Insuring No Rivals Develop', *New York Times*, 8 March 1992).

12 See, for example, The National Security Strategy of the United States of America, March 2006, p. 43.

13 H. Kissinger, *World Order* (Penguin Press, 2014), p. 275.

14 *Ibid.*, pp. 315–16.

15 S. Kinzer, *Overthrow: America's Century of Regime Change from Hawaii to Iraq* (Time Books, 2006), p. 34.

16 R. Sakwa, '"New Cold War" or twenty years' crisis?', *International Affairs*, 2008, Vol. 84, No. 2, p. 255.

17 Zhang Weiwei, *The China Wave: Rise of a Civilizational State* (World Century Publishing Corporation, 2011), p. 2.

18 *Ibid.*, p. 47.

19 V. Putin, 'Russia and the Changing World', *Moscow News*, 27 February 2012.

20 D. Trenin, *Russia and the World in the XXI Century* (E Publishing House, 2015), p. 36.

21 *Ibid.*

22 D. Simes, *After the Collapse: Russia Seeks its Place as Great Power* (Simon & Schuster, 1999).

23 *Ibid.*, p. 19.

24 *Ibid.*, p. 20.

25 S. Karaganov, *Op. cit.*

26 H. Védrine, *Le Monde au Défi* (Fayard, 2016), p. 123.

27 See, for example, D. Selbourne, *The Principle of Duty* (Sinclair-Stevenson, 1994).

28 A. de Tocqueville, *The Old Regime and the French Revolution (1856)*, translated by Stewart Gilbert (Anchor Books, 1955), p. 96.

29 M. Walzer, *Thick and Thin: Moral Argument at Home and Abroad* (University of Notre Dame Press, 1994), p. 8.

30 J. Haidt, *The Righteous Mind: Why Good People Are Divided by Politics and Religion* (Penguin, 2013), p. 116.

31 *Ibid.*, p. 368.

32 See an interesting, though unfortunately not widely commented work, on the advantages of the Chinese political system in Nicolas Berggruen & Nathan Cardels, *Intelligent Governance for the 21st Century: Middle Way between West and East* (Polity, 2013).

33 *The Economist* (7–13 July 2007), p. 39.

34 G. Malbrunot, 'En Iran, Hassan Rohani sous pression', *Le Figaro*, 26 November 2015).

35 H. Juvin, *Le Mur de l'Ouest n'est pas tombé* (Pierre-Guillaume de Roux, 2015), p. 71.

36 I. Morris, *Why the West Rules – For Now: The Patterns of History and What They Reveal about the Future* (Profile Books, 2011), p. 603.

37 Yoram Dinstain, Ugo Genesio, Rein Müllerson, Daniel Thürer, Rüdiger Wolfrum.

38 http://ectr.eu/en-projects-and-initiatives/national-statue-for-the-promotion-of-tolerance.

39 A. Chua, *Day of Empire: How Hyperpowers Rise to Global Dominance – and Why They Fall* (Doubleday, 2007), p. xxv.

40 H.-J. Chang, *Bad Samaritans. Rich Nations, Poor Policies & the Threat to the Developing World* (Random House Business Books, 2007), p. 18.
41 K. Popper, *The Open Society and Its Enemies*, vol. 2: *Hegel & Marx* (Routledge, 1996), p. 124.
42 J. Stiglitz, *The Price of Inequality: How Today's Divided Society Endangers Our Future* (W.W. Norton & Company, 2012); T. Piketty, *Le Capital au XXIe Siècle* (Les Livres du Nouveau Monde, 2013).
43 J. Dunn, *Setting the People Free: The Story of Democracy* (Atlantic Books, 2005), p. 127.
44 J. Stiglitz, *Op. cit.*, p. 38.
45 J. Dunn, *Op. cit.*, p. 130.
46 J. Stiglitz, *Op. cit.*, p. 38.
47 *Ibid.*, pp. 17–20, p. 119.
48 P. Krugman, 'Oligarchy, American Style', *New York Times*, 4 November 2011.
49 Zhang Weiwei, *The China Horizon: Glory and Dream of a Civilizational State* (World Century Publishing Corporation), 2016, p. 880.
50 J. Dunn, *Op.cit*, p. 134.
51 *Ibid.*, p. 129.
52 H. Arendt, *On Revolution* (Penguin Books, 1965), p. 74.
53 W. Streeck, 'The Crises of Democratic Capitalism', *New Left Review*, Vol. 71, September–October, 2011.
54 Hui Wang, *The End of the Revolution: China and the Limits of Modernity* (Verso, 2011), p. 103.
55 *Ibid.*
56 D. Dennett, *Breaking the Spell: Religion as a Natural Phenomenon* (Penguin Books, 2007), p. 23.
57 D. Dennet; *Op. cit.*, p. 69.
58 D. Held, *Models of Democracy*, 3rd edition (Polity Press, 2006), p. 231.
59 A. Etzioni, *Security First: For a Muscular, Moral Foreign Policy* (Yale University Press, 2007), p. 8.
60 See, for example, Jean-François Revel, *La Tentation Totalitaire* (Editions Robert Laffont, 1976).

61 Nobel economics prize winner Amartya Sen writes that 'famines are easy to prevent if there is a serious effort to do so, and a democratic government, facing elections and criticisms from opposition parties and independent newspapers, cannot help but make such an effort. Not surprisingly, while India continued to have famines under British rule right up to independence (the last famine, which I witnessed as a child, was in 1943, four years before independence), they disappeared suddenly with the establishment of a multiparty democracy and a free press' (A. Sen, 'Democracy as Universal Value', *Journal of Democracy*, 1999, No. 3, p. 8).

62 R. Rorty, *Philosophical Papers*, Vol. 1 (Cambridge University Press, 2007), p. 211.

63 S. Blackburn, 'Portrait: Richard Rorty', *Prospect Magazine*, Issue 85, April 2003.

64 President George W. Bush, *Commencement Address to the United States Coast Guard Academy*, 21 May 2003.

65 Quoted from H. Kissinger, *On China* (Penguin Books, 2011), p. 417.

66 J. Habermas, 'Interpreting the Fall of the Monument', in *Empire's Law. The American Imperial Project and the 'War to Remake the World'*, ed. by A. Bartholomew (Pluto Press, 2006), p. 51.

67 J. Gray, *Black Mass: Apocalyptic Religion and the Death of Utopia* (Allen Lane, 2007), p. 147.

68 A. Crooke, *Resistance. The Essence of the Islamist Revolution* (Pluto Press, 2009), pp. 29–30.

69 H. Védrine, *Op. cit*, p. 799. See also my article, R. Müllerson, 'Democratization through the Supply-Demand Prism', *Human Rights Review*, November 2009.

70 S. Karaganov, *Op. cit.*

Chapter 3 The West versus Russia or vice versa?

1 See, for example, G. Mettan, *Russie-Occident. Une guerre de mille ans: la russophobie de Charlemagne à la crise ukrainienne* (Éditions des Syrtes, 2015).

2 T. Shanker, 'Warning Against Wars Like Iraq and Afghanistan', *New York Times*, 25 February 2011.

3 Russia Today – a Russian English-language TV channel that gives alternative or different, which does not necessarily mean more correct, views and perspectives on many issues concerning people all over the world. It gives the Western viewer an opportunity to listen also to the other side (*audiatur et altera pars*). That is why the dominant elites in the West have become worried about 'Russian propaganda'.

4 A. Reichardt, 'Propaganda vs. Information Policy', *New Eastern Europe*, 27 April 2015.

5 E.L. Bernays, *Propaganda* (Routledge, 1928), pp. 9–10. Ten years ago this book was published in French as *Propaganda: comment manipuler l'opinion en démocratie* (Zones, 2007).

6 D. Moïsi, *La géopolitique des séries ou le triomphe de la peur* (Stock, 2016).

7 *Ibid.*, p. 191.

8 *Ibid.*, p. 270.

9 Ch. Guignon, *Heidegger and the Problem of Knowledge* (Hackett Publishing, 1983), pp. 125–6.

10 Zhang Weiwei, *The China Wave: Rise of a Civilizational State* (World Century Publishing Corporation, 2012), p. 68.

11 K. Popper, *Conjectures and Refutations: The Growth of Scientific Knowledge* (Routledge Classics, 2nd edition, 2002).

12 Mettan, *Op. cit*, p. 20.

13 F. Fillon, *Vaincre le Totalitarisme Islamique* (Albin Michel, 2016), p. 34.

14 'Joe Biden Says the PKK and the Islamic State are Equal Threats to Turkey' (https://news.vice.com/article/joe-biden-says-the-pkk-and-the-islamic-state-are-equal-threats-to-turkey).

15 C. Gorokhoff, 'Turquie-Kurdistan: deux pays en un', *Causeur*, 31 December 2015.

16 M.A. Reynolds, 'Vladimir Putin, Godfather of Kurdistan?', *The National Interest*, 1 March 2016.

17 *Ibid.*

18 *Le Figaro*, 25 November 2015.

19 *L'Obs*, 23 November 2015.

20 'Hadrien Desuin: l'Occident s'est trompé sur le modèle turc' (https://blogs.mediapart.fr/maxime-azadi/blog/281115/hadrien-desuin-loccident-sest-trompe-sur-le-modele-turc).

21 H. Dessuin, 'Comment la Turquie joue au poker menteur avec l'Union européenne', *Figaro Vox Monde*, 1 November 2015.

22 'A dark day for Europe: EU reaches agreement to send refugees back to Turkey despite legal concerns', *Independent*, 18 March 2016.

23 C. Schmitt, *The Concept of the Political* (University of Chicago Press, 1995), p. 54.

24 I. Lasserie, 'Porochenko: "Putin veut affablir l'Europe"', *Le Figaro*, 4 December 2015.

25 F. Fillon, 'Interview to Le Monde', *Le Monde*, 22 January 2016.

26 Club des Vingt, *Péchés capitaux. Les 7 impasses de la diplomatie française* (Cerf, 2016), p. 20.

27 *Ibid.* p. 33.

28 Badiou, *Op. cit.*

29 U. Gauthier, 'Après les attentats, la solidarité de la Chine n'est pas sans arrière-pensées', *L'Obs*, 18 November 2015.

30 A. Badiou, *Op. cit.*

31 In 1994, when I visited Baku, the capital of Azerbaijan, on a UN mission, I spoke to the then US Ambassador to Azerbaijan Richard Kauzlarich, who well and graphically explained to me what were Washington's interests in the Caucasus. In Azerbaijan it was obviously oil (no comment needed), in Armenia it was Armenians (for those who don't know, there is a sizable Armenian community in the US, a non-negligible part of the electorate) and in Georgia it was Shevardnadze (who had been rather pro-American even when working as the Soviet Foreign Minister, but who had come to the realisation that it would be impossible to return South Ossetia and Abkhazia, as well as Adjaria, which had also broken away from Georgia, without cooperation with Russia).

32 R. Girard, *Le monde en guerre. 50 clefs pour le comprendre* (Carnets Nords, 2016), p. 7.

33 A. Leclercq, *La Russie, puissance d'Eurasie: Histoire géopolitique des origines à Poutine* (Ellipses, 2012), p. 378.

34 As John Norris, Strobe Talbott's [then the US Deputy Secretary of State] Director of Communications during the Kosovo crisis, has written: 'it was Yugoslavia's resistance to the broader trends of political and economic reform – not the plight of Kosovar Albanians – that best explains NATO's war. Milošević had been a burr in the side of the transatlantic community for so long that the United States felt that he would only respond to military pressure' (J. Norris, *Collision Course: NATO, Russia, and Kosovo*, Foreword by Strobe Talbot (Praeger, 2005, p. XXIII)).

35 D. Treisman, 'Why Putin took Crimea? The Gambler in the Kremlin', *Foreign Affairs*, 18 April 2016.

36 N. White, *The Cuban Embargo under International Law* (El Bloqueo, Routledge, 2015), p. 29.

37 D. Acheson, 'The Cuban Quarantine – Implications for the Future', *Proceedings of the American Society of International Law*, 1963, p. 14.

38 *Statement of the President of the Russian Federation*, 18 March 2014 (official site of the President of Russia, http://eng.kremlin.ru/).

39 Independent International Commission on Kosovo, *The Kosovo Report: Conflict, International Response, Lessons Learned* (Oxford University Press, 2000).

40 The ICJ, Reports of Judgments, Advisory Opinions and Orders: Accordance with International Law of the Unilateral Declaration of Independence in respect of Kosovo Advisory Opinion of 22 July 2010, para. 84.

41 P. Péan, *Kosovo: une guerre 'juste' pour créer un État mafieux* (Fayard, 2013).

42 J. Hogard, *L'Europe est morte à Pristina: Guerre au Kosovo* (Hugo & Cie, 2014).

43 P. Péan, *Op. cit.*, p. 392.

44 *Ibid.*, p. 1038.

45 S. Rynning, 'The false promise of continental concert: Russia, the West and necessary balance of power', *International Affairs*, 2015, Vol. 91, No. 3, pp. 539–52.

46 *Second Abu Dhabi Strategic Debate*, 1–2 November 2015, Emirates Palace – Abu Dhabi, Conclusions (on file with the author).

47 'Washington's Cold War Containment Strategy is Stll Alive and Well', *Stratfor*, 23 January 2017.

48 D. de Villepin, *Mémoire de paix pour temps de guerre* (Bernard Grasset, 2017), p. 89.

49 H. Tiido, 'The Estonian Letter of Support for Washington was written in Washington', *Postimees*, 22 March 2013.

50 M. Burrows and R.A. Manning, 'Kissinger's Nightmare: How an Inverted US-China-Russia May Be Game-Changer' (http://valdaiclub.com/publications/valdai-papers/valdai-paper-33-kissinger-s-nightmare-how-an-inverted-us-china-russia-may-be-game-changer). A shorter version of the paper was published in *The National Interest* of 24 August 2015 (http://nationalinterest.org/feature/americas-worst-nightmare-russia-china-are-getting-closer-13661).

51 G-G. Moullec, *Pour une Europe de l'Atlantique à l'Oural: Les relations franco-soviétiques 1956–1974* (Max Chaleil, 2016).

52 *Ibid.*

53 R. Girard, 'La diplomatie française doit en finir avec le néo-conservatisme', *Figaro Vox Monde*, 29 March 2016.

54 Reuters, 19 February 2016.

55 Remarks on 'Strategic and Operational Innovation at a Time of Transition and Turbulence' at Reagan National Defence Forum, as delivered by Secretary of Defence Ash Carter, 7 November 2015.

56 'Critical Threats to Vital Interests of the US in the Next Ten Years', Gallup.com, 10 February 2016.

57 L. Imbert & M. Zerrouky, 'Les possibles conséquences de la reprise de Palmyre par le régime syrien', *Le Monde*, 25 March 2016.

58 T. Berthemet, 'L'Armée syrienne progresse dans la cité', *Le Figaro*, 26 March 2016.

59 http://www.rand.org/content/dam/rand/pubs/research_reports/RR1200/RR1253/RAND_RR1253.pdf.

60 *The National Interest*, 7 February 2016.

61 The 1991 referendum on sovereignty, as it was known, was held by the Crimeans when the very existence of the Soviet Union as a state had become questionable. The Crimeans were apprehensive lest in the case of the dissolution of the USSR they become a simple autonomous oblast within Ukraine. They would have preferred to stay within the USSR, as equal with other republics, or at least to have their say as to whether to become part of Russia or remain within Ukraine.

62 R. Girard, *Le monde en guerre. 50 clefs pour le comprendre* (Carnets Nords, 2016), p. 54.

63 R. Sakwa, *Frontline Ukraine: Crisis in the Borderlands* (I.B.Tauris, 2015), p. 30.

64 'Russia Expert Stephen Cohen Nails Terrorism, Syria, Ukraine and Russia: Washington's constant stubborn refusal to embrace new reality of multipolar world has become part of the problem and not part of the solution', *Russia Insider*, 7 December 2015 (Russia-insider.com).

65 http://carnegieeurope.eu/strategiceurope/?fa=63522.

66 T.L. Friedman, 'Foreign Affairs; Now a Word From X', *New York Times*, 2 May 1998.

67 H. Juvin, *Le Mur de l'Ouest n'est pas tombé* (Pierre-Guillaume de Roux, 2015), p. 18.

68 A. Leclercq, *La Russie, puissance d'Eurasie: Histoire géopolitique des origines à Poutine* (Ellipses, 2012), p. 378.

69 R. Sakwa,*Op. cit.*, p. 4.

70 M. Mandelbaum, *Mission Failure: America and the World in the Post-Cold War Era* (Oxford University Press, 2016).

71 *Ibid.*, Empl. 1388.

72 *Ibid.*, Empl. 1399.

73 B. Badie, *Nous ne sommes seuls au monde. Un autre regard sur l'ordre international* (La Dévouverte, 2016), p. 70.

74 R. Sakwa, *Op. cit.*, p. 22.

75 E. Todd, *Qui est Charlie? Sociologie d'une crise religieuse* (Seuil, 2015), p. 36.

76 Robert Cooper distinguishes three categories of states that exist side by side in the contemporary world: pre-modern, modern and post-modern states (R. Cooper, *The Post-Modern State and the World Order*, Demos, 1996).

Similarly, James Rosenau believes that 'one useful way of differentiating among the degrees to which states are able to manage their affairs is to classify them as pre-modern, modern, or post-modern entities' (J. Rosenau, *Along the Domestic-Foreign Frontier*, Cambridge University Press, 1997, p. 362), while Georg Sørensen distinguishes between post-colonial, Westphalian and post-modern states (G. Sørensen, 'An Analysis of Contemporary Statehood: Consequences for Conflict and Cooperation', *Review of International Studies*, 1997, Vol. 23, p. 255). The latter category, to which Western European states belong, is characterised, in the words of Robert Cooper, by the break-down of distinctions between domestic and foreign affairs; mutual interference in (traditional) domestic affairs; not only a formal rejection of the use of force for resolving disputes among themselves, but the very impossibility of foreseeing realistic scenarios for such use of force; the growing irrelevance of borders; security based on transparency, openness and interdependence. Modern states are more centralised, they are more concerned with their territorial integrity and non-interference in what they believe to be their internal affairs. Pre-modern states, in their efforts to create or maintain their statehood, are trying to become more centralised. The basic security problem in pre-modern states is qualitatively different from the security problems in Westphalian (modern) or post-modern states: for pre-modern states the most serious security threats are internal, not external.

77 R. Kagan, *Of Paradise and Power: America and Europe in the New World Order* (Alfred A. Knopf, 2003).

78 R.Y. Jennings, 'The Caroline and McLeod Cases', *American Journal of International Law*, 1938, Vol. 32, pp. 82–99.

79 'Fights against climate change, terrorism linked – Hollande', Reuters, 30 November 2015.

80 'If the 9/11 attacks against the United States came as a thunderbolt out of the blue, attacks of 13 November in Paris, on the contrary, happened when the security landscape had been already marked by multiple crises. During those fifteen years, not only had the geopolitical situation become much more tense, but Europe and particularly France had already been confronted by violent challenges, one worse than the other. At the end of 2015 all the lights were already in red'. 'Fin d'année préoccupante pour l'état de l'Europe', *Le Monde*, 30 November 2015.

81 O. Roy, 'Ces (nombreux) pays que l'existence de Daech arrange bien', *L'Obs*, 20 November 2015.

82 Remarks on 'Strategic and Operational Innovation at a Time of Transition and Turbulence' at Reagan National Defence Forum, as delivered by Secretary of Defence Ash Carter, 7 November 2015.

83 *Ibid.*

84 R. Soubrouillard, 'Chine, Russie: les Etats-Unis chérissent leur meilleur ennemis. Vous avez aimé la guerre froide?', *Causer*, 3 March 2016.

85 Z. Khalilzad, I. Lesser, *Sources of Conflict in the 21st Century: Regional Futures and US Strategy* (RAND Corporation, 1998).

86 D. Souchon, 'Quand les djihadists étaient nos amis', *Le Monde Diplomatique*, February 2016, pp. 14–15.

87 *Ibid.*, p. 15.

88 J. St Clair, A. Cockburn, 'How Jimmy Carter and I Started the Mujahideen', *Counterpunch*, 15 January 1998.

89 *Ibid.*

90 G. Aronson, 'Syria's ceasefire is impaired by opposition's pathologies', *Al-Jazeera*, 27 February 2016.

91 S.M. Hersh, 'The Redirection: Is the Administration's new policy benefitting our enemies in the war on terrorism', Annals of National Security, *New Yorker*, 5 March 2007.

92 A. Crooke, 'Obama and the legacy of the "dark side"', *Conflicts Forum*, 13 November 2015.

93 C. Chesnot and G. Malbrunot, *Nos très chers émirs. Sont-ils vraiment nos amis?* (Michel Lafon, 2016).

94 A. Codevilla, 'Romancing the Sunni: A US policy tragedy in three acts; Act I', *Asia Times*, 21 December 2015 (http://atimes.com/2015/12/romancing-the-sunni-a-us-policy-tragedy-in-three-acts-act-i/).

95 *Ibid.*, 'Act II', 23 December 2015 (http://atimes.com/2015/12/romancing-the-sunni-a-us-policy-tragedy-in-three-acts-act-ii/).

96 See full text in https://archive.org/stream/TheGlobalIslamicResistanceCall/The_Global_Islamic_Resistance_Call_-_Chapter_8_sections_5_to_7_LIST_OF_TARGETS_djvu.txt.

97 G. Kepel, *Terror dans l'Hexagone. Genèse du djihad français* (Gallimard, 2015), pp. 33–66.

98 See, for example, A. Rashid, *Jihad: The Rise of Militant Islam in Central Asia* (Yale University Press, 2002); O. Roy, *Globalised Islam: The Search for a New Ummah* (Hurst & Company, 2004); R. Müllerson, *Central Asia: A Chessboard and Player in the New Great Game*, 2nd edition (Routledge, 2009).

99 Müllerson, *Op. cit.*, p. 195.

100 G. Kepel, 'Il faut contrer la salafisation des esprit', *Le Figaro*, 22 March 2016.

101 '"Belgikistan": comment Bruxelles est devenu un plaque tournante du djihad', *L'Obs*, 23 March 2016.

102 R.F. Kennedy Jr, 'Why the Arabs don't want us in Syria: They don't hate our freedoms. They hate that we've betrayed our ideals in their own countries – for oil', *Politico*, 13 February 2016 (http://www.politico.eu/article/why-the-arabs-dont-want-us-in-syria-mideast-conflict-oil-intervention/).

103 *Ibid.*

104 *Ibid.*

Chapter 4 The Future of International Law

1 Anarchy in international relations theory is not associated with bomb-throwing anarchists or with a complete lack of order in the

international relations. This term emphasises the fact that the main actors of the system are independent states with no central authority over (above) them.

2 A. Watson, *The Limits of Independence: Relations Between States in the Modern World* (Routledge, 1997).

3 *Ibid.*, p. 150.

4 R. Müllerson, 'Anarchophilia, Hegemony and International Law', *Anuario Mexicano de Derecho Internacional*, 2004, Vol. IV, pp. 205–48.

5 A. Watson, *The Evolution of International Society* (Routledge, 1992), p. 291.

6 Mettan, *Op. cit*, p. 239.

7 *Ibid.*, 240.

8 L.F.L. Oppenheim, *International Law: A Treatise*, vol 1: *Peace* (London, 1905), p. 73.

9 See H. Bull, *Anarchical Society: A Study of Order in World Politics* (Macmillan, 1977).

10 *Ibid.*, p. 254.

11 Watson, *Op. cit*, p. 182.

12 See, for example, Krisch, *Op. cit*, pp. 369–408.

13 'The US Secretary of State Kerry condemns Russia's "incredible act of aggression" in Ukraine', Reuters, 2 March 2014.

14 H. Kissinger, *World Order* (Penguin Press, 2014), p. 303.

15 *Ibid.*, 372.

16 M. Koskenniemi, 'International Law and Political Theology', *Constellations*, 2004, Vol. 11, No. 4, p. 493.

17 R. Girard, *Le monde en guerre. 50 clefs pour le comprendre* (Carnets Nords, 2016), p. 35.

18 H. White, *The China Choice: Why America Should Share Power* (Black Inc., 2012), p. 1781.

19 H. Kissinger, *Op. cit*, p. 367.

20 T. Twiss, *The Law of Nations Considered as Independent Political Communities: On the Right and Duties of Nations in Time of Peace* (Oxford, 1861), p. 140.

21 This has been almost a perennial policy of dominant powers in international relations, starting from the attempts of Athens

to persuade the Melians to switch sides and ally with Athens instead of Sparta, as reported by Thucydides in his *Peloponnesian War*, to NATO membership for the former Soviet allies within the Warsaw Pact. Those who are able to break the balance usually try to do that, thereby threatening international peace and security.

22 M. Burrows, R.A. Manning, 'Kissinger's Nightmare: How an Inverted US-China-Russia May Be Game-Changer', Valdai Paper N. 33, 2015 (https://www.google.ee/search?q=kissinger%27s+nightmare&ie=utf-8&oe=utf-8&gws_rd=cr&ei=RlfEVu_oJ4Xi6ATs37T4AQ). See, also, a shorter version of their article 'America's Worst Nightmare: Russia and China are Getting Closer', *The National Interest*, 24 August 2015.

23 R. Higgins, The Place of International Law in the Settlement of Disputes by the Security Council, *American Journal of International Law*, 1970, Vol. 64, pp. 15–16.

24 See J. Meernik *et al.*, 'Judicial Decision Making and International Tribunals: Assessing the Impact of Individual, National, and International Factors', *Social Science Quarterly*, 2005, Vol. 86, p. 690.

25 See, for example, 'EJIL: Talk!, Danish Judge Blasts ICTY President', *European Journal of International Law*, 13 June 2013.

26 M. Markovic, 'International Criminal Trials and the Disqualification of Judges on the Basis of Nationality', *Washington University Global Studies Law Review*, 2014, Vol. 13, pp. 1–2.

27 L. Henkin, *How Nations Behave: Law and Foreign Policy* (Columbia University Press, 1979), p. 47.

28 Thucydides, *The Peloponnesian War* (W.W. Norton & Company, 1998), pp. 11–12.

29 *Ibid.*

30 *Ibid.*

31 A. Watson, *The Evolution of International Society* (Routledge, 1992), p. 10.

32 A. Nussbaum, *A Concise History of the Law of Nations*, revised edition (Macmillan, 1964), p. 11.

33 P. Allott, *The Health of Nations: Society and Law beyond the State* (Cambridge University Press, 2002), p. 416.

34 E. Vattel, *Le droit des gens, ou principes de la loi naturelle appliqués à la conduite et aux affaires des nations et des souverains* (1758); English translation used: *The Law of Nations, or The Principles of Natural Law Applied to the Conduct and the Affairs of Nations and of Sovereigns*, ed. by B. Kapossy & R. Whatmore (Liberty Fund, 2008), Book II, pp. xviii, 335.

35 I. Brownlie, *International Law and the Use of Force by States* (Clarendon Press, 1963), p. 41.

36 *Ibid.* pp. 55–65.

37 *Ibid.* p. 75.

38 See, for example, Abbe de Saint-Pierre, *Projet pour rendre la paix perpétuelle en Europe* (1713); E. Kant, *Toward Perpetual Peace* (1795).

39 See M. Nussbaum, *Op. cit.*, p. 217.

40 I. Brownlie, *Op.cit.*, p. 23.

41 *Ibid.* pp. 55–65.

42 *Ibid.* p. 75.

43 See, for example, W.V. O'Brien, 'Desert Storm: A Just War Analysis', *St. John's Law Review*, 1992, Vol. 66, Issue 3; G.R. Lucas Jr, '"New Rules for New Wars": International Law and Just War Doctrine for Irregular War', *Case Western Reserve Journal of International Law*, 2011, Vol. 43, Issue 3. A very interesting and detailed study of 'just war' problems can be found in *La retour de la guerre juste. Droit international, épistémologie et idéologie chez Carl Schmitt* by Celine Jouin (Editions de l'école des hautes études en sciences sociales, Librairie philosophique J. Vrin, 2013).

44 B. Badie, *Nous ne sommes seuls au monde. Un autre regard sur l'"ordre international"* (La Dévouverte, 2016), p. 215.

45 *Case concerning military and paramilitary activities in and against Nicaragua (Nicaragua vs. United States of America)*, ICJ Decision of 27 June 1986, para. 186.

46 F. Kirgis, 'Custom on a Sliding Scale', *American Journal of International Law*, 1987, p. 149.

47 O. Schachter, 'Entangling Treaty and Custom', in Y. Dinstein (ed.), *International law in a Time of Perplexity: Essays in Honour of Shabtai Rosenne* (Martinus Nijhoff Publishers, 1989), p. 731.
48 *Ibid.*
49 *Ibid.*, p. 734.
50 *Ibid.*
51 See, for example, T. Franck, 'Who Killed Article 2(4) or Changing Norms Governing the Use of Force by States', *American Journal of International Law*, 1970, Vol. 64; but see also L. Henkin, 'The Reports of the Death of Article 2(4) Are Greatly Exaggerated', *American Journal of International Law*, 1971, Vol. 65.
52 J. Moore, 'The Caroline', *Digest of International Law*, Vol. 2, p. 412. See also R.Y. Jennings, 'The Caroline and McLeod Cases', *American Journal of International Law*, 1938, Vol. 32.
53 Y. Dinstein, *War, Aggression, and Self-Defence*, 2nd edition (Cambridge University Press, 1994), pp. 213–45.
54 T. Franck, 'Terrorism and the Right of Self-Defence', *American Journal of International Law*, 2001, Vol. 95, p. 841.
55 G.M. Travalio, 'Terrorism, International Law, and the Use of Military Force', *Wisconsin International Law Journal*, 2000, Vol. 18, p. 165.
56 *The National Security Strategy of the United States of America* [hereinafter National Security Strategy], September 2002 (http://www.whitehouse.gov/nsc/nss.pdf).
57 M. Sapiro, 'Iraq: The Shifting Sands of Pre-emptive Self-Defence', *American Journal of International Law*, 2003, Vol. 97, p. 599; R. Falk, 'What Future of the UN Charter System of War Prevention', *American Journal of International Law*, 2003, Vol. 97, p. 598.
58 M. Reisman, *Self-defense in an Age of Terrorism* (ASIL Proceedings, 2003), p. 142.
59 M. Bothe, 'Terrorism and the legality of pre-emptive force', *European Journal of International Law*, 2000, Vol. 14, No. 2, p. 227.
60 SC Res. 487 (19 June 1981).

61 A. Armstrong, M. Reisman, 'The Past and Future of the Claim of Pre-emptive Self-Defense', *American Journal of International Law*, 2006, Vol. 100, p. 549.

62 T-H. Cheng, E. Valaitis, 'Shaping an Obama Doctrine if Pre-emptive Force', *Temple Law Review*, 2009, Vol. 82, p. 737.

63 J.-Y. Le Drian, *Qui est l'ennemi?* (Les éditions du Cerf, 2016), p. 139.

64 *Military and Paramilitary Activities in and against Nicaragua (Nicaragua vs. The United States of America)*, Merits, ICJ Reports 1986, para. 191.

65 Y. Dinstein, *Op. cit.*, p. 192.

66 See 1974 UN Definition of Aggression, 29 UN GAOR, Supp. 31, Art. 3(g), UN Doc. A/RES/3314 (XXIX) (1975).

67 D. Bethlehem, 'Principles Relevant to the Scope of a State's Right of Self-Defense Against an Imminent or Actual Armed Attack by Non-State Actors', *American Journal of International Law*, 2012, Vol. 106, p. 5.

68 *Ibid.*

69 Address Before a Joint session of the Congress on the United States Response to the Terrorist Attacks of September 11, *Weekly Compilation of Presidential Documents*, Vol. 37, 1347 (20 September 2001).

70 R. Girard, 'La diplomatie française doit en finir avec le néo-conservatisme', *Le Figaro Vox Monde*, 29 March 2016.

71 http://www.un.org/en/ga/search/view_doc.asp?symbol=S/RES/2249 (2015).

72 D. Akande/M. Milanovic, EJIL Talk, 'The Constructive Ambiguity of the Security Council's ISIS Resolution (http://www.ejiltalk.org/the-constructiveambiguity-of-the-security-councils-isis-resolution).

73 M. Weller, 'Permanent Imminence of Armed Attacks: Resolution 2249 (2015) and the Right to Self-Defence Against Designated Terrorist Groups' (http://www.ejiltalk.org/permanent-imminence-of-armed-attacks-resolution-2249-2015-and-the-right-to-selfdefence-against-designated-terrorist-groups).

74 http://www.securitycouncilreport.org/atf/cf/%7B65BFCF9B-6D27-4E9C-8CD3-CF6E4FF96FF9%7D/s_2014_691.pdf.
75 P. Hilpold, 'The Security Council and the Fight against Terrorism: Does SC Resolution 2249 (2015) lead to a more Hobbesian or a more Kantian international society?' (http://ssrn.com/abstract=2704467 or http://dx.doi.org/10.2139/ssrn.2704467 or http://papers.ssrn.com/sol3/papers.cfm?abstract_id=2704467).
76 See, for example, K.M. Kenkel, 'Five Generations of Peace Operations: From the "Thin Blue Line" to "Painting the Country Blue"', *Rev. Bras. Polit. Int.*, 2013, Vol. 56 (1).
77 See, for example, A. Abass, 'The Security Council and the Challenges of Collective Security in the Twenty-First Century: What Role for African Regional Organisations?' in D. Lewis (ed.), *Global Governance and the Quest for Justice*, vol. 1: *International and Regional Organisations* (Hart Oxford, 2006), pp. 91–112.
78 E. De Witt, M. Wood, 'Collective Security', *Max Planck Encyclopedia of Public International Law* (http://www.mpepil.com/).
79 L.R. Schumacher, 'The Eastern Question as a Europe question: Viewing the ascent of "Europe" through the lens of Ottoman decline,' *Journal of European Studies*, March 2014, pp. 64–80; N. Ronzitti, *Rescuing Nationals Abroad Through Military Coercion and Intervention on Grounds of Humanity* (Springer, 1985).
80 R. Plant, 'Rights, Rules and World Order', in *Global Governance: Ethics and Economics of the World Order*, ed. by M. Desai, P. Redfern (Pinter, 1995), p. 207.
81 R. Higgins, *Problems and Process: International Law and How We Use It* (Clarendon Press, 1994), p. 247.
82 See, for example, 'Draft Articles on Responsibility of States for Internationally Wrongful Acts', with commentaries, 2001, *Yearbook of the International Law Commission*, 2001, Vol. II, Part Two, p. 112.
83 *Ibid.*, pp. 112–13.
84 O. Schachter, 'International Law in Theory and Practice: General Course in Public International Law', *Recueille des Cours de l'Académie de Droit International*, 1982, Vol. V, p. 43.
85 *Ibid.*

86 Article 1 of the Convention on the Prevention and Punishment of the Crime of Genocide provides that 'The Contracting Parties confirm that genocide, whether committed in time of peace or in time of war, is a crime under international law which they undertake to prevent and to punish' (http://www2.ohchr.org/english/law/genocide.htm). It is necessary to reiterate that crimes against humanity and systemic war crimes are often no less serious crimes than acts of genocide. Crimes against humanity are, by definition, 'widespread and systematic', while war crimes, if not individual excesses but state policy (or policy of other organised groups), are also always massive and heinous. For an act to be considered as genocide, the massiveness of the crime is not an obligatory requirement. What matters most is the genocidal intent.

87 In December 1971, immediately after the Indian intervention had started, the Indian Ambassador to the UN declared: '[W]e have on this particular occasion absolutely nothing but the purest of intentions: to rescue the people of East Bengal from what they are suffering' (UN Doc. S/PV.1606, 4 December 1971, p. 86). Soon, however, the Indian government denounced this statement of its Ambassador and referred to the right of self-defence instead.

88 Press Release, SC/6686, 4011th Meeting (PM), 10 June 1999.

89 D. Sharnak, *Jimmy Carter, Cambodia, and the United Nations: Human Rights in a Cold War Climate* (University of Wisconsin-Madison, April 2010).

90 ECOWAS forces entered Liberia on 23 August 1990. The first reaction of the Security Council came in January 1991 when the Council lauded ECOWAS for working to bring peace to Liberia and encouraged all parties to co-operate with ECOWAS. Note by the Press Office of the Security Council, S/22133, 23 January 1991.

91 See more in R. Higgins, 'Some Thoughts on the Evolving Relationship between the Security Council and NATO', in *Boutros Boutros-Ghali Amicorum Discipulorumque Liber* (Bruylant, 1998), p. 521.

92 'International Commission on Intervention and State Sovereignty, the Responsibility to Protect' (http://www.iciss.ca/report-en.asp).

93 'A More Secure World: Our Shared Responsibility, Report of the High-Level Panel on Threats, Challenges and Change', UN Doc. A/59/565, at 56–7, para. 201 (2004) (http:ll//www.un.org/secureworld/report. pdf).

94 'In Larger Freedom: Towards Development, Security and Human Rights for All', Report of the Secretary-General, UN Doc. A/59/2005, paras. 16–22 (2005) http://www.un.org/largerfreedom/contents.htm).

95 '2005 World Summit Outcome', GA Res. 60/1, paras. 138–9 (24 October 2005).

96 'International Commission on Intervention and State Sovereignty, the Responsibility to Protect', paras 4.18, 4.32–48.

97 *Ibid.*, paras 6,39; 6,40.

98 Press Release, SG/SM 6949, 7 April 1999.

99 *Financial Times*, 26 May 1999, p. 2.

100 Press Release, SG/SM/6997.

101 *The Economist*, 18 September 1999.

102 SG/SM/7136, 20 September 1999.

103 *Ibid.*

104 A.J. Bellamy, 'The Responsibility to Protect and the problem of military intervention', *International Affairs*, 2008, Vol. 84, No. 4, p. 638.

105 C. Stahn, 'Responsibility to Protect: Political Rhetoric or Emerging Legal Norm?', *American Journal of International Law*, 2007, Vol. 101, p. 111.

106 G. Evans, 'Russia, Georgia and the Responsibility to Protect', *Amsterdam Law Forum*, 2009, Vol. 1, No. 2.

107 *Ibid.*

108 *Ibid.*

109 A. de Waal, 'How to End Mass Atrocities', *New York Times*, 9 March 2009.

110 Present Problems of the Use of Armed Force in International Law – Humanitarian Action (Rapporteurs Mr Reisman/Owada),

Institut de Droit Internationale, Session de Santiago – 2007 (http://justitiaetpace.org/resolutions_chrono.php?start=2001&end=2007).

111 10th Commission: Humanitarian Action, Traveaux de la session de Tallinn (http://justitiaetpace.org/annuaire_resultat.php?id=16).

112 See, for example, an insightful analysis of reasons of successes and failures of different interventions in Rory Stewart & Gerald Knaus, *Can Intervention Work?* (W.W. Norton & Company, 2011). One of the main conclusions of the authors is that the success or failure of outside interventions depend less on what the intervenors do, on their characteristics and staying-power and much more on the characteristics of societies where interventions take place. The greatest problem is that intervenors are often rather ignorant of the latter.

113 M. Burrows, R.A. Manning, 'Kissinger's Nightmare: How an Inverted US-China-Russia May Be Game-Changer', *Valdai Paper*, N. 33, 2015.

114 M. Mandelbaum, *Mission Failure: America and the World in the Post-Cold War Era* (Oxford University Press, 2016), p. 248.

115 G. Chaliand, *Pourquoi perd-on la guerre? Un nouvel art occidental* (Odile Jacob, 2016), p. 17.

116 E. Luce, 'David Petraeus: Général déchu', *La Revue*, July–August 2016, p. 68.

Instead of Conclusions

1 'To Paris, US Looks Like a "Hyperpower"', *New York Times*, 5 February 1999.

2 S. Kinzer, 'Stop Complaining about Trump – we earned him', *The Boston Globe*, 1 February, 2017

3 I. Morris, *War! What Is It Good For? Conflict and the Role of Civilization from Primates to Robots* (Profile Books, 2015).

4 *Ibid.*, p. 8.

5 *Ibid.*, p. 9.

6 *Ibid.*, p. 339.

7 F. Fukuyama, *Our Posthuman Future: Consequences of Biotechnological Revolution* (Picador, 2003).

8 *Ibid.*, p. 386.

9 L. Ferry, *La révolution transhumaniste. Comment la technomédecine et l'uberisation du monde vont boulverser nos vies* (Plon, 2016), p. 11.

Further Reading

Bethlehem, D., 'Principles Relevant to the Scope of a State's Right of Self-Defense Against an Imminent or Actual Armed Attack by Non-State Actors', *American Journal of International Law*, 2012, Vol. 106.

Boniface, P., *La Géopolitique: 40 fiches thématiques et documentées pour comprendre l'actualité* (Eyrolles, 2014).

Brzezinski, Z., *The Grand Chessboard: American Primacy and Its Geostrategic Imperatives* (Basic Books, 1998).

Burrows, M., Manning, R.A., 'Kissinger's Nightmare: How an Inverted US-China-Russia May Be Game-Changer' (http://valdaiclub.com/publications/valdai-papers/valdai-paper-33-kissinger-s-nightmare-how-an-inverted-us-china-russia-may-be-game-changer). A shorter version of the paper was published in *The National Interest* of 24 August 2015 (http://nationalinterest.org/feature/americas-worst-nightmare-russia-china-are-getting-closer-13661).

Chaliand, G., *Pourquoi perd-on la guerre? Un nouvel art occidental* (Odile Jacob, 2016).

Deudney, D., Ikenberry, G.J., 'The Myth of the Autocratic Revival. Why Liberal Democracy Will Prevail', *Foreign Affairs*, January–February 2009.

Dinstein, Y., *War, Aggression and Self-Defence* (fifth edition) (Cambridge University Press, 2012).

Eltchaninoff, M., *Dans la tête de Vladimir Poutine* (Actes Sud, 2015).

Ferry, L., *La révolution transhumaniste: comment la technomédecine et l'uberisation du monde vont bouleverser nos vies* (Plon, 2016, p. 222).

Fillon, F., *Vaincre le totalitarisme islamique* (Albin Michel, 2016).

Girard, R., *Le Monde en guerre. 50 clefs pour le comprendre* (Carnets Nords, 2016).

Haidt, J., *The Righteous Mind: Why Good People Are Divided by Politics and Religion* (Penguin, 2013).

Higgins, R., *Themes and Theories: Selected Essays, Speeches, and Writings in International Law* (Oxford University Press, 2009).

Hui Wang, *The End of the Revolution: China and the Limits of Modernity* (Verso, 2011).

Independent International Commission on Kosovo, *The Kosovo Report: Conflict, International Response, Lessons Learned* (Oxford University Press, 2000).

Juvin, H., *Le Mur de l'Ouest n'est pas tombé* (Pierre-Guillaume de Roux, 2015).

Kaplan, R., *The Revenge of Geography: What the Map Tells Us About the Coming Conflicts and the Battle Against Fate* (Random House, 2012).

Kepel, G., *Terreur dans l'Hexagone: Genèse du djihad français* (Gallimard, 2015).

Kinzer, S., *Overthrow: America's Century of Regime Change from Hawaii to Iraq* (Time Books, 2006).

Kissinger, H., *World Order* (Penguin, 2014).

Koskenniemi, M., 'International Law as Political Theology', *Constellations*, 2004, Vol. 11, No. 4.

———, *The Gentle Civilizer of Nations* (Cambridge University Press, 2001).

Krisch, N., 'International Law in Times of Hegemony: Unequal Power and the Shaping of the International Legal Order', *European Journal of International Law*, 2005, Vol. 16, No. 3.

Le Drian, J.-Y., *Qui est l'ennemi?* (Les éditions du Cerf, 2016).

Leclercq, A., *La Russie puissance d'Eurasie: Histoire géopolitique des origines à Poutine* (Ellipses, 2012).

Mandelbaum, M., *Mission Failure: America and the World in the Post-Cold War Era* (Oxford University Press, 2016).

Mead, W.R., 'The Return of Geopolitics: The Revenge of the Revisionist Powers', *Foreign Affairs*, May/June 2014.

Moïsi, D., *La Geopolitique des series ou le triomphe de la peur* (Stock, 2016).

Morris, I., *War! What Is It Good For? Conflict and the Role of Civilization from Primates to Robots* (Profile Books, 2015).

———, *Why the West Rules – For Now: The Patterns of History and What They Reveal About the Future* (Profile Books, 2010).

Müllerson, R., 'Ideology, Geopolitics and International Law', *Chinese Journal of International Law*, 2016, Vol. 15, No. 1.

———, 'F.F. Martens – Man of the Enlightenment: Drawing Parallels between Martens' Times and Today's Problems', *European Journal of International Law*, 2014, Vol. 25, No. 3.

———, *Regime Change: From Democratic Peace Theories to Forcible Regime Change* (Brill, 2013).

Niebuhr, R., *The Irony of American History* (University of Chicago Press, 2008).

———, *Moral Man and Immoral Society* (Continuum, 2005).

Putin, V., 'Russia and the Changing World', *Moscow News*, 27 February 2012.

Sakwa, R., *Frontline Ukraine: Crisis in the Borderlands* (I.B.Tauris, 2015).

Saunders, P.J., 'Barack Obama is not a realist', *The National Interest*, 26 August 2014.

Schachter, O., International Law in Theory and Practice (Martinus Nijhoff Publishers,1991).

Schmitt, C., *The Nomos of the Earth in the International Law of the Jus Publicum Europaeum* (Telos, 2006).

Simes, D., *After the Collapse: Russia Seeks its Place as Great Power* (Simon & Schuster, 1999).

Slama, M., *La guerre des mondes: Réflexions sur la croisade idéologique de Poutine contre l'Occident* (Editions de Fallois, 2016).

Trenin, D., *Russia and the World in the XXI Century* (E Publishing House, 2015).

Védrine, H., *Le monde au défi* (Fayard, 2016).

Villepin, D. de, *Mémoire de paix pour temps de guerre* (Bernard Grasset, 2017).

White, H., *The China Choice: Why America should Share Power* (Black Inc., 2012).

Zhang Weiwei, *China Horizon: The Glory and Dream of a Civilizational State* (World Century Publishing Corporation, 2016).

———, *The China Wave: The Rise of Civilizational State* (World Century Publishing Corporation, 2012).

Index

References in **bold** type indicate detailed discussion.
n = footnote.
R2P = Responsibility to Protect.